Joomla!® Explained

Joomla!® Explained

Your Step-by-Step Guide

Stephen Burge

✦✦Addison-Wesley

Upper Saddle River, NJ · Boston · Indianapolis · San Francisco
New York · Toronto · Montreal · London · Munich · Paris · Madrid
Cape Town · Sydney · Tokyo · Singapore · Mexico City

Many of the designations used by manufacturers and sellers to distinguish their products are claimed as trademarks. Where those designations appear in this book, and the publisher was aware of a trademark claim, the designations have been printed with initial capital letters or in all capitals.

The author and publisher have taken care in the preparation of this book, but make no expressed or implied warranty of any kind and assume no responsibility for errors or omissions. No liability is assumed for incidental or consequential damages in connection with or arising out of the use of the information or programs contained herein.

The publisher offers excellent discounts on this book when ordered in quantity for bulk purchases or special sales, which may include electronic versions and/or custom covers and content particular to your business, training goals, marketing focus, and branding interests. For more information, please contact:

U.S. Corporate and Government Sales
(800) 382-3419
corpsales@pearsontechgroup.com

For sales outside the United States please contact:

International Sales
international@pearson.com

Visit us on the Web: informit.com/aw

3 9547 00369 5066

Library of Congress Cataloging-in-Publication Data:

Burge, Stephen, 1978-
  Joomla! explained : your step-by-step guide / Stephen Burge.
     p. cm.
  Includes index.
  ISBN-13: 978-0-321-70378-1 (pbk. : alk. paper)
  ISBN-10: 0-321-70378-2 (pbk. : alk. paper)
  1. Joomla! (Computer file) 2. Web sites—Authoring programs. 3. Web site development. I. Title.
  TK5105.8885.J86B87 2012
  006.7'8—dc23

                              2011014788

ISBN-13: 978-0-321-70378-1
ISBN-10: 0-321-70378-2

Text printed in the United States on recycled paper at RR Donnelley, Crawfordsville, Indiana.

Second printing December 2011

❖

This book is dedicated to the generations of wonderful women in my family:

Irene and Miriam
Lynne
Nicky and Katie
Stacey
Eshun and Evelyn

❖

Contents

Preface

This book was written for my Dad and for people like you.

I teach Joomla! classes all across the United States and talk with people like you who have tried to learn Joomla and other software.

They order books, watch videos, read online documentation, and go to other classes. Many are frustrated and say the same thing: "Geeks create this training, and geeks don't speak our language."

So when I was asked to write this book, I wanted to write it in plain English. I wanted to write a book that my Dad could read, understand, and enjoy.

My Dad was a teacher and only took up Web sites after retiring. Maybe you're in a similar situation and Joomla is a hobby for you.

Maybe you went to work one day and your boss said "Surprise! You're learning Joomla."

Maybe you're a Web professional who's looking to make a career from building Joomla sites.

It doesn't matter. We all want to spend more time building Web sites and less time struggling with complicated instructions. After all, the whole point of using Joomla is to allow you to take control of your site quickly and easily.

This book worked for my Dad. He read the manuscript and has now built several Joomla sites.

I hope this book works for you also and that you can create Joomla Web sites that make you proud.

Joomla! Press Mission Statement

The mission of Joomla! Press is to enhance the Joomla! experience by providing useful, well-written, and engaging publications for all segments of the Joomla! Community from beginning users to framework developers. Titles in Joomla! Press are authored by leading experts and contributors in the community.

Acknowledgments

Wonderfully, this book stands on the shoulders of the entire Joomla community. Every month, 7 million people visit Joomla.org, which is more people than live in London. Every one of those visitors plays his or her role in helping Joomla grow, from those who drop in once to those who volunteer dozens of hours per week.

Practically, this book was written thanks to the undying patience and support of Debra Williams-Cauley and Songlin Qiu. Thanks also to my Dad, my wife, my friends, and all those who gave feedback on the unfinished chapters.

About the Author

Stephen Burge grew up in and around Portsmouth in southern England. He comes from a long line of teachers and soon became one himself. Teaching never made him rich, but it did pay the bills during years living abroad in Wales, Mexico, Japan, Australia, and the United States.

During his travels he dabbled with building Web sites and in 2003 discovered Mambo, the predecessor to Joomla! Three years later, his evening job as a Web designer was making him more money than this day job as a teacher. Now living in Atlanta, Georgia, in the United States, he founded Alledia.com, a company dedicated to building Joomla Web sites.

After a few years and few dozen Joomla Web sites, Stephen started to feel the urge to teach again. A friend asked him to teach a Joomla class in Chicago: He tried it and loved it. The reintroduction to teaching lead to more Joomla classes in Atlanta, New York, Washington, and other cities. They went well enough that Stephen ended up combining his two careers and became a full-time Joomla teacher. He now runs OSTraining.com, which helps thousands of people learn Joomla every year.

1

Joomla! Explained

You can build great Web sites with Joomla!

My name is Steve Burge, and I'm a full-time Joomla trainer. During the hundreds of Joomla classes I've taught in many cities and countries, I've met a lot of different types of Joomla learners:

- **Joomla learners come from many different backgrounds.** They are accountants, florists, photographers, secretaries, factory workers, stay-at-home mothers, and people from all walks of life. Two of our best students have been an undertaker and a travel agent.

- **Joomla learners don't need to know anything about Web sites.** Some Joomla learners are professional Web designers, but many others have never built a site before and don't know any Web site code or jargon.

- **Joomla learners don't need any experience.** We've trained people who went to work the previous week and found their boss saying "Surprise! You're running our Joomla site!" They often still wore their look of shock.

- **Joomla learners are of all ages.** We've taught 15-year old students skipping class all the way up to retirees in their 80s.

If any of those descriptions sounds like you, you've picked up the right book. Using plain English and straightforward instructions, we enable you to build great Web sites using Joomla.

Before you start, you probably need to know something about Joomla. This chapter is a brief introduction.

The What, When, Where, and Who of Joomla

Here are four key things to know about Joomla:

- **What is Joomla?** It's Web-publishing software. It's designed for people to publish content online: news, blogs, photos, products, documents, events, or 1,001 other things. Because it allows you to manage your content, you often hear it called a Content Management System or CMS for short.

- **When did Joomla start?** Joomla has been around in various forms since 2000, which makes it one of the most established software projects on the Web. Initially it was called Mambo, and in 2005 the name changed to Joomla.

- **Where did Joomla start?** It was created by Australians, which according to some people, explains many of the quirks. It now has developers based all over the world with particularly strong representation coming from Europe, North America, Southeast Asia, and of course Australia.

- **Who runs Joomla?.** Rather than being run by a company, Joomla is operated by a nonprofit organization staffed by volunteers. Those volunteers are of course wonderful, kind-hearted people like myself. However, they do still need to keep a roof over their heads and eat. Many of them have Joomla businesses in the daytime and volunteer in their spare time helping to keep the project running.

Why Joomla?

Why should you use Joomla rather than other web-publishing software?

- **It's easier.** I can't promise that your Joomla experience will be 100% frustration-free. You will have some moments when you get stuck and wish you'd taken up knitting instead. However, Joomla is much easier than most other types of Web site software, and really there's not much to learn. Once you've mastered the basics in this book, you can go out and build great Joomla sites.

- **It's quicker.** Joomla provides many ready-built features. If you want a new site design or to add a calendar or shopping cart to your site, you can often do it with just a few clicks. It may take a few days or even weeks to build a really great Joomla site, but you'll be able to develop and launch more quickly than with many alternatives.

- **It's cheaper.** Building a Joomla site is unlikely to be completely cost-free because at a certain point you may need to spend some money: You may have purchased this book or other training, and you might buy a new design or feature for your site. A good Joomla site may cost you between a few dollars and thousands of dollars at the top end. However, commercial alternatives to Joomla often cost tens or hundreds of thousands of dollars.

- **It has more options.** If you want extra features on your Joomla site, http://extensions.joomla.org is the place to go. It currently lists more than 7,000 options. For example, if you want a calendar, there are around 20 options; and if you want a photo gallery, you can choose from around 60 options. All those numbers will probably go up by the time you read this, so there really are a lot of options. Though at some point you may have to hire a developer if you have unusual or specific requirements, many of the things you need for your site have already been built.

How Much Is Joomla?

Joomla is free. Yes, 100% free.

The software is free to use, free to download, free to use on your sites, and free to use on your customers' sites.

Thousands of free extensions also are available. You can find designs that people have created and are giving away. You can also find free shopping carts, calendars, photo galleries, and much more.

However, there are companies that make a living by selling products for Joomla. If you want a very impressive design or feature, there are companies that sell them, typically for a price between $5 and $150.

What Does the Joomla Name Mean?

Yes, Joomla is a silly name. We admit it. Why was it chosen? Because the domain name was available. Okay, that sounds like a joke, but it's partially true. It was also chosen because the alternatives were so bad: They included Zegris and Feenix.

You might have guessed that Joomla isn't a real word. It's the phonetic spelling of a Swahili word "Jumla," which means "all together" or "as a whole."

The logo is shown in Figure 1.1 and was chosen during a competition in 2005.

The winning designer started with several letter J's for "Joomla" and rotated them until they fit together smoothly.

Adding the circles to each J gave the impression of people, and the multiple colors gave the impression of different races, peoples, and cultures.

The Joomla logo has the same meaning as the name: People all together as one.

Figure 1.1   The Joomla logo

How Many Versions of Joomla Are There?

At least three. We are using version 1.6 in this book, but other versions are
widely used.

- Joomla 1.0 was released in September 2005. Though many Web sites still
  use this version, and it is safe and secure, Joomla no longer officially sup-
  ports this version, and companies are no longer releasing products for it.

- Joomla 1.5 was released in January 2008. Millions of Web sites use it, and it
  is still being actively supported and updated by the Joomla team. However,
  there are no plans for new features for this version.

- Joomla 1.6 was released in January 2011. This latest and greatest version
  offers many improvements over both 1.0 and 1.5. It's the version we use
  in this book.

In the future, more versions will be released, and they will be released regularly. In fact, there's a good chance that by the time you're reading this book, the
latest version of Joomla will be 1.7, 1.8, or something even higher. Don't let that
put you off. New versions of Joomla are like new models of cars. This year's
Toyota, Ford, or Honda might have small improvements or tweaks over last year's
model, but it's instantly recognizable as the same car, and you'll have little problem moving from one to the other.

The key concepts of Joomla don't change, and in this book we focus on
those key concepts. After you're finished reading, you should be able to pick up a
site using 1.0, 1.5, 1.6, or even a future version and be able to successfully use it.

It really is like learning to drive. You learn to drive in one type of car, but
once you understand how to do it, you can quickly adapt to driving any other
type of car.

Who Uses Joomla?

Corporations: Joomla is used by many businesses, including world-leading corporations. McDonald's, Sony, General Electric, eBay, Palm, Ikea, Kellogg's, Porsche, and more are all Joomla users. Danone, the French corporation, has a particularly exciting Joomla Web site at http://www.danone.com, shown in Figure 1.2.

Figure 1.2   Danone.com built with Joomla

Governments: Joomla is used by more national government sites than any other software. International organizations such as United Nations and the European Union use Joomla, and so do governments from the U.S., the U.K., and Portugal to Indonesia, Sri Lanka, and Mongolia. One example is http://www.presidencia.gov.ar, the official site of the president of Argentina, shown in Figure 1.3.

Figure 1.3   The Joomla Web site for the president of Argentina

Media: Joomla powers many TV, entertainment, and news Web sites and can handle large amounts of traffic. Leading newspapers in Chile, Italy, Nigeria, the Philippines, and many other countries use Joomla. Sony is using Joomla for the Web site of their popular TV program: *The Nate Berkus Show* at http://www.thenateshow.com (see Figure 1.4).

Education and Cultural Groups: Joomla is particularly popular in education with groups ranging from large universities to small schools. Many charities and nonprofit organizations rely on Joomla. One of the most famous is the Guggenheim museum with branches in New York, Venice, Bilbao, Berlin, and Abu Dhabi. Its Web site is http://www.guggenheim.org, shown in Figure 1.5.

Famous Places: Tourist destinations and attractions around the world use Joomla to show their best side to tourists. One of the most famous is the Eiffel Tower, whose beautiful Web site is available in both English and French at http://www.tour-eiffel.com (see Figure 1.6).

Figure 1.4   *The Nate Berkus Show* built with Joomla

Figure 1.5   The Guggenheim Web site built with Joomla

Figure 1.6   The Eiffel Tower Web site built with Joomla

This Book Explained

Now that you know a little about Joomla, here's what you should know about this book.

What You'll Need

You only need two things to follow along with this book:

- A computer with an Internet connection
- A Web hosting account to install Joomla

What This Book Covers

- **Chapter 1, "Joomla! Explained"**—You've almost finished reading it!
- **Chapter 2, "Joomla! Installations Explained"**—You install Joomla and set it up correctly.
- **Chapter 3, "Joomla! Sites Explained"**—You learn how to navigate the two halves of every Joomla site: the visitor area and the administrator area.

- **Chapter 4, "Joomla! Content Explained"**—You practice the three-step workflow that makes creating a Joomla site really easy.

- **Chapter 5, "Joomla! Content Editing Explained"**—You add articles to your site, together with images, links, and formatting.

- **Chapter 6, "Joomla! Menus Explained"**—You create your site's navigation.

- **Chapter 7, "Joomla! Components Explained"**—You add powerful extra features to your site such as contact forms, advertising banners, and a directory of links to other sites.

- **Chapter 8, "Joomla! Modules Explained"**—You add extra boxes of information to your site. These allow people to do many different things, including how to use the search form, see your latest articles, or register on your site.

- **Chapter 9, "Joomla! Plug-ins Explained"**—You add smaller extra features to your site such as allowing people to vote on articles or blocking e-mail addresses from being seen by spammers.

- **Chapter 10, "Joomla! Templates Explained"**—You change your site design choosing the colors and graphics that you want.

- **Chapter 11, "Adding Joomla! Extensions Explained"**—You learn how to find, evaluate, install, and use extra features on your Joomla site.

- **Chapter 12, "Putting It All Together: Personal Site"**—You put together everything you've learned in previous chapters to build a personal Web site for yourself.

- **Chapter 13, "Putting It All Together: Business Company Site"**— You use the same skills you practiced in Chapter 12, but this time you build a fully featured business site.

  Chapters 1 to 13 teach you the absolute essentials you need to know to build a Joomla site. This book also has three extra chapters that take you further. Not every user will need to learn and use the information in these chapters, but many will.

- **Chapter 14, "Joomla! Users Explained"**—You learn how a Joomla site can enable many different users to have access to different areas of the site.

- **Chapter 15, "Joomla! Languages Explained"**—You translate your site into more than one language.

- **Chapter 16, "Joomla Site Management Explained"**—You manage your site successfully and safely, ensuring that it is regularly updated and backed up.

This Book Is Concise

Big books often written in long, complicated sentences and paragraphs and chapters that go on and on while the text grows and the words grow longer and more obscure as the author tries to show their verbosity and vocabulary, examining the thesaurus for words that describe, narrate, and impress and fill up space but never quite get to the point so that the reader ends up going back to the beginning of the long confusing text and tries to reread, but then they start wondering what's for dinner or what's on TV instead....

This book is concise because it contains only what a Joomla beginner really needs to know.

This Book Is Active

You don't learn to ride a bicycle by reading a book: You learn by actually riding.

You don't learn to drive a car by reading a book: You learn by actually driving.

A book might help and give some advice, but without actually riding a bike or driving a car, you'll never really learn.

The same is true with Joomla. So throughout every chapter of this book, you're going to be asked to work with Joomla.

This Book Uses Specific Examples

Once you've mastered the techniques in this book, you'll be able to build your own Web sites for companies, charities, schools, sports, or whatever else you need.

However, in this book we use specific example sites. Using specific examples makes it really easy to follow along together and know for certain that you're doing things right. At every step you'll have a clear screenshot to look at and compare with what you're seeing on your site. If it's not identical, you will easily know you've made a mistake, and you can try the steps one more time.

The first example we use is a city Web site. Starting in Chapter 2 and going through to Chapter 11, we create a site with information about a fake city called Joomlaville. That's going to be the project we use to show you how to build and run a Joomla site.

The end result of this process should look like http://
www.joomlaexplained.com/joomlaville, as shown in Figure 1.7. I've been
through all the chapters from 2 to 11 and created this site as an example for you.
Whenever you get stuck, you can look at that site for guidance. We also have a
lot of information, including detailed instructions, updates, and (in all probabil-
ity) corrections for each chapter at http://www.joomlaexplained.com.

Figure 1.7   The completed Joomlaville Web site built in this book

What's Next?

In this chapter, you learned some really important information about Joomla:

- Joomla is easier, cheaper, quicker, and has more options than many of the alternative ways to build Web sites.
- Joomla is widely used by businesses, governments, and nonprofit organizations.
- People of all backgrounds, ages, and technology experience have learned Joomla.
- You're going to join them by following clear, step-by-step instructions.
- When you've finished this book you'll have built our example Web sites, but you'll be ready to build your own Joomla sites on many more topics.

The next step is to get you a Joomla site. Are you ready? If you are, turn the page, and we'll install a new Joomla site for you to use.

2

Joomla! Installations Explained

In Chapters 2-11, we introduce you to the workflow we recommend that all beginners use for building a Joomla site:

Step 1: Installation

Step 2: Content

Step 3: Extensions (Components, Modules and Plugins)

Step 4: Templates

Over those chapters we take you through the Joomla workflow and explain each step.

- During those chapters, we build an example site—an information site for a city called Joomlaville. We add details about the city, its attractions, festivals, transport, and more.

- Once we've practiced, we go through the workflow putting all the pieces together.

After you have more experience, you may find that this workflow is too basic. Great—that means you're on your way to becoming a Joomla expert. However, when getting started with Joomla, following these four steps in this order will make your life much easier.

This chapter shows you where and how to install Joomla. When you've finished, you should have a complete Joomla site. That is where you can practice everything else we do in this book.

Things You Can Do After Reading This Chapter

- Choose the best place to install Joomla
- Choose the best way to install Joomla
- Install Joomla automatically
- Install Joomla manually
- Get help if you're stuck with installing Joomla

Choose the Best Place to Install Joomla

Joomla is not like many other software programs. It can't just run on any computer. It requires a server to run successfully. That means you normally have the choice of installing Joomla in one of two places:

- A local server installed on your computer
- A Web server

Choosing the best place to install Joomla is important, so here is an explanation of the difference between the two options.

Your Computer

There are several useful advantages to working on your computer:

- **Working offline.** You can work without an Internet connection.
- **Privacy.** Your Joomla site will be safe and private, accessible only to people who can access that computer.
- **Free.** There are no fees to pay.

However, there are also several important disadvantages to using a computer:

- **Extra installations needed.** You need to download and configure special software for your computer.
- **Difficult to get help.** You can't easily show it to other people and ask for help.
- **Only one computer.** You can only access it from the computer you used to install it.
- **Need to move in order to launch.** When you're ready to make your site public, you need to move everything to a Web server and adjust for any differences between the two locations

Because of these disadvantages, installing Joomla on your computer can present significant obstacles for a beginner. I'm going to recommend that you don't take this route until you have more experience.

However, if you do feel comfortable overcoming these obstacles, we provide instructions on how to install Joomla on a PC at http://www.joomlaexplained.com/pc and on a Mac at http://www.joomlaexplained.com/mac.

A Web Server

Unlike your computer, a Web server is specifically designed for hosting Web sites so they are easy to visit for anyone who's online.

If you work for a company, they may be able to provide a server. However, for most of us we need to rent space from a hosting company. There are two common types of Web servers, Linux and Microsoft. Both require PHP because that is the language Joomla is written in and MySQL because it is the type of database Joomla uses. These are the minimum versions needed:

- PHP 5.2 or above
- MySQL 5.1 or above

Linux servers also require Apache, a type of Web server software. The minimum version for that is 1.3 and above.

When it comes to running Joomla, Linux has long been the favorite choice. Microsoft is working hard to make Joomla run as smoothly as possible on its Web server software, but for now Linux is still my recommendation.

Most hosting companies now support Joomla, but it's worth choosing carefully. Some hosting companies are much better than others. Here is some advice before picking your host:

- Search forum.joomla.org for other people's experiences with that host.
- Contact the host's customer support and ask what they know about Joomla. One of our training students actually called the phone numbers of several hosts and timed their responses. After all, in an emergency you don't want to be on hold for an hour or be talking to someone who knows nothing about Joomla.
- Check prices. Most good hosting companies will charge around $6 to $10 per month for approximately 1 GB of space (enough for a 2,000-page site) and 50 GB of bandwidth (enough for about 100,000 visitors per month).

For more Joomla hosting advice, visit http://www.joomlaexplained.com/hosting.

Choose the Best Way to Install Joomla!

For people who choose to install Joomla on a Web server, there are two common ways to install:

- Use a "One-Click" installation.
- Upload the files and create the database manually.

The One-Click installation method is the fastest and easiest way to install Joomla, but you do need to make sure it is supported by your hosting company.

If you choose to install Joomla manually, you'll be moving Joomla files to the Web server. For that you need FTP (File Transfer Protocol) software. One good choice is Filezilla, which is free to download and can work on Windows, Mac, or Linux computers. To download it, go to http://www.filezilla-project.org and click Download Filezilla Client.

We show you both ways to install Joomla. If you're in a hurry, use the One-Click option explained under the heading "Install Joomla Automatically."

If you want to be a little geeky and take the time to install Joomla yourself, use the steps explained later in the chapter under the heading "Install Joomla Manually."

Install Joomla Automatically

Automatic installers are often called One-Click installers. To tell the truth, "One Click" is a bit of an exaggeration because installing Joomla this way really takes about five clicks. However, the idea is that this is an easy and quick way to install Joomla. There are many different versions of One-Click installers. We use perhaps the most popular version, which is called Fantastico. Your hosting company may offer an alternative that looks a little different but works similarly. Here are the steps to install Joomla automatically:

1. Log in to your Web hosting account. Each hosting account looks a little different, but there are often similarities. CPanel and Plesk are two popular types of software used for accounts. In this example we use CPanel as shown in Figure 2.1.

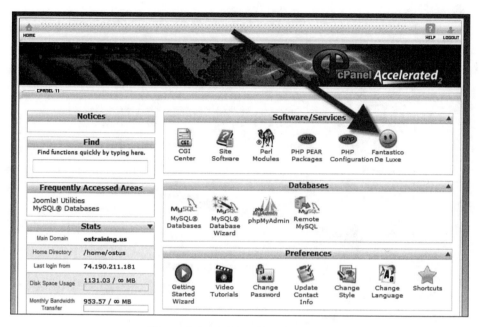

Figure 2.1   CPanel hosting account

2. Find the Fantastico button and click it. The button may be found on any of the rows, but you can normally find it by looking for the blue smiley face as shown in Figure 2.2.

Figure 2.2   Fantastico button

3. View the Fantastico Control Panel. After clicking on the Fantastico button, you are taken to the main Fantastico Control Panel. You see a screen like the one shown in Figure 2.3. Click Joomla on the left.

4. Choose to install Joomla. You now see a screen like the one in Figure 2.4 with a brief introduction to Joomla. Click on New Installation to proceed.

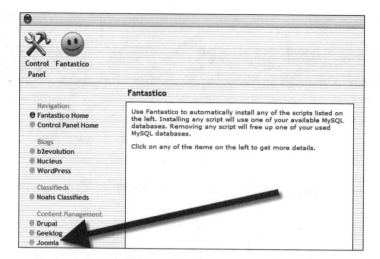

Figure 2.3   Fantastico Control Panel

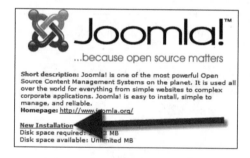

Figure 2.4   Joomla screen in Fantastico

5. Enter your new site details. Fantastico now asks for the details of your new site. Here's what you need to know:

   - **Install on Domain.** Unless you're an experienced Web site builder, you can leave this field alone.

   - **Install on Directory.** You can leave this blank if you want the site to be accessible directly via your domain, for example: http://www.joomlaexplained.com. The alternative that I recommend for learning with this book is to use a subfolder. For example, as we're building a site about Joomlaville, we can place the site at http://www.joomlaexplained.com/joomlaville/. If you do this, it's not difficult to move your site if you later want to make it accessible directly via your domain. So go ahead and enter **joomlaville** into this field.

- **Administrator.** This is the username you will use on your site. Please don't use "admin" as that is too easy for other people to guess.

- **Password.** This is the password you'll use to log in. Please don't use "admin" here either! Don't use "password," "1234," or "iloveyou." A good combination of numbers, punctuation, and uppercase and lowercase letters is vital.

- **Admin Email.** Enter your own e-mail address here. If you do happen to forget your password, this is where it will be sent.

- **Admin Full Name.** Enter your own name here.

- **Site Name.** Enter **Joomlaville** here. This is what people see when they get e-mails from your site. For example, the e-mail will say "Thank you for registering at Joomlaville."

- **Install Sample Data.** Make sure that this box is unchecked. We are not going to use any sample data for our Joomla sites in this book.

Enter those details in the screen you see. It should look like the one in Figure 2.5.

Figure 2.5   Joomla installation screen in Fantastico

6. Confirm your installation details. Once you've entered all your information and clicked Install, you are taken to a confirmation screen like the one in Figure 2.6. Click Finish Installation to complete the install.

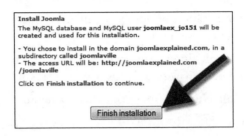

Figure 2.6   Joomla confirmation screen in Fantastico

7. Bookmark your new site addresses. You now are taken to the final Joomla screen in Fantastico. Your installation is complete. There are two links as shown in Figure 2.7.

   - The full URL to the admin area (Bookmark this!)
   - The full URL to this installation of Joomla

Take their advice and click on both links; then bookmark them in your browser. You'll be using both of those links often!

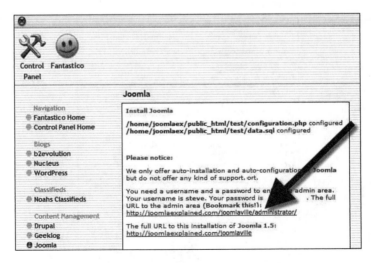

Figure 2.7   Final Joomla screen in Fantastico

8. Visit your new site. Go ahead and click the links shown in Figure 2.7. The links take you to http://www.joomlaexplained.com/joomlaville. You now see a new Web site like the one shown in Figure 2.8.

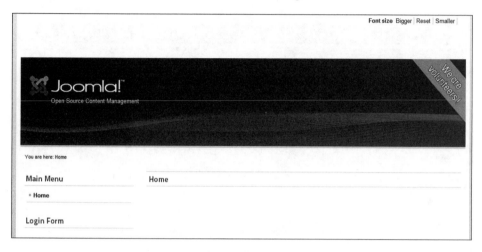

Figure 2.8   Your new Joomla site

9. Try logging in to your new site. You can log in to your site by typing in the location of your site and then the word /administrator/ at the end. So in the example you saw previously, the login area is at http://www.joomlaexplained.com/joomlaville/administrator. If you're in the right place, you should see a login screen like the one in Figure 2.9. Log in using the username and password you created earlier.

Figure 2.9   Joomla Administrator Login screen

10. View the Joomla Control Panel. If you remembered your username and password correctly, you are taken to the main control panel for your Joomla site, and it will look like the image displayed in Figure 2.10.

Figure 2.10   Joomla administrator control panel

11. Congratulations. You can now go straight to the end of this chapter. Most of the rest of this chapter is spent installing Joomla manually, but even many experienced Joomla users prefer to do things automatically using a One-Click installer.

Install Joomla Manually

An old-fashioned HTML Web site consists only of one part: files. It doesn't need anything else to run.

However, a Joomla Web site is a little different because it consists not only of files but also includes a database to store all the site's information. We're going to have to set up both the files and the database and then connect them together. So the process of installing Joomla manually is like this:

Step 1: Create a database.

Step 2: Download the Joomla files and upload them to the Web server.

Step 3: Complete the Joomla installation by connecting the database and files together.

Step 1: Create a Database

Our first step is going to be to create a database to store all the unique information about our site.

Joomla uses a particular type of database known as MySQL. Like all other databases, MySQL is basically a group of tables with letters and numbers stored in its rows and columns. Think of it as several spreadsheets. There's a spreadsheet with all the articles you write. There's another for all the users who register on your site. The database makes it easy for Joomla to handle large amounts of data. If a new article or user is added, Joomla just needs to add an extra row to the appropriate spreadsheet.

Let's go ahead and set up a database for our new Joomla site:

1. Log in to your Web hosting account. Each hosting account looks a little different, but there are often similarities. CPanel and Plesk are two popular types of software used for hosting accounts. In this example we're going to use CPanel, as shown in Figure 2.11.

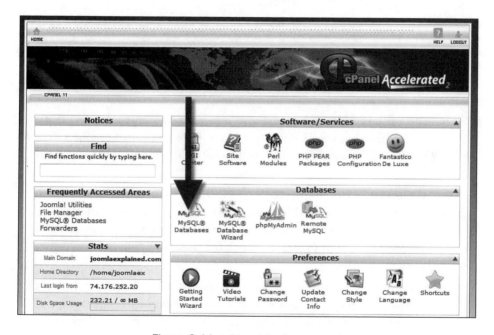

Figure 2.11   CPanel hosting account

2. Find the button that says MySQL Databases and click it. The button may be on any of the rows, but you can normally spot it by looking for the MySQL name and the blue dolphin logo (see Figure 2.12).

Figure 2.12   MySQL Databases button

3. Create a new database. Choose a name that is relatively easy to remember and click Create Database. Be sure to write down this name and note that it's likely to have your hosting account name before it. In Figure 2.13, our new database is called joomlaex_joomla.

Figure 2.13   Create a new database

4. Create a database user. Our next step is to create a user account so that we can access the database. Without password protection, anyone might be able to log in and see our site's important information. Here's what you need to do:

- **Choose a username.** Enter a short username here, different from anything you've used before. In this example, I'm using dbuser. The username is a little confusing because our hosting account name is added also, so in Figure 2.14, our full username will be joomlaex_dbuser.

- **Choose a password.** Some versions of CPanel help you choose a password that is difficult to guess. If you set your own, please use a combination of numbers, punctuation, and uppercase and lowercase letters so that the password is hard to guess.

- **Be sure to record both your username and password safely.** You're going to need them again soon.

- **Click Create User.** You should see a message saying the user has been created successfully.

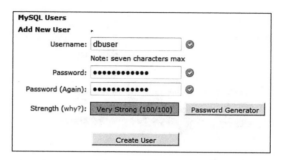

Figure 2.14   Creating a new database user

5. Allow the new user access to the database. Now we need to allow our new user to be able to log in to the database. There should be an area called Add User To Database. Choose your database name and then your username before clicking Add as in Figure 2.15.

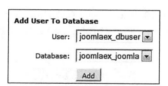

Figure 2.15   Adding user to database

6. Give our user permission to modify the database (see Figure 2.16). The final step in this process is to decide what our new user can and cannot do with the database. We're going to give them All permissions so that our Joomla site can make whatever changes it needs to the database. Click on Make Changes to finish the process.

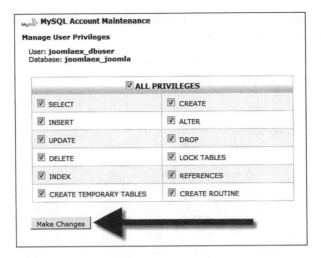

Figure 2.16   Giving user permissions to modify the database

Step 2: Download the Joomla Files and Upload Them to Our Web Server

Now that we have the database ready, we're going to upload the Joomla files. These contain all the code and images that Joomla needs to run.

1. Find the Joomla download area. Go to http://www.joomla.org and click on the Download Joomla Get the Latest Version button (see Figure 2.17).

Figure 2.17   Download Joomla button

2. Find the Joomla download link. You now see a page with two download links as shown in Figure 2.18. Click on the ZIP link next to Full Package.

Figure 2.18   Download Joomla link

3. Download Joomla. Click on the ZIP link, and a download starts. You receive a .zip file with a name like this: Joomla_1.6.0-Stable-Full_Package.zip. It contains all the files you need to install Joomla, so look after it! Save it to your desktop, your downloads folder, or somewhere you can find it easily.

4. Uncompress the .zip file. On a Windows computer you can right-click on the file and choose Extract Here. On a Mac you can click on File then Open With and choose Archive Utility. When that's complete you should have a folder on your desktop.. The folder will have a name similar to Joomla_1.6.0-Stable-Full_Package. To make sure that you have the correct folder, open it, and the contents should look like Figure 2.19. To make this process easier, let's rename the folder to something easier and simpler than Joomla_1.6.0-Stable-Full_Package. To rename the folder, right-click on the folder icon and change the name to /joomlaville/.

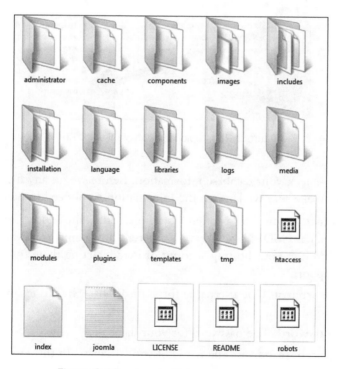

Figure 2.19   Joomla files on your computer

5. Access your Web server. We're now going to start the process of moving our files onto our Web server.

   The first step is to open your FTP software, such as Filezilla. Then log in to your FTP account and browse to the folder where you want to install Joomla. Often this is the root directory, which has a name such as /public_html/, /www/, or /htdocs/.

6. Move the Joomla files to your Web server. Select the folder that you just downloaded, extracted, and renamed. Move them via your FTP software into the folder where you're installing Joomla. With Filezilla this is as simple as dragging-and-dropping the files as shown in Figure 2.20. Uploading might take from 5 to 30 minutes or more depending on the speed of your Internet connection.

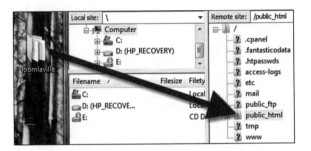

Figure 2.20   Uploading Joomla files by FTP

7. Double-check your database information. Before we go any further, let's stop to make sure we have all the information we'll need in Step 3:

   - **Host name.** This is often "localhost," but some hosting companies such as GoDaddy will have a different host name. You'll be able to find it in your hosting account or by contacting their customer support.
   - **Username.** The username for your database. In this example it was joomlaex_dbuser.
   - **Password.** The password for your database.
   - **Database name.** The name of your database. In this example it was joomlaex_dbuser.

   Got all that? Then let's move on to Step 3 and wrap up your Joomla installation.

Step 3: Complete the Joomla Installation by Connecting the Database and Files Together

We've now successfully set up the two halves of our Joomla site: the database (Step 1) and the files (Step 2). Our final step is to connect those two halves together. Let's do that now:

1. Joomla Web Installer Step 1: Language. Start your browser and visit the URL where you uploaded the files. In the example I've been using, that was to http://www.joomlaexplained.com/joomlaville/.

   You should see an installation screen like the one in Figure 2.21. This is the first step in Joomla's easy-to-use installation manager. There are seven steps to go through. The first one is simple: You just need to choose the main language for your Web site and then click Next.

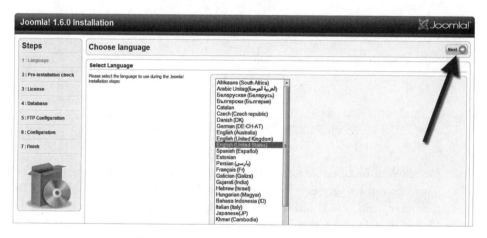

Figure 2.21   Joomla Web Installer Step 1

2. Joomla Web Installer Step 2: Pre-Installation Check. This step verifies whether your hosting account is correctly set up to run Joomla. You see a screen like the one in Figure 2.22. If items are marked with a green Yes or On, then they're fine. However, if items are marked with a red No or Off, you may need to fix them.

   The items at the top are essential, and Joomla can't run unless they're green. The items at the bottom are recommended but not essential: Joomla will still run if they're red.

What do you do if items are red? The bad news is that you can't fix many of these problems, even if you were a geek genius because many hosting companies won't give you access. The good news is that the solution is easy: Copy-and-paste the items in red into a support ticket and ask your hosting company to fix them.

When the essential settings are green, click Next to move on.

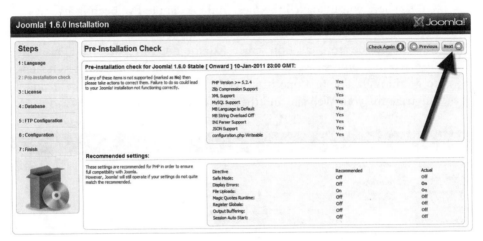

Figure 2.22   Joomla Web Installer Step 2

3. Joomla Web Installer Step 3: License. Your screen will look like Figure 2.23. This step can be very easy: You simply need to click Next and move on. On the other hand, you could stop to read the 2,978 words of the license that Joomla uses. In short, that license is called the General Public License (GPL) and allows you to reuse Joomla for anything you want. There's just one major limitation: You can't pass on Joomla to someone else and impose extra restrictions. You have to be as nice to other people as Joomla is to you.

4. Joomla Web Installer Step 4: Database. This is the most important step. This is where you connect your files and database together. For this step, we're going to need the details we collected when we created the database earlier. You see a screen like Figure 2.24, and most of the six fields will be similar:

   - **Database Type.** Leave this as the default setting.
   - **Host Name.** Enter the details you collected earlier.
   - **Username.** Enter the details you collected earlier.
   - **Password.** Enter the details you collected earlier.

- **Database Name.** Enter the details you collected earlier.
- **Table Prefix.** For security reasons it is good to change this away from _jos to something unique.

Click Next when you're done. If you've made a mistake, Joomla sends you back here to try again.

There are also some advanced settings. If you already have a database installed with information inside, you can use these settings to make sure Joomla doesn't overwrite that older data.

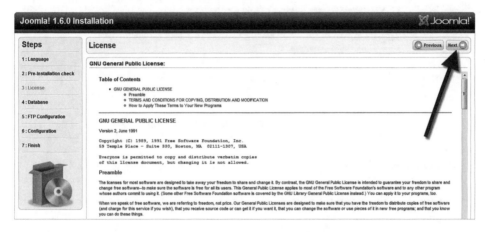

Figure 2.23   Joomla Web Installer Step 3

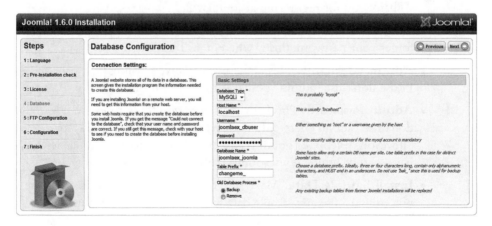

Figure 2.24   Joomla Web Installer Step 4

5. Joomla Web Installer Step 5: FTP Configuration (see Figure 2.25). It is nearly always best to skip Step 5 and just click Next.

    If you're later having problems uploading files to Joomla, you can go back and fix this. Otherwise it's better left empty for security reasons: It's not ideal to have your hosting account login details stored this way.

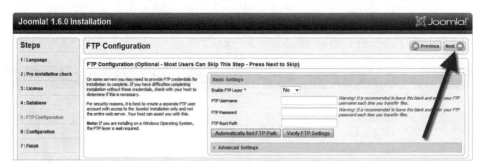

Figure 2.25   Joomla Web Installer Step 5

6. Joomla Web Installer Step 6: Configuration. The screen shown in Figure 2.26 is the final place where you need to enter any information. Please be sure to make a careful note of the e-mail, username, and password that you enter:

    - **Site Name.** Enter **Joomlaville** here. This is what people see when they get e-mails from your site. For example, the e-mail will say "Thank you for registering at Joomlaville."

    - **Your Email.** Enter your own e-mail address. If you do happen to forget your password, this is where it will be sent.

    - **Admin Username.** This is the username you will use on your site. Please don't use "admin" as that is too easy for other people to guess.

    - **Admin Password.** This is the password you'll use to log in. Please don't use "admin" here either! Don't use "password," "1234," or "iloveyou." Plenty of good free password generators are available. We have a list at http://www.joomlaexplained.com/passwords.

    - **Install Sample Data.** Make sure that this box is unchecked. We are not going to use any sample data for our Joomla sites in this book.

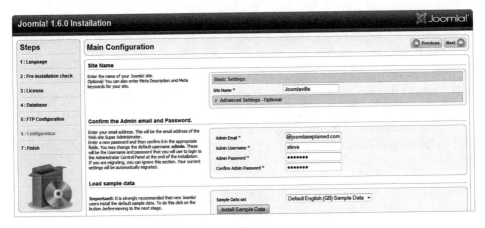

Figure 2.26   Joomla Web Installer Step 6

7. Joomla Web Installer Step 7: Finish. You've finished the Joomla Web installer and you should see a screen like Figure 2.27! Just a couple more things, and then you can log in and start working with Joomla.

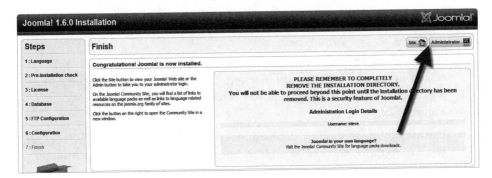

Figure 2.27   Joomla Web Installer Step 7

8. Delete the installation folder.

Notice that big red message in Figure 2.27?

"PLEASE REMEMBER TO COMPLETELY REMOVE THE INSTAL-LATION DIRECTORY. You will not be able to proceed beyond this point until the installation directory has been removed. This is a security feature of Joomla!"

We need to listen to Joomla's advice here. The reason behind this is that someone might be able to go through the installation process after us and mess with our site. We need to burn our bridges.

Remember when we logged in to our FTP program such as Filezilla to upload the Joomla files? We need to log in there just one more time. Click on the joomlaville folder, and you should see a list of all the folders and files we uploaded earlier. This time select the /installation/ folder and click Delete (see Figure 2.28).

Figure 2.28   Delete the installation folder.

9. Go visit your new site! Go to the location where you installed Joomla, which in the preceding example was http://www.joomlaexplained.com/joomlaville/. You now can see a Web site like the one shown in Figure 2.29.

Browse around and enjoy the feeling. Over the next few chapters you learn what everything does. Make sure to bookmark this page in your browser so that it's easy to find.

Also go ahead and add the word **/administrator/** to the end of your site name, for example: http://www.joomlaexplained.com/joomlaville/administrator. If you're in the right place, you'll see a login screen like the one in Figure 2.30. Log in using the username and password you created a few steps earlier.

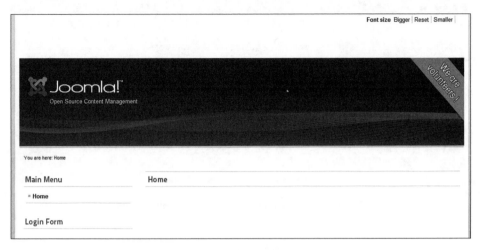

Figure 2.29   Your new Joomla Web site

Figure 2.30   Joomla Administrator Login screen

10. View the Joomla Control Panel. If you remembered your username and password correctly, you'll be taken to the main control panel for your Joomla site, and it will look as shown in Figure 2.31.

11. Pat yourself on the back! You've just installed your first Joomla site!

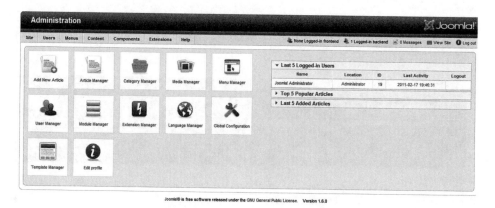

Figure 2.31   Joomla Administrator Control Panel

Get Help If You're Stuck Installing Joomla!

There are three places I recommend going for help if you get stuck at any point during this chapter:

- **The Joomla Forum.** It's almost guaranteed that someone has experienced the same Joomla installation problem as you and has asked about it on http://forum.joomla.org. It's a great place to search for solutions and ask for help.

- **The Joomla help site.** There's an installation manual available for Joomla 1.6 at http://docs.joomla.org.

- **JoomlaExplained.com.** The site has video tutorials and more to help with your installation.

What's Next?

You now have a Joomla site ready to use. It should like Figure 2.32.

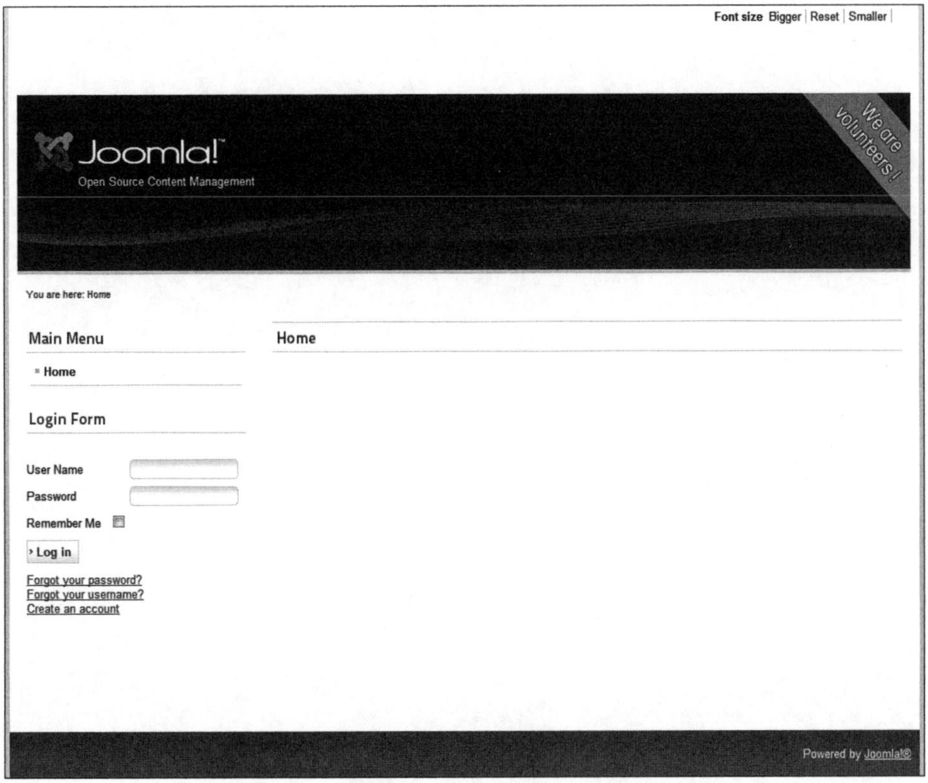

Figure 2.32 Your Joomla site at the end of Chapter 2

In the next chapter, we introduce you to the most important things you need to know about your new site. We also make the first changes to the site. Are you ready? Turn the page, and let's get started.

3

Joomla! Sites Explained

This chapter explains the basic concepts of your Joomla site. After you've finished this chapter, you'll understand how users see your site and how administrators manage your site.

Things You Can Do After Reading This Chapter

- Understand the two areas of your Joomla site
- Understand the visitor area of your Joomla site
- Understand the administrator area of your Joomla site
- Make your first Joomla site changes
- Know the following words:

    Article

    Extension

    Component

    Template

    Module

    Plug-in

Understand the Two Areas of a Joomla Site

Every Joomla Web site has two areas: a public area for visitors and a private area for administrators.

Visitor Area

Absolutely everything you want visitors to see on your site can be accessed from here.

You can always access the visitor area simply by visiting the Web address where you installed Joomla. You should see the same Web site as in Figure 3.1.

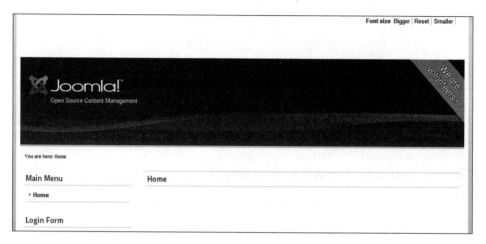

Figure 3.1   The visitor area of your Joomla site

Administrator Area

The other half of your Joomla site is the private area for administrators. Absolutely everything you want to change about your site can be changed from here. It is the Control Panel of your site, where you go to add content, create navigation, or modify your site layout.

This area is always accessible by adding /administrator/ to your site's home page. So if your site was http://joomlaexplained.com/joomlaville, you'd add /administrator to visit the administrator area. Thus, you'd type in http://joomlaexplained.com/joomlaville/administrator.

You see a login screen like the one in Figure 3.2. Enter the username and password you created in Chapter 2, "Joomla Installations Explained," during the final stages of installing your site.

If you've lost those details already (pay more attention at the back), you can click Go to Site Home Page and then click either Forgot Your Password? or Forgot Your Username? on the left-hand side.

Figure 3.2   The administrator login for your Joomla site

Once you've logged in, you are taken to the screen in Figure 3.3. This is your top secret headquarters. This is the main Control Panel for your entire site. Absolutely everything you want to change about your site can be changed from here.

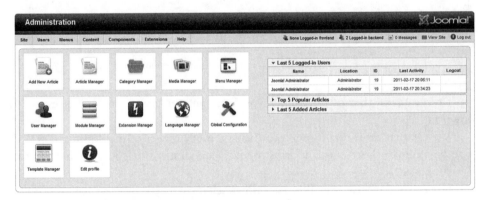

Figure 3.3   The administrator area of your Joomla site

In this chapter, you get an overview of both areas of your Joomla site, and we start right here in the administrator area.

Understand the Administrator Area of Your Joomla Site

In the administrator area of your Joomla site, you see four distinct sections outlined in Figure 3.4:

1: Drop-down menu. This has all the key links you need to manage your site.

2: Quick links. This allows you to easily logout or click View Site to see the public area of your site.

3: Latest updates. This area includes information about what's currently happening on your site.

4: Short-cuts. These buttons give you quick access to really common administrator tasks like adding a new article.

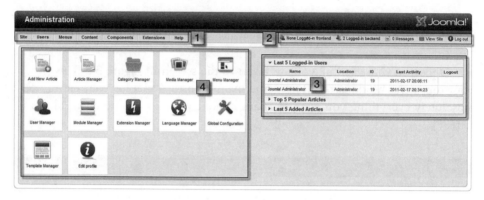

Figure 3.4   The four sections of your Joomla administrator area

I recommend that, as a beginner, you focus all your attention on the drop-down menu.

We use that drop-down menu to manage every aspect of our Joomla site. The quick links, short-cuts, and latest updates are all just other ways of getting to the same place.

Hover your mouse over the drop-down menu, and you see the same options as in Figure 3.5.

Figure 3.5   The administrator drop-down menu

Because the drop-down menu is so important, we base this entire book on it. Every time we ask you to visit a page in the administrator area, we go via this drop-down menu. The drop-down menu contains the following options:

- **Site** (Chapter 16). Contains all the main configuration options for your site. The good news is that most of these configuration options will be set up correctly when you first install your site.

- **Users** (Chapter 14). Contains one of the major new features in Joomla 1.6. Here you can give different permissions to different users and groups of users. For example, if you are running a school Web site, you could decide that the history teacher could only write articles about history, the science teacher could only write about science, and the sports teacher could only enter game results.

- **Menus** (Chapter 6). Contains the navigation for your visitors. Remember the menu links you were clicking on in the visitor area of the site? We can control and create these from this area.

- **Content** (Chapters 4 and 5). Contains all of your text articles. Any text you write goes here, from news and blog posts to essays and book chapters.

- **Components** (Chapter 7). The powerful extra features you can add to your site. Social networking, photo galleries, shopping carts, event calendars, and much more are all called components.

- **Extensions**. The extra features you can add to your site. The Extensions drop-down menu includes links to the following types of extensions:

    - **Module Manager** (Chapter 8). Modules are the small boxes around the outside of your site. They show visitors little snippets of information such as the latest or most popular five articles.

    - **Plug-in Manager** (Chapter 9). Plug-ins are tiny scripts that make small improvements to your site. One example of a plug-in adds a small row of stars to the top of articles so that visitors can vote for articles. Another example loads a small piece of code to protect e-mail addresses from spammers.

    - **Template Manger** (Chapter 10). Templates are the design of your site. If you want a red, blue, pink, green, yellow, white, or orange site, you need to find a template of the right color.

- **Language Manager** (Chapter 15). Joomla has been translated into more than 40 languages. You can upload Spanish, French, German, Japanese, Arabic, and many other languages. All Joomla's site functions will be automatically translated. However, you still need to manually translate any articles you write—Joomla isn't that clever unfortunately.

- **Help**. Provides answers to your questions. I hope this book is useful, but you're certain to have more questions that we can't answer here. The Joomla Help link leads to documentation you can view inside your site. The other links take you to the most important parts of the official Joomla site, http://joomla.org.

Things You'll See All the Time in Joomla

It's confusing when things change. The good news is that Joomla is good at keeping things consistent. There are many things you'll see all the time in Joomla. The following sections discuss some examples.

Language

Joomla uses similar language on each page. For example, you see the phrase "… Manager" ten times in just those seven drop-down links. This makes it easy for you to navigate your way around. If you want to manage anything on your Joomla site, you know where to go:

- If you want to manage your articles, go to the Article Manager.
- If you want to manage your users, go to the User Manager.
- If you want to manage your menus, go to the Menu Manager.
- If you want to manage your languages, go to the Language Manager.

I could go on, but you get the picture.

Page Layouts

Joomla also uses similar layouts for every page you visit from the drop-down menu. For example, take a look at Joomla's Article Manager by clicking on Content and then on Article Manager as in Figure 3.6.

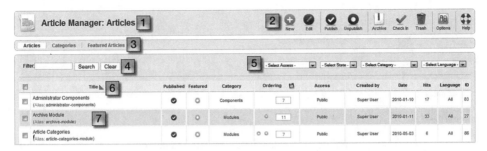

Figure 3.6   Joomla's Article Manager

You see the following:

1: Page title. This tells you where you are in your administrator area.

2: Action buttons. These buttons allow you to modify any of the items you see.

3: Submenu. These links give you access to important, related parts of your administrator area.

4: Search box. This searches for the title of something and allows you to quickly find what you're looking for.

5: Filters. These are preset searches. They filter out the content, allowing you to focus your search.

6: Column titles. These are clickable titles you can use to sort the items you are looking at. For example, click on Title to search alphabetically or Date to search chronologically.

7: Items. These vary throughout the site and can be many different things, depending on what part of the site you are currently using. For example, if you are in the User Manager, the items show the users. If you are in the Menu Manager, this shows the menus, and if you are in the Article Manager, this shows the articles as in Figure 3.6.

Next, visit Joomla's Template Manager by clicking on Extensions and then Template Manager. You see a screen like the one in Figure 3.7.

Let's take a look at one more example. Go to Joomla's User Manager by clicking on Users and then User Manager. The screen you see looks like Figure 3.8 and should be increasingly familiar.

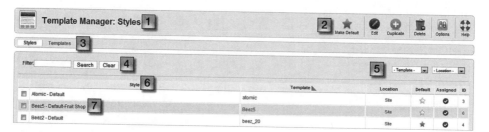

Figure 3.7   Joomla's Template Manager

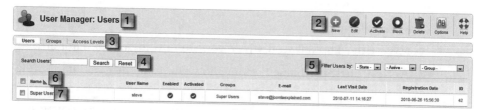

Figure 3.8   Joomla's User Manager

Go ahead and click on some other links, especially those under Components and Extensions. You see the same layout almost everywhere you go. Hopefully this makes your life easier in several ways:

- **Not sure where you are?** Look at the title and submenu.
- **Can't find an item?** Just use the search box or the filters.
- **Need to modify or create an item?** Look for all the action buttons in the top-left corner.

Individual Page Layouts

It's not only the pages from the drop-down menu that nearly always look the same. When you click through to an individual page, the layout is also consistent.

Let's go back to Joomla's Article Manager by clicking on Content, then Article Manager, and finally Administrator Components. When you open it, the page looks like Figure 3.9.

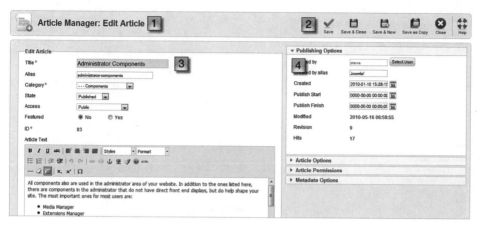

Figure 3.9   Joomla's Article layout

You see the following:

1: Page title. This tells you where you are in your administrator area.

2: Action buttons. These buttons allow you to modify any of the items you see.

3: Most important content. This is why you're visiting this part of the site. For example, if you're in an article, this will be the main article text. If you're in a user's profile, this will be the user's name, e-mail, and password. If you're in a menu link, this will be the text people click on and the URL the link will send them to.

4: Extra options. These are extra settings, but they're not as important as those on the left-hand side. For example, one option in an article may allow you to turn voting on or off. Another example is an option in a contact form to show or hide the e-mail address that the e-mail will be sent to.

Let's also go back to Joomla's Template Manager by clicking on Extensions, then Template Manager, and finally Beez2 – Default. You see a screen like the one in Figure 3.10.

Let's take a look at a final example. Go back to Joomla's User Manager by clicking on Users, then User Manager, and finally Super User. The screen you see looks like Figure 3.11.

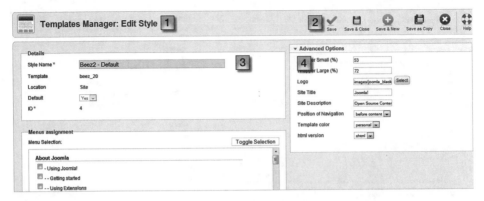

Figure 3.10   Joomla's Template layout

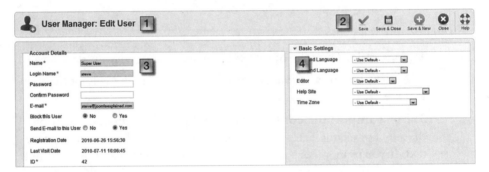

Figure 3.11   Joomla's User layout

Joomla is easy to use because it's consistent:

- **Not sure where you are?** Look at the title.

- **Need to modify this page?** Look for all the action buttons in the top-right corner.

- **Need to edit the important parts of the page?** Look to the left-hand side.

- **Need to make a small tweak to the page?** Look to the right-hand side.

Now that we've seen the administrator area in more detail, let's look at the visitor area.

Understand the Visitor Area of Your Joomla Site

This visitor area is why you build your site. It shows all the information that you want to share with people.

Your visitor area looks similar to Figure 3.12.

Figure 3.12   The visitor area of your Joomla site

Every Joomla page is put together using several types of extensions. Currently you're able to see two types of extensions, modules and templates:

- **Template: Beez2.** You're currently using this blue and white design.

- **Module: Breadcrumbs.** Remember the Hansel and Gretel fairy tale? They used a trail of breadcrumbs to find their way home. The small You are here: Home text shows where you are on the site.

- **Module: Main Menu.** This menu links to information about your site.

- **Module: Login Form.** This allows people to log in and to also register and recover lost account details.

All these items in your visitor area can be modified, moved, or replaced from your administrator area.

Earlier in this chapter we saw that the administrator area is where you change your site. Now that we've seen that the visitor area is what you change on your site, let's go and actually make our first changes.

To make changes, we need to go the administrator area. To do this, add /administrator to your site's URL or click on your bookmark for the Joomla administrator area.

Make Your First Joomla Site Changes

Now that you know a little about navigating through the Joomla administrator area, let's see how easy it is to make some changes to your site.

Changing Your First Article

Let's add a welcome article on the visitor page so that people can find out about your city.

1. In the drop-down menu, click on Content, then Article Manager, and then click on New. You see a screen like the one in Figure 3.13. This is where you will write all your articles in Joomla.

Figure 3.13   Creating a new Joomla article

2. There are only three settings that we need to use for this article:

   1: Title. A good choice would be "Welcome to Joomlaville."

   2: Featured. Select Yes so that this will appear on the front page.

   3: Article Text. http://www.joomlaexplained.com/chapter3 has some text that you can use for this article. You can copy and paste the text from that site into your new article. Before you do so, I have a note of caution: Copying and pasting text is always somewhat tricky. Some programs such as Microsoft Word are notorious for creating a lot of bad formatting with their articles. My suggestion would always be to type directly into Joomla. However, if you do copy-and-paste, always start by copying from the article and pasting into a text editor like WordPad or Notepad. That clears away the formatting. You can then copy the code out of the editor and paste into Joomla.

Figure 3.14 shows you how your screen looks once these three settings are applied.

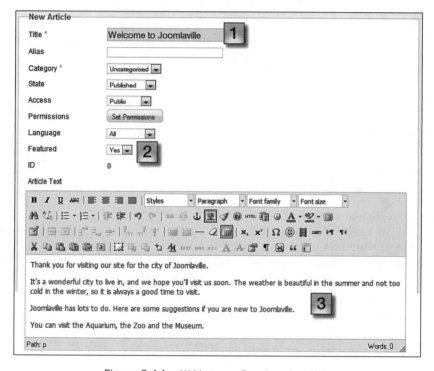

Figure 3.14   Writing your first Joomla article

3. When you're happy with the article, click Save & Close in the top-right corner. This saves all the changes you made.

4. Then in the very top-right corner, above the Save & Close button, click on View Site. This sends you to the visitor area of your site. You can see both the Save & Close and the View Site buttons in Figure 3.15.

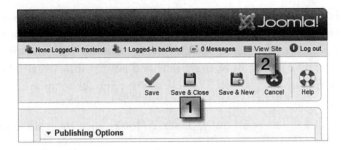

Figure 3.15   Saving your first Joomla article

In the visitor area, you now can see your first Joomla article live on your site. Figure 3.16 shows how it will appear.

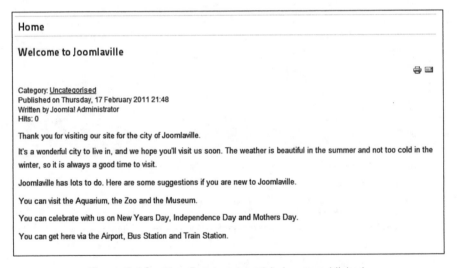

Figure 3.16   Your first Joomla article is now published.

Great! You now know how to welcome people to your new Joomlaville site. However, the heading across the top of the site still reads "Joomla! Open Source Content Management." Let's go ahead and change that to reflect our new content.

Changing Your First Template

Now let's change the design of the site so that visitors can clearly see the word Joomlaville.

1. Go back to the administrator area of your site.

2. In the drop-down menu, click on Extensions and then Template Manager.

3. Either click on the Beez2-Default name or select the box next to Beez2-Default and click Edit in the top-right corner. You see a screen like Figure 3.17.

Figure 3.17   Editing a Joomla template

4. On the right-hand side under Advanced Options there are several things you can change. Here are some first steps:

   - **Logo.** Click Clear to remove the Joomla logo from the header.

   - **Site Title.** Enter **Joomlaville**.

   - **Site Description.** Enter **A great place to live!**

   Figure 3.18 shows how your screen looks once these three settings are saved.

Figure 3.18   Editing a Joomla template

5. When you're happy with the changes, click Save & Close in the top-right corner. This saves all the changes you made.

6. In the very top-right corner, above the Save & Close button, click on View Site. This sends you to the visitors area of your site.

You can see both the Save & Close and the View Site buttons in Figure 3.19.

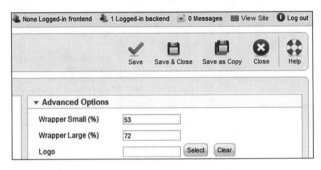

Figure 3.19   Saving your Joomla template

In the visitors area, you now can see your template changes live on your site. Figure 3.20 shows how it will appear.

Figure 3.20   Your Joomla template changes are live.

Your whole site at the end of Chapter 3 should now look like Figure 3.21.

Great! You made your first Joomla site changes. You published an article and modified the template. You're ready for the next step—to start building your first Joomla site.

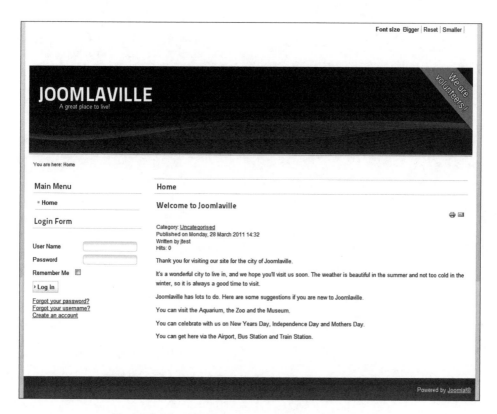

Figure 3.21   Your Joomla site at the end of Chapter 3

What's Next?

There is one indispensable workflow for building Joomla sites. If you understand the workflow and follow it, you'll find Joomla much easier than if you try to do things in any other way. This book is dedicated to teaching you that workflow.

Turn the page, and let's learn how.

4

Joomla! Content Explained

This chapter explains the easiest and fastest way to add content to a Joomla site. If you follow this workflow, it will make your Joomla life very easy.

The workflow for adding Joomla content is simple:

Step 1: Categorize. Create organization for your articles.

Step 2: Add. Write your articles.

Step 3: Show. Make menu links so that people can click through and see your articles.

I like to call this the *CASh* workflow. CASh is short for Categorize, Add, Show. It does take a little bit of practice to follow the workflow correctly. But once you run through the workflow a few times, it should become easy to add content to your Joomla site.

Things You Can Do After Reading This Chapter

- Organize your Joomla content into categories
- Add new content to Joomla
- Show your content in various ways, including a full page, a blog with intro text, or a long list of articles

Step 1: Categorize

The first step in the Joomla content workflow is to categorize our content. We need to make sure that our information can be usefully organized.

Let's think about the Joomlaville project we started in the previous chapters. What do we need to include on the Web site for our visitors? To plan our site's organization, grab a piece of paper and a pen and brainstorm.

Go ahead and write down all the articles you want on your site. For this small site, your list might look like this one:

Joomlaville Overview

Joomlaville Location

Joomlaville History

Museum

Zoo

Aquarium

New Year's

Independence Day

Mother's Day

Train Station

Bus Station

Airport

Now that we know what information we want to have on our site, let's organize it. Joomla uses categories to organize articles. Let's create one category for each group of related articles and name it appropriately.

About

Joomlaville Overview

Joomlaville Location

Joomlaville History

Attractions

Museum

Zoo

Aquarium

Festivals

New Year's

Independence Day

Mother's Day

Transport

Train Station

Bus Station

Airport

We can then draw a table so that we can see which articles are in which categories. Figure 4.1 shows how this table would look.

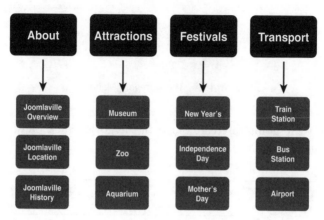

Figure 4.1   The categories and articles for our first Joomla site

Things can get much more advanced, but this is a nice straightforward example to get us started.

Now that we've finished our plan, we are ready to start implementing that plan in Joomla. We use the CASh workflow to create the first category called About and the three articles inside called Joomlaville Overview, Joomlaville Location, and Joomlaville History. Here's the process we use:

Step 1: Categorize. Create the About category.

Step 2: Add. Write your three articles.

Step 3: Show. Make menu links so that people can click through and see your articles.

Ready? Let's get started and use Joomla's CASh workflow for the first time:

1. Go to your administrator area and then click on Category Manager under the Content drop-down. You'll see a page like the one in Figure 4.2. Uncategorized is already an option. The Uncategorized category is used for articles that really don't fit inside any other category. It's most commonly used for small sites with only five or six articles. With so few articles, you wouldn't really need to divide them into categories. However, we're going to have at least a dozen articles, so we need to create categories.

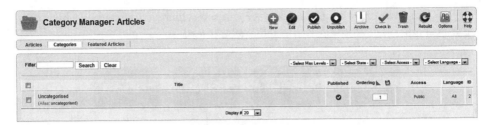

Figure 4.2   The Category Manager

2. Because we're going to create our own categories, click New, which is on
    the left in Figure 4.3.

Figure 4.3   Creating a new category

3. To get started, we only need to fill in one field: Title. The text in this field
    should simply be **About**. However, to help our visitors, it might be worth
    entering a short description, explaining what's in this part of the site. For
    example, you could say *This category contains information about Joomlaville.*

    Your category should look like Figure 4.4.

4. Click Save & Close. You should see that your category has been added as in
    Figure 4.5.

    Now that we have a category to organize our articles, let's go and write
    those articles.

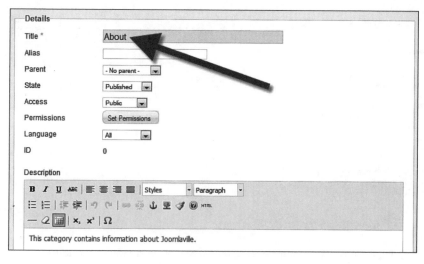

Figure 4.4   Creating a new category

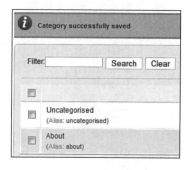

Figure 4.5   Your new category

Step 2: Add

To start writing, click on Article Manager under the Content drop-down. You should be looking at a page like the one in Figure 4.6.

Remember earlier when we said that all the important stuff was on the left-hand side? That's true almost everywhere in Joomla, and it's true here. You can ignore the right-hand side for now.

Figure 4.6   This is the screen you always see when writing new articles.

There are only three fields you must fill in, and they are on the left-hand side: Title, Category, and Article Text (see Figure 4.7).

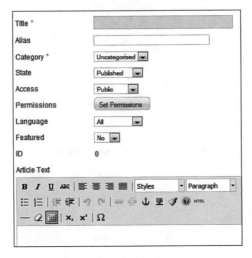

Figure 4.7   The Title, Category, and Article Text fields are required when you're writing an article.

Let's fill in those three fields from top to bottom:

1. Enter a title for your article. Let's start with the first article on our list, Joomlaville Overview. Type that into the Title field as shown in Figure 4.8.

When you save the article, the Title is copied automatically into the Alias field. This Alias field forms part of the URL, so our Joomlaville Overview will have a URL that contains joomlaville-overview. You can find out more about how Joomla creates URLs in Chapter 16, "Joomla Site Management Explained."

Figure 4.8   Writing a title for your article

2. Now place this article into the correct category. Click the Category drop-down and choose the About category that you created earlier (see Figure 4.9).

Figure 4.9   Choosing a category for your article

3. Finally, write the article. Put your cursor into the large text area at the bottom and start typing as shown in Figure 4.10. There is some sample text at http://www.joomlaexplained.com/chapter4 that you can use for this article.

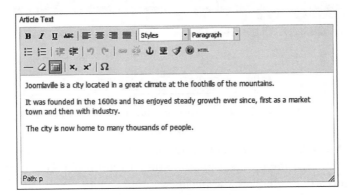

Figure 4.10   Writing your Joomlaville Overview article

4. Click Save & Close, and your Joomlaville Overview article will be complete.

Let's go ahead and repeat that process again for the article titled Joomlaville location. Here are the details for our second article in the About category:

1. **Title:** Joomlaville Location

2. **Category:** About

3. **Article Text:** Describe where the city is. There is some sample text at www.joomlaexplained.com/chapter4 to help you out.

When you've filled in those three fields, your article should look like the one in Figure 4.11.

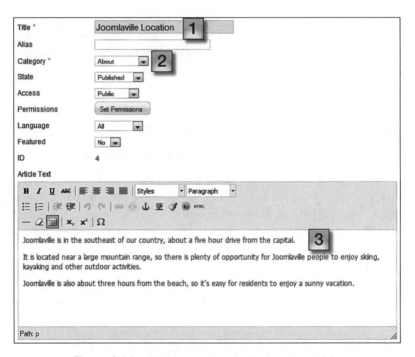

Figure 4.11   Writing your Joomlaville Location article

Click Save & Close to finish creating this article.

Let's go through the process one more time to finish our About category with the third article. Here are the details we use:

1. **Title:** Joomlaville History

2. **Category:** About

3. **Article Text:** As before, there is some sample text at www. joomlaexplained.com/chapter4 to help you out.

Our Joomlaville History article should look like Figure 4.12.

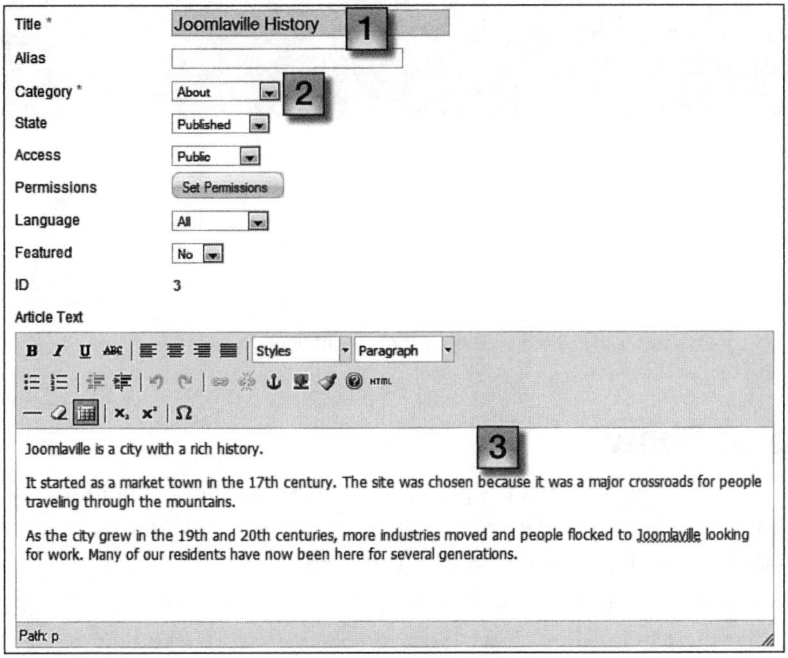

Figure 4.12   Writing your Joomlaville History article

Click Save & Close to finish creating this article.

Wonderful! We now have one new category on our site called About, and it contains three new articles: Joomlaville Overview, Joomlaville Location, and Joomlaville History.

There's only thing left to do.

Go and visit the front of your site. Have a look at your site and Figure 4.13. What's missing?

You can't see your new articles anywhere!

One solution would be to choose Featured for these articles so that we could see them on the front page. However, imagine what will happen when you have 100 articles or more—you can't put them all on the front page. We need another solution. That solution is to create menu links to the articles.

We've done two steps of our Joomla workflow: Categorize and Add. The third and final step is Show.

Figure 4.13   The visitor area of your Joomla site

Step 3: Show

To see pages on any Web site, people need to click through to them.

Joomla is no different. We need to allow people to click and see our articles. We do that by making menu links to the articles:

1. In the main drop-down on your administrator area, click on Main Menu under the Menus drop-down, and you a see a screen like Figure 4.14. This is the Menu Manager, and currently it's showing the links in your Main Menu.

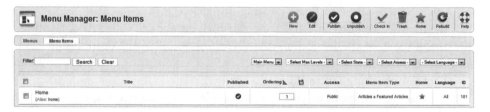

Figure 4.14   The Menu Manager showing the Main Menu
of your Joomla site

Let's go ahead and create some more menu links in our Main Menu. We're going to link to the articles we created earlier.

2. In the Main Menu screen (refer to Figure 4.14), click New in the top-right corner. You see a screen like Figure 4.15. Whenever you create a menu link to any part of your site, you'll always see this same screen. To get started, click Select next to Menu Item Type.

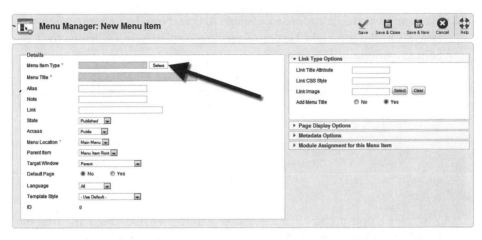

Figure 4.15   Creating a new Joomla menu link

3. You see a pop-up screen like in Figure 4.16 with all sorts of different options. Each one allows you to link to a different part of your Joomla site. You could link to a contact form, a search box, a registration form, or many other things. We want to link to one of the articles we created earlier, so choose Single Article.

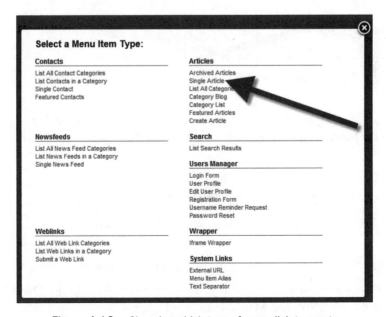

Figure 4.16   Choosing which type of menu link to create

4. We have just chosen to link to a Single Article. Now let's choose *which* article. On the top-right corner of the screen, click Select/Change to Select Article as in Figure 4.17.

Figure 4.17   Choosing on the Select/Change button to choose which article to link to

5. You'll see a pop-up box like the one in Figure 4.18. Go ahead and find the Joomlaville Overview article that you wrote earlier. Click on the Joomlaville Overview name.

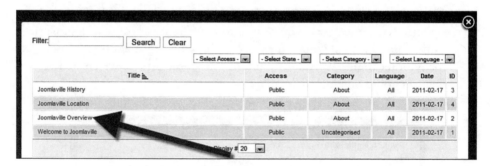

Figure 4.18   Choosing to link to the Joomlaville Overview article

6. After clicking the article name, you should see the screen in Figure 4.19. Enter **Joomlaville Overview** in the Menu Title field.

Figure 4.19   Choosing a title for your menu link

7. Click Save & Close to complete the creation of your menu link.

8. Visit the front of your site, and you see your new Joomlaville Overview link on the left in the Main Menu (see Figure 4.20).

Figure 4.20   Your new menu link

9. Click on the Joomlaville Overview link, and you see your new article published on your site as in Figure 4.21.

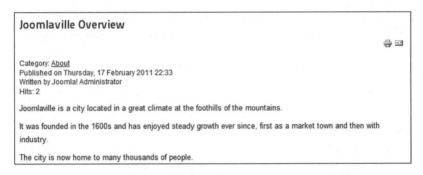

Figure 4.21   Your Joomlaville Overview article published on the site

That's it. You've done it! Both you and your visitors can see that new article on your site.

Now that we've created a menu link once, let's go back and do it again while it's still fresh in your mind. Let's link to our Joomlaville Location article. Go ahead and follow these steps:

1. Click on Main Menu under the Menus drop-down.

2. Click New in the top-right corner on the main menu page.

3. Click Select next to Menu Item Type, and you see a pop-up screen.

4. Click on Single Article in the pop-up screen.

5. On the right-hand side, click Select/Change next to Select Article.

6. You see a pop-up. Go ahead and find the Joomlaville Location article that you wrote earlier. Click on the Joomlaville Location name.

7. Enter **Joomlaville Location** in the Menu Title field.

8. Click Save & Close to complete the creation of your menu link.

9. Visit the front of your site and see your new Joomlaville Location link on the left in the Main Menu.

10. Click on the Joomlaville Location link, and you see your new article published on your site as in Figure 4.22.

Figure 4.22   Your Joomlaville Location article published on the site

Congratulations, you've done it again! You and your visitors can see two of your new articles on the site.

You've done great so far. Are you feeling brave? I'm going to set you a challenge: See if you can make a menu link to your Joomlaville History article. You're going to follow exactly the same process as we just did for the Joomlaville Location article. Figure 4.23 shows the end result that we're aiming for. If you get stuck, the specific steps you should take to complete this task are at www.joomlaexplained.com/chapter4.

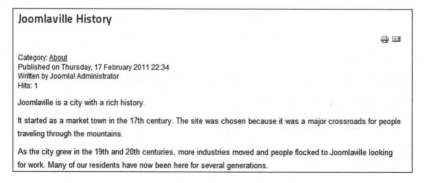

Figure 4.23   Your Joomlaville History article published on the site

The Joomla CASh Workflow—Why Do It This Way?

Step 1: Categorize

Step 2: Add

Step 3: Show

Those are three steps for adding content to a Joomla site.

However, why is it this way? Why not make our menu links first? Why not write our articles first? Why bother making links at all?

Here are answers to some of the questions you might have at the moment:

- **Why not make our menu links first?** Because we wouldn't have anything to link to. We wouldn't have any articles to show.

- **Why create our categories first?** Imagine you build a big Joomla site. You might be planning 50, 500, or even 5000 articles. I've seen Joomla sites with more than 100,000 articles. How would you organize that many articles? Categories allow us to organize all our articles. Our restaurant review goes in the Restaurants category. Our Zoo article goes in the Attractions category. We don't have to get them mixed up.

- **Why bother making links at all?** Remember when we first added our articles but couldn't see them on our site? Menu links are what allows people to see our articles. If people can't click through to the articles, they can't see them.

We regularly meet Joomla students who have tried to teach themselves and got stuck. Most of the time it's because they didn't know about this workflow:

- Some of them tried to make their menu links first and wondered why they had so few choices.

- Some people wrote all their articles first and then ended up with a big mess of unorganized articles.

- Some people added their categories and articles and then stopped. They looked at their site and got frustrated because they couldn't see what they'd written.

Follow the workflow, and creating your Joomla content will be easy. Here it is one more time:

Step 1: Categorize. Create categories so that you can organize your articles.

Step 2: Add. Write your articles.

Step 3: Show. Make menu links so that people can click through and see your articles.

Now that we've learned the Joomla CASh workflow, let's practice it.

Practicing the CASh Workflow

Think back to the categories and pages we planned earlier:

About
Joomlaville Overview
Joomlaville Location
Joomlaville History

Attractions
Museum
Zoo
Aquarium

Festivals
New Year's
Independence Day
Mother's Day

Transport
Train Station
Bus Station
Airport

We've done that first category, and here's what we're going to do now. We're going to give you a full step-by-step guide to creating the Attractions category, articles, and menu links. Then we're going to let you try and do the Festivals and Transport categories by yourself. I've provided sample text for all of them at http://www.joomlaexplained.com/chapter4.

Step 1: Categorize

1. Go to Category Manager under the Content drop-down menu and click New.

2. Enter **Attractions** in the Title field and click Save.

Step 2: Add

1. Go to Article Manager under the Content drop-down menu and click New.

2. Enter **Museum** in the Title Field.

3. Choose Attractions from the Category drop-down.

4. Copy and paste the text from www.joomlaexplained.com/chapter 4 into your article.

5. Click Save & New and then add the Zoo and Aquarium articles. After the final article, click Save & Close.

Step 3: Show

1. Go to Main Menu under the Menus drop-down and click New.

2. Click Select next to Menu Item Type, and you see a pop-up screen. Click on Single Article.

3. On the right-hand side, click Select/Change next to Select Article.

4. You see a pop-up. Go ahead and find the Museum article that you wrote earlier. Click on the Museum name.

5. Enter **Museum** in the Menu Title field.

6. Click Save & New to complete the creation of your menu link.

7. Now add the Zoo and Aquarium articles. After the final menu link, click Save & Close.

8. Visit the front of your site, and you see your three new menu links on the left in the Main menu.

Now that you've finished using the CASh workflow, your Main Menu should look like Figure 4.24. Click on the links, and you see all the articles you've written.

Figure 4.24   Your Attractions articles published in your Main Menu

Congratulations. Hopefully that wasn't too bad! If you're ready, let's see if you can do that again but without step-by-step directions.

Your task is to create the Festivals and Transport categories, articles, and menu links. If you get stuck, don't worry. Full instructions are online at http://www.joomlaexplained.com/chapter4.

When you are done, your Main Menu should look like Figure 4.25.

Main Menu

- Home
- Joomlaville Overview
- Joomlaville Location
- Joomlaville History
- Museum
- Zoo
- Aquarium
- Airport
- Bus Station
- Train Station
- New Years Day
- Mothers Day
- Independence Day

Figure 4.25   Your Festivals and Transport articles
published in your Main Menu

If we take a step back and look at your whole site, it should look like what you see in Figure 4.26.

Figure 4.26   Your Joomla site at the end of Chapter 4

Congratulations! You've done an excellent job to get this far, and by understanding the CASh workflow you've unlocked the key to building a Joomla site.

If you put this chapter down and don't remember anything but Joomla's CASh workflow, you'll be in good shape. Write it down, print it on a T-shirt, sing it in the shower, tattoo it on your arm, or do whatever else you need to do to remember it. This is how you add content to your Joomla site:

Step 1: Categorize. Create categories so that you can organize your articles.

Step 2: Add. Write your articles.

Step 3: Show. Make menu links so that people can click through and see your articles.

What's Next?

We now know how to organize, create, and show our articles.

That's great, but currently those articles aren't very interesting. The articles are just plain text—there's no formatting, no images, and no links to other pages. That's the problem we're going to solve in Chapter 5, "Joomla Content Editing Explained."

Turn the page to learn how to create articles with formatting, images, links, and more.

5

Joomla! Content Editing Explained

We currently have about a dozen articles on our site. It's now time to make those articles more interesting. In this chapter, we focus on making your articles more exciting. Specifically, we work on formatting the text, adding images and links, and choosing the best publishing, article and metadata options for your articles.

Things You Can Do After Reading This Chapter

- Format the text of your Joomla articles
- Add images to your content
- Add links between different articles and to other sites
- Choose the best publishing, article, and metadata options for your articles

Formatting Your Text

In the previous chapters, we added articles to our site. However, we only wrote in plain text. We didn't use any bold text, italics, bullet points, or indeed any type of formatting.

Fortunately formatting text is easy in Joomla. If you can do formatting in your e-mail or in Microsoft Word, you can do it in Joomla.

Let's start by editing our front page article "Welcome to Joomlaville." Go to Content, then Article Manager, and then Welcome to Joomlaville. It should look like the screen shown in Figure 5.1.

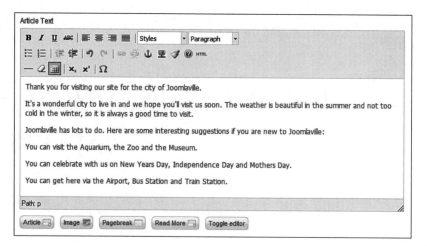

Figure 5.1   Our Welcome to Joomlaville article

Your formatting options are all above the text. Let's take a closer look at them. The buttons are in Figure 5.2, and many will be familiar if you've done any word processing before. The workflow is simple: Select text you want to format and then click the formatting button.

Figure 5.2   Joomla article formatting buttons

The Joomla formatting buttons work in the same way as e-mail and Microsoft Word buttons. Let's show you how to use them.

To start, we're going to look at the first set of buttons that include **B**, *I*, U̲, A̶B̶C̶, and more.

Bold, Italic, Underline, and Strikethrough

Here's an example of how to use the formatting buttons to make some text bold:

1. Using your cursor, select the first text in the article: "Thank you for visiting our site for the city of Joomlaville."

2. Choose the **B** button in the top-left of the formatting options. This is the button to make your text bold. As you're doing this, your screen looks like Figure 5.3.

Figure 5.3   Adding bold formatting to Joomla text

3. When you're finished, your text will be in bold as shown in Figure 5.4.

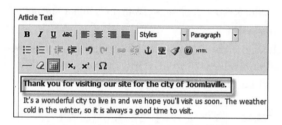

Figure 5.4   Joomla text with bold formatting added

Let's repeat that process but with the italics option. Here's how we do it:

1. We need to highlight the text we want to format. Start by selecting the word "wonderful." Why? Because our city of Joomlaville is really, really wonderful, we want to highlight that word.

2. Click on the *I* button in the top-left of the formatting options. This is the button to make your text italic. As you're doing this, your screen looks like Figure 5.5.

Figure 5.5   Adding italic formatting to Joomla text

3. When you're finished, your text will be in italic as in Figure 5.6.

Figure 5.6   Joomla text with italic formatting added

We can do the same thing with the U (underline) and ~~ABC~~ (strikethrough) buttons. Go ahead and select some text and then click on those buttons. You should get a result like Figure 5.7.

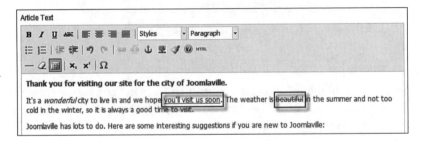

Figure 5.7   Joomla text with underline and strikethrough formatting added

Aligning Your Text

Next up is the option to align your text. You can choose from left, center, and right alignments. As before, select the text you want to align and click the appropriate button. Your results will look like Figure 5.8.

Finally, along the top row are the Style and Format options. Style only has a couple of features that are difficult to use at the beginner level, so for now let's focus on Format, a much more useful option. The Format feature allows you to create headings and subheadings in your text.

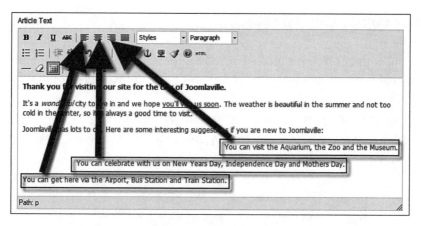

Figure 5.8   Joomla text aligned left, center, and right

For example, the second half of the Welcome to Joomlaville article we are working with deals with suggestions for site visitors. We can put a subheading in there to break up the text and make it easier to read. Here's how we do it:

1. Use normal text to write your subheading. For this example, we write "Joomlaville Visitor Suggestions" and then select it.

2. Click the drop-down that has Paragraph as the first choice. Scroll down in the drop-down and select Heading 2. We choose Heading 2 because Heading 1 is normally associated with the article title—the most important heading on the page. When formatting headings, it can be useful to have a line space above and below the text you're formatting; otherwise, you might accidentally format the lines above and below also. As you're doing this, your screen looks like Figure 5.9.

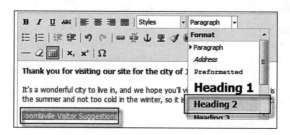

Figure 5.9   Adding a heading format to Joomla text

3. You should now see "Joomlaville Visitor Suggestions" in larger text.

Bullet Points and Indentation

The first thing you see on the second row of formatting options is the ability to make bullet points. You can make either an unordered list with bullet points or an ordered list with numbers. The process is similar to the previous ones: Select and click:

1. Highlight all the suggestions for Joomlaville visitors.

2. Choose the unordered bullet list. As you're doing this, your screen looks like Figure 5.10.

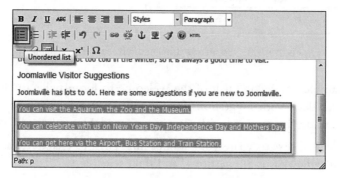

Figure 5.10   Adding bullet points to Joomla text

Your results will look like Figure 5.11.

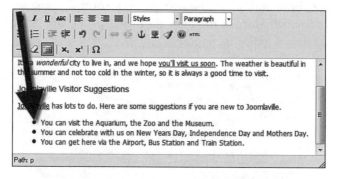

Figure 5.11   Joomla text with bullet points

You also have the option to indent sections of text. Because text indentation is often used for quotes, we use quotes as our example here. We're going to add a quote from a resident of Joomlaville:

1. First, write a subheading at the bottom of your article. For example: **"A Quote from a Joomlaville Residents."**

2. Highlight your subheading.

3. Choose Heading 2 from the Format drop-down. As you're doing this, your screen looks like Figure 5.12.

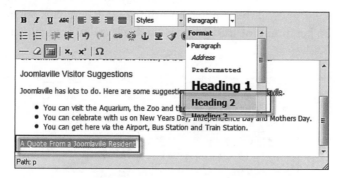

Figure 5.12   New Joomla subheading

4. Enter a quote from a resident. For example, I'm going to use this line: **"I love living here. Homes are cheap and there are lots of nice parks for our children."**

5. Highlight your entire quote.

6. Choose the second of the two indent buttons. As you're doing this, your screen looks like Figure 5.13.

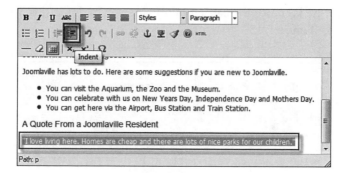

Figure 5.13   Indenting a quote

What if I Made a Mistake?

There's no need to worry if you made a mistake while working on your article. There are two ways you can undo any mistake:

Option 1: The Undo button. Click on the back arrow, the Undo button, which is in the middle of the second row. Clicking this will undo the last change you made. It has a long memory, so you can keep clicking and undoing changes all the way back to the point where you opened the article at the beginning of this chapter. The back arrow is highlighted in Figure 5.14.

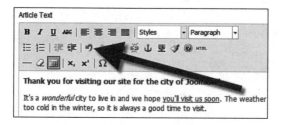

Figure 5.14   Using the Undo button

Option 2: The Remove Formatting button. Unlike the Undo button, this works on any text whether or not you changed it during this particular session. The process for removing formatting is the same as for adding formatting:

1. Highlight the text you want to return to plain text.

2. Choose the Remove formatting button. As you're doing this, your screen looks like Figure 5.15.

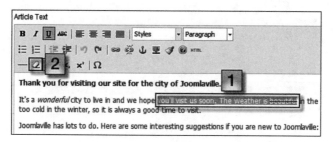

Figure 5.15   Using the Remove Formatting button

Finally, let's see what our article looks like live on the site. Click Visit Site in the top-right corner, and you see your article on the front page (see Figure 5.16).

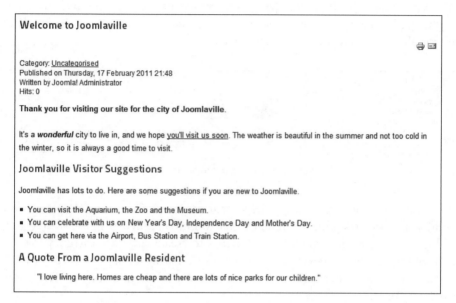

Welcome to Joomlaville

Category: Uncategorised
Published on Thursday, 17 February 2011 21:48
Written by Joomla! Administrator
Hits: 0

Thank you for visiting our site for the city of Joomlaville.

It's a **wonderful** city to live in, and we hope you'll visit us soon. The weather is beautiful in the summer and not too cold in the winter, so it is always a good time to visit.

Joomlaville Visitor Suggestions

Joomlaville has lots to do. Here are some suggestions if you are new to Joomlaville.

- You can visit the Aquarium, the Zoo and the Museum.
- You can celebrate with us on New Year's Day, Independence Day and Mother's Day.
- You can get here via the Airport, Bus Station and Train Station.

A Quote From a Joomlaville Resident

"I love living here. Homes are cheap and there are lots of nice parks for our children."

Figure 5.16   Seeing your first formatted article

We formatted our text some, but the article still looks a little plain. That may be because it lacks images. Let's add some images to our Joomlaville articles and show our visitors what Joomlaville looks like.

Adding Images to Your Content

Remember the CASh workflow we used in Chapter 4, "Joomla Content Explained," to add content?

1. Categorize
2. Add
3. Show

We use exactly the same CASh workflow for adding images.

Categorize Images

To categorize our articles, we went to Content and then Category Manager. To categorize our images, we now go to Content and then Media Manager.

When you're in the Media Manager, you see a screen like the one in Figure 5.17. It contains all the images you uploaded to your site. At the moment, all you should see are a few sample images.

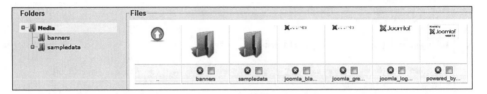

Figure 5.17   The Media Manager

Next, we create some categories so that we can organize our images. If we build a large site, it's going be much easier to find a particular image if they are all logically organized. One logical choice is to create an image category for each of our article categories. For our example, that means all the images we use in our Attractions articles go into an image folder of the same name. Here's how we create that folder:

1. Enter the folder name **"attractions"** into the "create folder" field at the bottom-right of the screen. I recommend using all lowercase letters with no spaces or punctuation.

2. Click Create Folder. As you're doing this, your screen looks like Figure 5.18.

Figure 5.18   Creating folders in Media Manager

3. Repeat the process until you have one image folder for each article category. For our example, you would create image folders called festivals, about, and transport. Your screen should look like Figure 5.19.

You can also add your images via the Media Manager using the Upload files area at the bottom of the page. However, it's possible and even easier to upload your image files when you're writing your articles.

Figure 5.19 New folders in Media Manager

Before we leave the Media Manager screen, let's turn on a feature that allows bulk uploading of images. Here's how we do it:

1. Click Options in the top-right corner of the Media Manager.

2. Set Enable Flash Uploader to Yes and click Save, as in Figure 5.20.

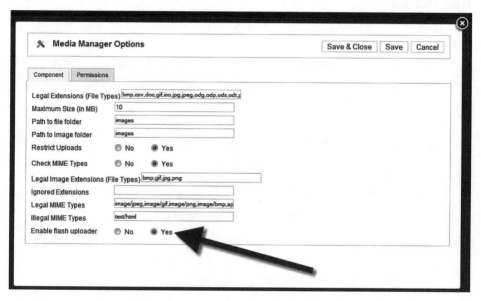

Figure 5.20 Enabling the bulk upload of images

You'll know you've enabled the Flash Uploader for bulk uploads of images successfully if you see a new version of the Upload Files area on your screen as shown in Figure 5.21.

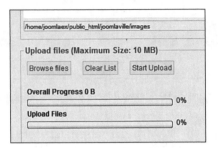

Figure 5.21   Joomla's bulk uploader for images

Add Images

Let's start by opening our Welcome to Joomlaville article and getting an image ready to place inside it:

1. Go to Content, then Article Manager, and then Welcome to Joomlaville.

2. Go to http://www.joomlaexplained.com/chapter5, and you see an image called Town Hall.

3. Download the Town Hall image to your desktop. To do this, click the Download link under the image. Some computers automatically download the image file to your desktop. On other computers you see the image and need to right-click on it and use the "Save Image As" option to download it to your desktop. Before you move on, check to make sure that the image has actually been downloaded to your computer.

Now we can upload and add that image to our article. Here's how we do it:

1. Select the place where you want to insert the image. Do this by putting your cursor into the text at the appropriate point.

2 Click the Image button below the article. As you're doing this, your screen looks like Figure 5.22.

3. You see a pop-up screen like the one in Figure 5.23.

4. To upload your own images, click Browse Files at the bottom of the pop-up screen as in Figure 5.24. Then choose your image from the desktop.

5. Click Start Upload.

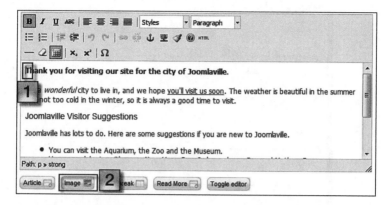

Figure 5.22   Using the Image button inside Joomla articles

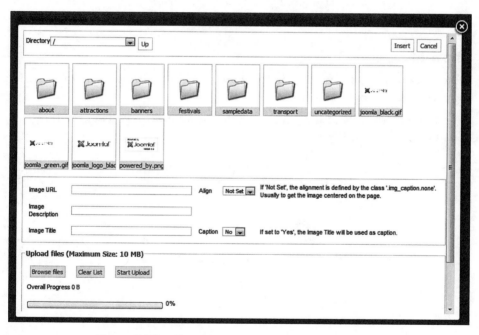

Figure 5.23   Choosing an image to insert into an article

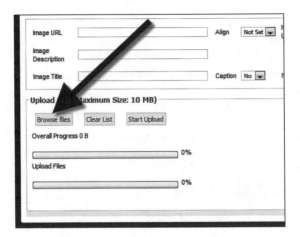

Figure 5.24   Browsing for an image

Show Images

Now that our images have been uploaded to our Joomla site, we can start insert-ing them. Here's how we do it:

1. Click on the townhall.jpg image so that its location appears in the Image URL field as in Figure 5.25.

Figure 5.25   Choosing your new image

2. There are now four options for you to choose, as seen in Figure 5.26. Here's what they do:

- **Image Description.** This appears if people are browsing your site with images turned off. I normally use a short, accurate description of the image. In this case, I use "Joomlaville Town Hall."

- **Image Title.** This text pops up when you hover over an image. I often use exactly the same text as for the Image Description.

- **Align.** This is similar to the text alignment we did earlier. If you set this to Right, your image will be on the right side of the page, and the text will wrap around to the left. If you set this to Left, your image will be on the left of the page, and the text will wrap around to the right.

- **Caption.** If you set this to Yes, then the text in Image Title will appear directly under your image.

Figure 5.26   Setting the options for your new image

3. Now we can finish inserting the image by clicking Insert as in Figure 5.27.

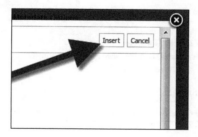

Figure 5.27   Inserting your new image

4. You should now see the image inside your article as in Figure 5.28.

5. Click Save and then Visit Site so you can see how your new image looks to visitors. It should look like Figure 5.29.

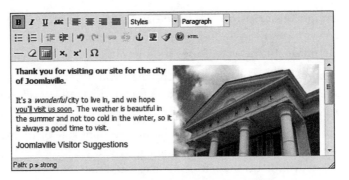

Figure 5.28   An image placed inside a Joomla article

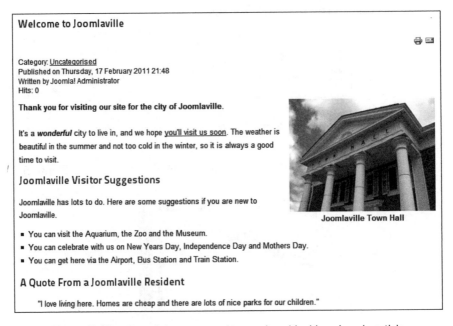

Figure 5.29   How visitors see an image placed inside a Joomla article

What If I Made a Mistake?

If you don't like the size of the image or how it's placed in your article, you have three ways to fix the mistake:

1. **Resize the image.** You can dynamically resize images inside your article. Click the image inside your article, and you see a small square on each

corner and edge of the image. You can click on these squares and drag them to resize the image as shown in Figure 5.30.

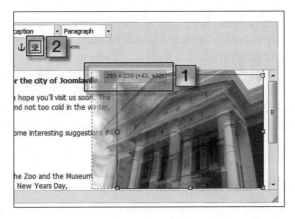

Figure 5.30   Resizing an image inserted into an article

2. **Change the image options.** Click the image inside your article, and the small picture button becomes highlighted as shown previously in Figure 5.30. Click on that button, and you see a pop-up screen where you can edit the image settings as in Figure 5.31. You can edit alignment, width, and height. It may take a couple of trials before you get the image placed in the position you want it to appear for visitors.

Figure 5.31   Editing your image settings

3. **Delete the image.** You might decide to remove this image entirely. To do this, as in the first two options, click the image inside your article, and you see a small square on each corner of the image. Now click the Delete or Backspace button on your keyboard.

So we now have a formatted article with images. However, there are still many more useful things we can do with our content.

To take just one example, we have sentences like this on our site's home page: "You can visit the Aquarium, the Zoo and the Museum."

However, how do visitors find the information pages for the Aquarium, Zoo, or Museum? They need links to those pages, and that's what we're going to do next.

Adding Links to Your Content

There are three types of links that you can add to your Joomla articles:

- **Internal links.** Links to other articles on your Web site.
- **External links.** Links to pages on other people's Web sites.
- **Internal article links.** Links that divide up the article you're reading.

Let's see how to make all three types of links.

Internal Links

Let's start by editing the article we've been using throughout this chapter: "Welcome to Joomlaville." Go to Content, then Article Manager, and then Welcome to Joomlaville.

The process for adding links to text is the same as for adding formatting: Select and then Click.

1. Select the text that you want to be linked. In this example, let's choose the word "Aquarium."

2. Click the Article button below the article. As you're doing this, your screen looks like the one in Figure 5.32.

3. You see a pop-up window with a list of all your articles. Find the article you want to link to and click on the article title. It should look like Figure 5.33.

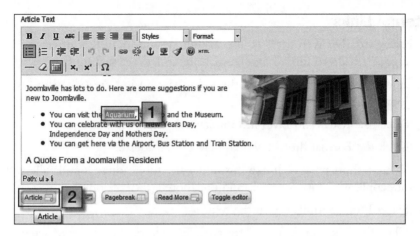

Figure 5.32   Inserting an internal link into an article

Figure 5.33   Choosing which article to link to

That's it. There will now be a link to the article you chose. Two things to note:

- If the article title is different from the text you selected, the article title will be used. If you don't want to use the article title, you can put your cursor on the text and edit it.

- These links won't work in the Article Editor, but they will when you go to the visitor area of your site.

Now see if you can add more links to our Welcome to Joomlaville articles. Go ahead and add links from these words to the appropriate articles: Zoo, Museum, New Year's Day, Independence Day, Mother's Day, Airport, Bus Station, Train Station.

External Links

For linking to other Web sites, we use a different button. In this article, we also need a good reason to link to an external site, so let's set that up first:

1. Add a new subheading under the links that you just created: Who Lives in Joomlaville?

2. Select the text: Who Lives in Joomlaville?

3. Click the Format drop-down and choose Header 2.

4. Write a short paragraph like this under the subheading: Joomlaville is full of people who love Joomla! Find out more at http://joomla.org.

5. Select http://joomla.org in the text.

6. Click the link icon in the editor area. Just before clicking, your screen looks like Figure 5.34.

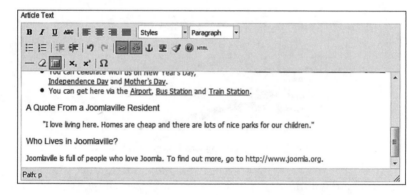

Figure 5.34   Adding an external link from a Joomla article

7. You see a pop-up screen like the one in Figure 5.35. Go ahead and enter the URL of the page you want to link to. The most accurate way to do this is to visit the page you want to link to and copy and paste the URL. The text in the Title field is what appears if people hover over the link.

8. Click Insert to create the link.

You can now click Save to save all your new links. Also click Visit Site in the top-right corner of the screen to see all your links. It should look like Figure 5.36.

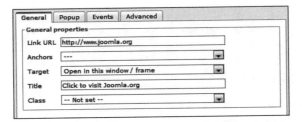

Figure 5.35   Entering an external link

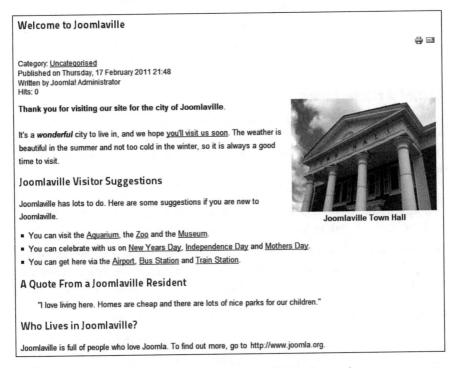

Figure 5.36   A Joomla page with links inserted

What If I Made a Mistake?

The process for removing an incorrect link is similar to the process we've been using so far: Select and Click.

1. Select the text you want to remove the link from.

2. Click the small unlink icon in the editor area. As you're doing this, your screen should look like Figure 5.37.

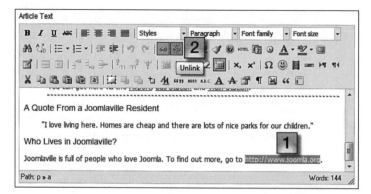

Figure 5.37   Removing a link from a Joomla article

Internal Article Links

In addition to the internal links to our site's pages and external links to other sites' pages, there is one more type of link we can create.

If we have a long article, we can divide it into different sections to make it easier to read.

There are two ways we can do this:

- **Pagebreak.** Divides one article into separate pages such as Page 1, Page 2, Page 3. Pagebreak links are ideal for use with very long articles.

- **Read More.** Divides a single article into a teaser text and the rest of the article. Visitors have to click on the internal Read More link to view the rest of the article. Read More links are ideal for news and blog articles.

Both of these are set up using the workflow we used earlier:

1. Put your cursor in the text where you want to split the article.

2. Choose either Pagebreak or Read More at the bottom of the article, and a dotted line is inserted into the article where your cursor is placed. As you're doing this your screen looks like Figure 5.38.

Unlike Read More internal links, which only allow you to insert one per article, you can insert as many Pagebreaks as you want. Each time you insert a new Pagebreak, Joomla shows a pop-up screen that asks you what you want the new page to be called. Give the new page an appropriate title. If you are unsure of what title to give it, add page 1, page 2, page 3, and so on to the article's title.

Figure 5.38   Inserting a Pagebreak link or a Read More link

After inserting a Read More or Pagebreak link, you see a dotted line inside your article, as shown in Figure 5.39.

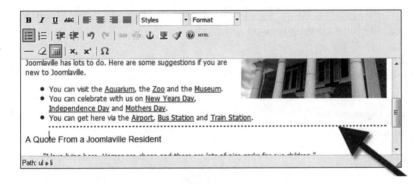

Figure 5.39   A Read More link inside an article

The Read More link creates teaser text as shown in Figure 5.40. It's an ideal solution for the front page of your site because it means you can show many articles without needing to show every last word of every article.

Let's see the steps needed to add a Read More link to the Welcome to Joomlaville article:

1. Put your cursor where you want the teaser to end and the Read More link to appear, essentially where you want to split the article.

2. Select the Read More button at the bottom of the article. A dotted line is inserted into the article where your cursor is placed.

Save the article and go to the visitor area. The screen your visitors see will looks like Figure 5.40.

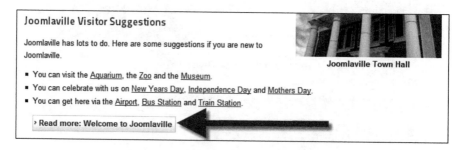

Figure 5.40   A Read More link in a Joomla article

Examples of Pagebreak links are Table of Contents links and Previous and Next links. Figure 5.41 shows what an article looks like with these two Pagebreak links inserted. It should be noted though that unlike the Read Move links, these Pagebreak links are not suited for the front page of your site. They are, however, more ideal for long, insed pages on your site.

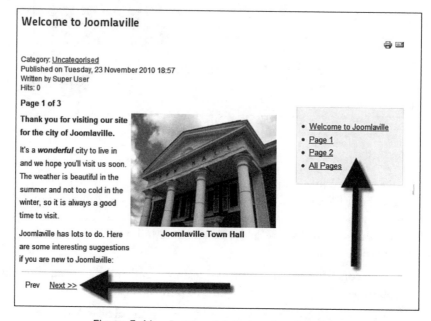

Figure 5.41   Pagebreak links in a Joomla article

What If I Want to Remove a Link?

If you want to remove either a Read More or Pagebreak link, do the following:

1. Put your cursor into your article, just after the Read More or Pagebreak line.

2. Press the backspace or back button on your keyboard.

This can be a little fiddly unfortunately, so after deleting the line, you may have to add some formatting again.

Now that we can create content with formatting, images, and links, there's one more thing to show you about Joomla articles: the options. These control whether information such as the author's name and the publication date appear on the page.

Choosing Your Article Options

Back in Chapter 3, "Joomla Sites Explained," we explained that all the important stuff about your Joomla site is on the left side of the page, and all the extra options are on the right.

When you are creating an article in Joomla, there are three types of options we can change. These options are located on the right-hand side of your article. You can see them in Figure 5.42.

- **Publishing Options.** These control when your article will be published and who is shown as the author.

- **Article Options.** These options control the information about the article that is displayed to visitors.

- **Metadata Options.** These help search engines categorize and display your pages.

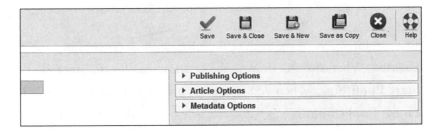

Figure 5.42   Options on a Joomla article

Let's see how to configure all these options.

Publishing Options

Learning how to do what's in this Publishing Options part of the chapter is useful but not essential for the site we're building during this book.

On the right-hand side under the Publishing Options tab, there are options for how to display the article author's name:

- **Created by.** This option allows you to choose which user is displayed as the author of an article. By default the author is the person who created the article. Click on Select User to choose another user to be shown as the author.

- **Created by alias.** This option allows you to override the author setting with any text you choose.

There are also options for when to publish the article. For example, if you have information about the New Year's Party in Joomlaville, you might want to unpublish it automatically on January 1st. After all, you don't want to be getting out of bed early just to unpublish it. Let Joomla do the hard work. The process of automatically unpublishing an article is simple: Just click on the small calendar icon next to Finish Publishing and choose a date. As you're doing this, your screen looks like Figure 5.43.

Figure 5.43   Automatically unpublishing an article

More specifically, there are three options for when to publish the article:

- **Created.** What date will show as the creation date for the article?

- **Start Publishing.** When will the article first be published on your site?

- **Finish Publishing.** When will the article be unpublished from your site?

If you leave these fields blank, the Created date will be today, and the article won't be automatically published or unpublished.

Article Options

The next set of options after Publishing options is called Article options. These control whether visitors see different types of information about your article. For example, take a good look again at your Welcome to Joomlaville article in the visitor area. You can see several extra pieces of information about the article (see Figure 5.44):

- Category: Uncategorised
- Published on Thursday, 17 February 2011 21:48
- Written by Joomla Administrator
- Hits: 0

Category: Uncategorised
Published on Thursday, 17 February 2011 21:48
Written by Joomla! Administrator
Hits: 0

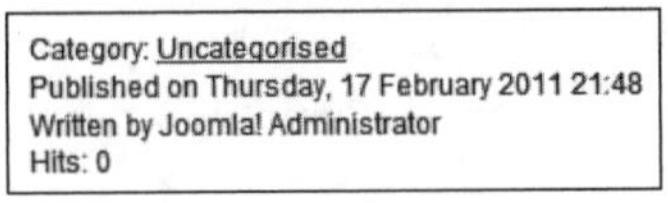

Figure 5.44   Article Options on a Joomla article

Let's look at some of these article options in more detail so that you get a better understanding of what they are and how to control them:

- **Category.** This option controls whether visitors see the category that the article is organized into.
- **Published.** This option controls whether visitors see the date when the article was published.
- **Written by Super User.** This option controls whether visitors see the article's author. Super User is the name that is given to the main site administrator account. If you are the site administrator and you choose this option, your name will be published as the author of the article. You can change the Super User name by going to the administrator area and clicking My Profile under the site link in the main drop-down menu.
- **Hits: 1.** This option controls whether visitors see how many times the article has been visited.

Whether you decide to turn these options off depends on the type of content you are writing. For our example, it's probably best to turn them off. It's not really important for visitors to the Welcome to Joomlaville page to know who wrote the article or when. However, if you are writing blog articles that contain your own strong opinions or if you are writing time-sensitive information, it's probably best to turn these options on.

Now that you have a better idea what these options do, let's see how we turn them off:

1. Click on Article Options on the right-hand side of the article, as in Figure 5.45.

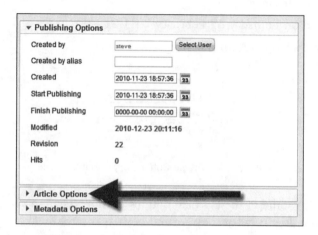

Figure 5.45   Click to open the Article Options area

2. The options tab on the right-hand side slides up and down. For example, if you click on the Article Options tab, you see a set of options that can change for the article you are viewing as in Figure 5.46.

Global Options

We can choose our options right here inside our article. However, notice that most of the options are set to Use Global. In other words, there is a default setting for all articles. By editing that, we turn off these settings in one go, rather than having to edit every article. Here's how we do it:

1. Click Save and Close, and you'll be back at the Article Manager.

2. Click Options in the top-right corner as shown in Figure 5.47.

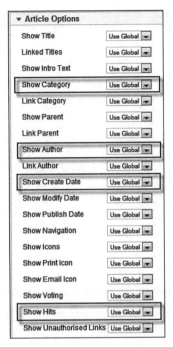

Figure 5.46   The Article Options area

Figure 5.47   The Article Options button

3. You see a pop-up screen as in Figure 5.48. This is where you can set the global options for your whole site. Turn off the author name here, and it will be turned off on every article, unless you open that article and edit that article's options, changing Global to Show.

4. Set the following to Hide:

   - Show Category
   - Show Author
   - Show Publish Date
   - Show Hits

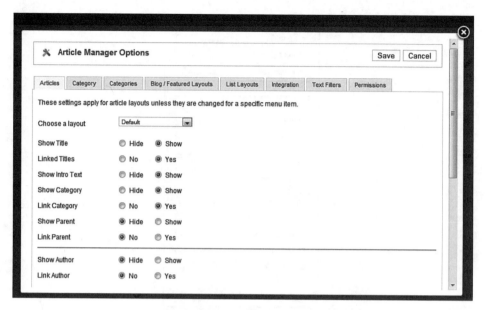

Figure 5.48   Global settings for your Article Options

5. Click Save in the top-right corner, and you'll be back at the Article Manager.

6. Click Visit Site in the top-right corner, and you should see your article with all four options disabled as in Figure 5.49.

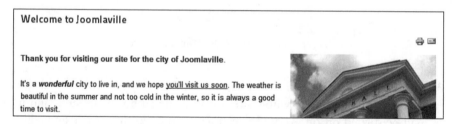

Figure 5.49   Article with options turned off

Metadata Options

Metadata options are the last set of options on the right-hand side of your articles. These options allow you to give information to the search engines about your page. Let's take a look at how we set them up:

1. Go to Content, then Article Manager, and open up your Welcome to Joomlaville article.

2. Click Metadata Options on the right-hand side, and you see an area like the one shown in Figure 5.50.

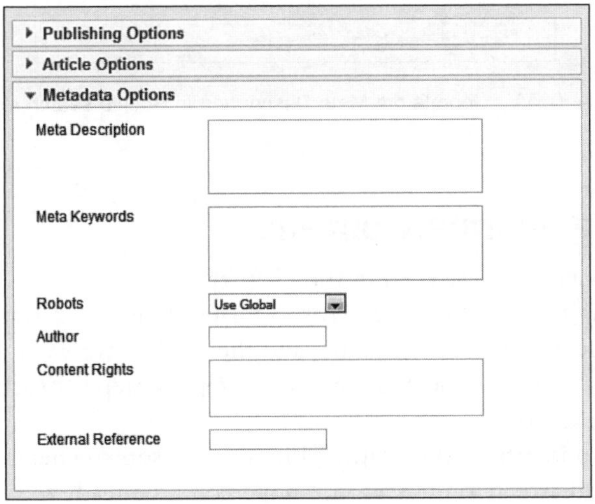

Figure 5.50   Article Metadata options

To be honest, these options have become less and less useful over the years. Previously, search engines needed a lot of help working out what your article was about. However, search engines are now smart enough to do most of that work for themselves. For example, they almost entirely ignore keywords included in your metadata because so many people tried to misuse that feature for spam. It's much more important to have keywords in your main article text instead.

For this reason, there is really only one option here that is worth spending time discussing: Meta Description. This is what may appear under your site title in the search engine results as shown in Figure 5.51. You have a maximum of about 160 characters to describe this page. Google sometimes uses this, but it's also common for Google to create its own description from the text on the page.

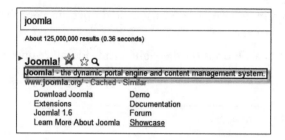

Figure 5.51   Joomla.org Meta Description in Google search results

Practicing Joomla Content

Let's practice what we've learned in this chapter.

We're going to fill in our empty Airport, Bus Station, and Train Station articles with text, formatting, images, links, and the options we want.

For the first article, Airport, there will be step-by-step instructions for everything you need to do.

For the second article, Bus Station, I'll give you some general guidance.

For the third article, Train Station, I hope you'll be ready to create that article on your own.

Airport

Let's go ahead and add some text to the Airport article. We'll then format the text and insert images and links.

1. Go to Content, then Article Manager, then Airport.

2. Go to http://www.joomlaexplained.com/chapter5, and you'll see some text called "Airport Sample Text."

3. Select that text and click Copy in your browser.

4. Paste that text into your Airport article.

After you've added the text, your article should look like Figure 5.52. Now that we have the Airport text, let's add formatting:

1. Turn Europe, Asia, Africa, and North and South America into a list of bullet points.

2. Write some subheadings. Suggestions are Terminals, Destinations, Food, and Location. As we mentioned earlier, to avoid formatting other text, make sure that you have space both above and below the headings.

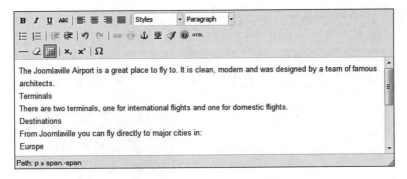

Figure 5.52   Airport article with text

3. Highlight the subheadings one-by-one.

4. Choose Heading 2 from the drop-down in the editor.

After you've added the formatting, your article should look like Figure 5.53. Now let's add an image next to our formatted text:

1. Go to http://www.joomlaexplained.com/chapter5 and download the Airport Sample Image.

2. Place your cursor in the article where you want to insert an image.

3. Click the Image button at the bottom of your article.

4. Click the Transport folder so the image will be uploaded there.

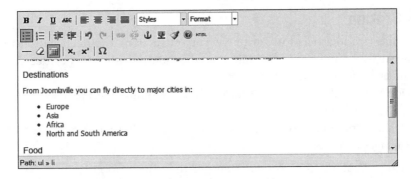

Figure 5.53   Airport article with formatted text

5. Click Browse files, select the airport image, and click Start Upload.

6. Double-click on the airport image. Enter an Image Title and Image Description; then set Align to Right and Caption to Yes. Click Insert.

After you've added the image, your article should look like Figure 5.54.

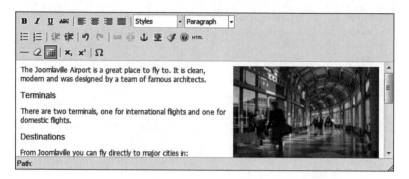

Figure 5.54   Airport article with image formatted text

Finally, let's add some links into our Airport article:

1. Highlight the text for Zoo in the Airport article.

2. Use the image button below the article. Find and click on the Zoo article name (created in Chapter 4).

3. Now, click Save & Close to save your changes and then click View Site in the top-right corner of the page. You can see your Airport article by clicking on the Airport menu link on the left.

Your finished Airport article should look like Figure 5.55.

Bus Station

Here's the second article for you to try. The instructions are much shorter than for the Airport article, but hopefully now that you've had more practice you will remember how to do these tasks.

Don't worry if you can't; full instructions are online at http://www.joomlaexplained.com/chapter5.

Let's add some text to the Bus Station article. We'll then format the text and insert images and links:

1. Go to Content, then Article Manager, then Bus Station.

2. Go to http://www.joomlaexplained.com/chapter5, and you see some text called "Bus Station Sample Text."

3. Add that text to your Bus Station article.

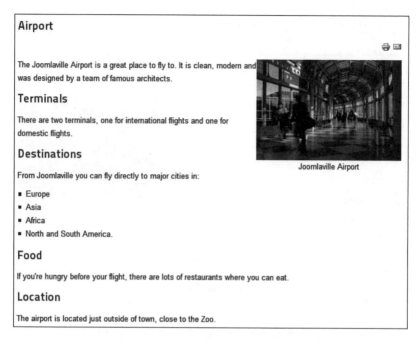

Figure 5.55   Finished Airport article

Now that we have the Bus Station text, let's add formatting:

1. Turn TV, Toilets, and Food and drink service into a list of bullet points.

2. Write some subheadings. Suggestions are Services, Schedule, Location, and Tickets and make them stand out by using the Heading 2 setting.

3. Add bold text formatting to Please Remember.

Let's add an image next to our formatted text:

1. Go to http://www.joomlaexplained.com/chapter5 and download the Bus Station Sample Image.

2. Upload the image to the Transport folder.

3. Insert the image into your article.

Finally, let's add some links into our Bus Station article:

1. Link the word Museum to the Museum article (created in Chapter 4).

2. Click Save & Close to save your changes and then click View Site in the top-right corner of the page. You can see your Bus Station article by clicking on the Bus Station menu link.

Your finished Bus Station article should look like Figure 5.56.

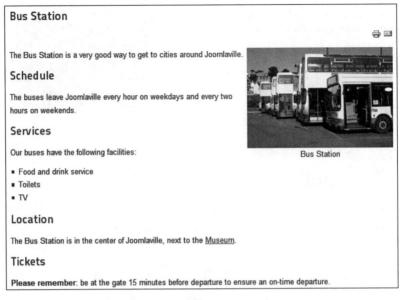

Figure 5.56   Finished Bus Station article

Train Station

Here's the third article for you to try. This time there are no instructions, but hopefully with the practice you've just done, you are feeling more confident. Again, don't worry if you can't complete the task on your own—full instructions are online at http://www.joomlaexplained.com/Chapter5.

Here are your tasks:

1. Text: Go to http://www.joomlaexplained.com/chapter5, and you'll see some text called "Train Station Sample Text." Move that text to your Train Station article.

2. Formatting: Add subheadings to your article. Add bullet points to the Types of Train, and add numbered bullet points to the Buying Tickets instructions.

3. Image: Go to http://www.joomlaexplained.com/chapter5 and download the Train Station Sample Image. Add it to your article.

4. Link: Link the word "Aquarium" to the Aquarium article (created in Chapter 4).

Figure 5.57 is what your article should look like at the end.

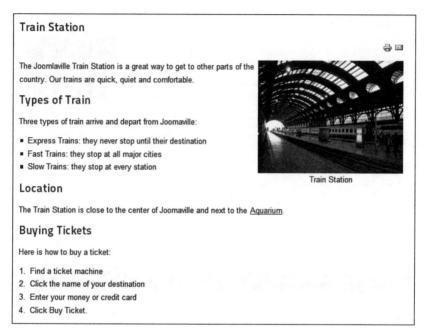

Figure 5.57   Finished Train Station article

Congratulations! You now have four great articles on your Joomla site. Each article has text, formatting, images, and links. Your Joomla site should look like Figure 5.58. Don't worry if it's not an exact copy. As long as you're comfortable with the categorize/add/show workflow that we've practiced here to create content, you're ready move on to the next chapter.

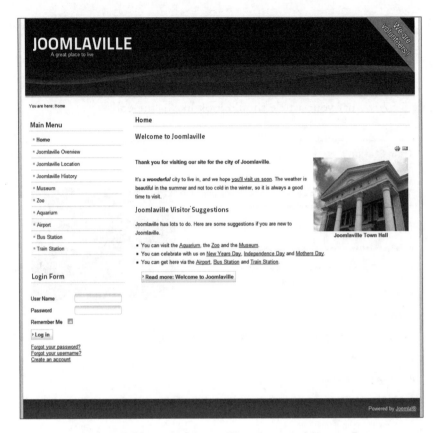

Figure 5.58   Your Joomla site at the end of Chapter 5

What's Next?

We've added great articles to our site, but there's a problem. As we add more and more articles, it becomes harder to find them all.

We need some better navigation so that people can easily find all of our wonderful articles.

In Joomla, navigation is created with menus. So that's what we're going to do next—get a better understanding of menus and menu links so we can create really good navigation on our site. Turn to Chapter 6, "Joomla Menus Explained," to learn more about menus.

6

Joomla! Menus Explained

Joomla has menus for two really good reasons:

- They allow visitors to find pages on your site. Without menus, all your visitors would be stuck on the home page.
- They have substantial control over how your page is laid out and displayed.

Remember the workflow we used for creating Joomla content? There's an almost identical CASh workflow for creating menus:

- **Categorize.** Create organization for your menu links.
- **Add.** Create your menu links.
- **Show.** Display your menu links on the site.

Things You Can Do After Reading This Chapter

- Understand how Joomla menus work
- Categorize your menu links
- Add your menu links
- Show your menus
- Understand more advanced menu layout options

Why Do you Need Menus?

Joomla menus are for easy, organized navigation. At the simplest level, links allow us to browse easily around a Web site. That means not only must we have links to all our important pages, but they must be organized clearly.

Remember back in Chapter 4, "Joomla Content Explained," when we created categories for our articles? This is the same: Menus are categories for our links.

We need to categorize our links because otherwise we'll just end up with one big, long disorganized list of links. In fact, that's what we have right now. We've been creating menu links already, and yours probably look like Figure 6.1.

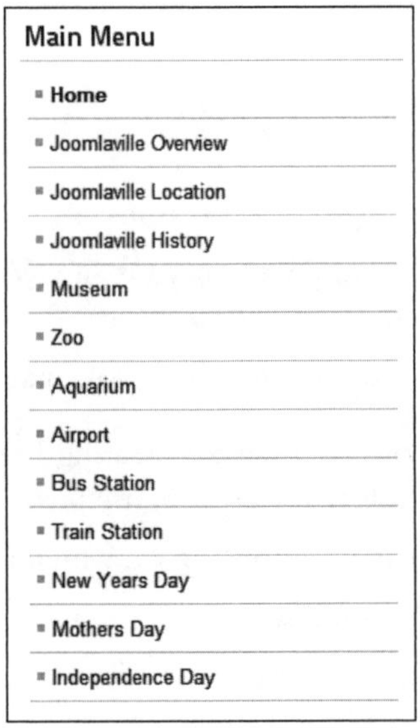

Main Menu

- Home
- Joomlaville Overview
- Joomlaville Location
- Joomlaville History
- Museum
- Zoo
- Aquarium
- Airport
- Bus Station
- Train Station
- New Years Day
- Mothers Day
- Independence Day

Figure 6.1   The links on your Joomla site

It makes sense to break up those links into different areas. Rather than lumping them all in together, we can have one menu for About Joomlaville articles, one for Attractions, one for Transport, and one for Festivals.

Let's go ahead and show you how do that.

Step 1: Categorize Your Menu Links

Creating menus requires us to use Joomla's CASh workflow. Here's how it works for menus.

- **Categorize.** This is done by going to the Menus tab in the drop-down, and then clicking on Menu Manager and creating a new menu.
- **Add.** This is done by going to Menus, clicking on the name of the menu, and creating a new link.

- **Show.** Our final step is to publish that menu on the site. We do that by using a module.

The first step is to categorize our links. Let's show you how it's done and set up an Attractions menu to list links to the Zoo, Aquarium, and Museum:

1. Go to Menus and then Menu Manager; you see a screen like Figure 6.2. This is the Menu Manager and is similar to the Category Manager we saw earlier. At the moment there is only one menu: Main Menu.

   You can actually see the three steps of the CASh workflow laid out here from left to right:

   1. **Categorize:** The details of the menu

   2. **Add:** The details of the menu links

   3. **Show:** The details of the module

Figure 6.2   The Menu Manager

2. Click New, and you see a screen like Figure 6.3.

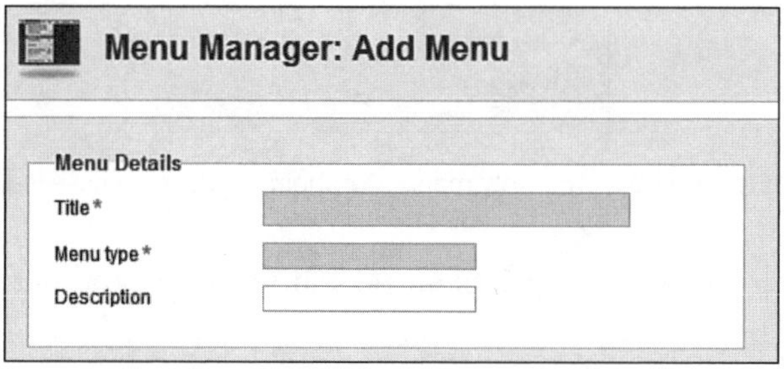

Figure 6.3   Adding a new Menu

3. To make things as easy as possible, let's put the same thing in each field. Enter **Attractions Menu** into each of the three fields as shown in Figure 6.4. Here's what the fields mean:

   - **Title.** This is really useful because it's the name of the menu that you'll see in the administrator area and visitors will see in the visitor area.

   - **Menu Type.** This is much less useful for you. It's a name that Joomla uses for technical stuff, but you'll rarely need to use it, if ever.

   - **Description.** As if the name Attractions Menu wasn't clear enough, we can use this box to spell out the menu's purpose even more clearly.

Figure 6.4   Setting up a new menu

4. Click Save & Close in the top-right corner, and you see that the menu has been created as in Figure 6.5.

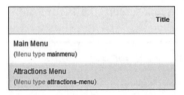

Figure 6.5   The new menu after being successfully saved

Now we can go on to Step 2 of the CASh workflow and put links inside the menu.

Step 2: Adding Your Menu Links

There are two ways we can fill our Attractions Menus. Which one to choose depends on whether we've already made menu links to our Attractions articles.

If You Already Have the Links

We've already created links to our Aquarium, Zoo, and Museum pages in the
Main Menu, so the lazy way is simply to move those links into the Attractions
Menu.

1. Go to Menus and then Main Menu.

2. Check the boxes next to your Aquarium, Zoo, and Museum menu links
   (see Figure 6.6).

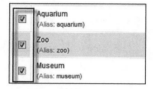

Figure 6.6   Selecting menu links

3. Look at the Batch Process the Selected Menu Items area at the bottom of
   the page and make sure that Move is checked as in Figure 6.7.

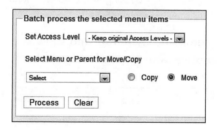

Figure 6.7   Moving menu links

4. Click the drop-down menu and select Add to This Menu under Attractions
   Menu as in Figure 6.8.

5. Complete the move of the three menu links by clicking Process underneath the drop-down menu.

6. Let's check that it worked. At the top of the list, look for the first
   drop-down and change it from Main Menu to Attractions Menu as in
   Figure 6.9.

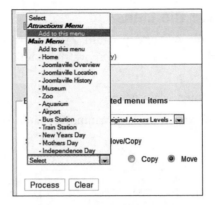

Figure 6.8   Choosing where to move menu links

Figure 6.9   Looking at a different menu

7. The page should automatically refresh and show you the Attractions Menu with your links in place as in Figure 6.10.

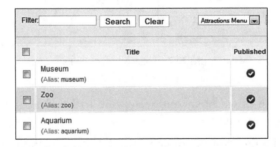

Figure 6.10   The Attractions Menu

If You Haven't Already Created the Links

If we hadn't already created the menu links, we'd need to create them now. Think back to Chapter 4 when we did this multiple times to see our articles. Here's the process we used to create the menu links:

1. Go to Menus, Attractions Menu, and click New.

2. Click Select next to Menu Item Type, and you see a pop-up screen. Click on Single Article.

3. On the right-hand side, click Select/Change next to Select Article.

4. You see a pop-up screen. Go ahead and find the Aquarium, Museum, or Zoo article that you wrote earlier. Click on the Museum name.

5. Enter the article name in the Menu Title field.

6. Click Save & Close to complete the creation of your menu link.

Whichever route you choose, you should be able to click on Menus and then Attractions Menu and see your Aquarium, Museum, and Zoo links.

There's only one remaining problem: Your visitors can't see those links. Let's go and solve that problem now.

Step 3: Showing Your Menu Links

We show our menus to visitors by using a module. We manage our categories in the Category Manager, our Articles in the Article Manager, and our Menus in the Menu Manager, so hopefully you can guess where we're going now. That's right: the Module Manager.

1. Go to Extensions, Module Manager, and you see a screen like Figure 6.11.

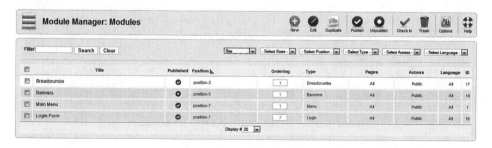

Figure 6.11   The Module Manager

2. Click New in the top-right corner, and you see a pop-up like Figure 6.12. Click on Menu.

Figure 6.12   Choosing which type of module to create

3. You see a screen as in Figure 6.13. This is where you can decide how to show this menu to your visitors.

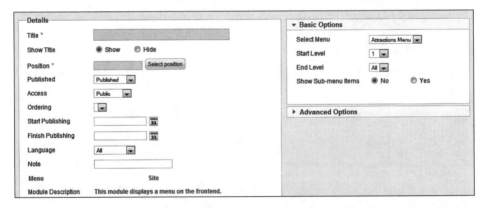

Figure 6.13   Choosing the options for a module

There are three things you need to check here:

- **Title.** Enter **Attractions Menu**. This is the name of the menu that you'll see in the Module Manager and also the name visitors will see.

- **Position.** Click Select Position, and you get a pop-up. Chapter 10, "Joomla Templates Explained," talks more about what these positions mean, but for now just find and click on Position-7. To find this, you may have to use the filter box in the top-left or use the Next button at the bottom.

- **Select Menu.** Make sure this is set to Attractions Menu rather than Main Menu. This option controls the category of links that appears.

Before you click Save & Close, your screen will look like Figure 6.14.

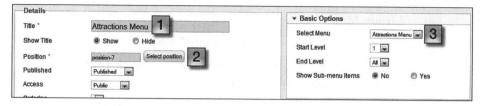

Figure 6.14   Options for the module to display your Attractions Menu

4. If everything looks like Figure 6.14, click Save & Close and then click View Site. You should see your new menu on the left-hand side of the site as in Figure 6.15.

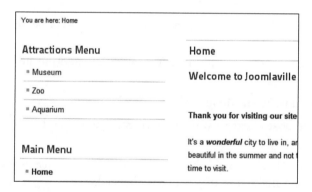

Figure 6.15   Your Attractions Menu as visitors will see it

That's it. You did it. You used the CASh workflow to categorize, add, and show your menu links to visitors.

Practicing the CASh Workflow with Menus

You might have already guessed what's next. We're going to practice the CASh workflow with menus.

As with the previous chapters, we're going to practice three times: For the first walkthrough, there will be step-by-step instructions for everything you need to do. For the second walkthrough, we give you some general guidance. For the third walkthrough, I hope you'll be ready to do that on your own.

Transport Menu

Categorize: Let's create the menu to organize our links:

1. Go to Menus, Menu Manager.

2. Click New and enter **Transport Menu** into each field.

3. Click Save & Close in the top-right corner and check to see that the menu has been created as in Figure 6.16.

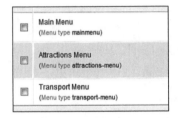

Figure 6.16   The Menu Manager with the Transport Menu created

Add: We can go on to step 2 of the CASh workflow and put links inside the menu:

1. Go to Menus, Main Menu.

2. Check the boxes next to your Airport, Bus Station, and Train Station menu links.

3. Look at the Batch Process the Selected Menu Items area at the bottom of the page and make sure that Move is checked.

4. Click the drop-down menu and select Add to This Menu under Transport Menu.

5. Complete the move of the three menu links by clicking Process underneath the drop-down menu.

6. At the top of the list, look for the first drop-down and change it from Main Menu to Transport Menu. You should be able to see your links inside the menu as in Figure 6.17.

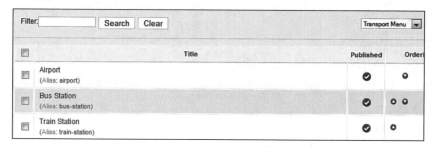

Figure 6.17   The Transport Menu with links

Show: We can now complete the CASh workflow by showing the menu to our visitors:

1. Go to Extensions, Module Manager.

2. Click New in the top-right corner and click Menu inside the pop-up.

3. There are three things you need to write in here:

    - **Title.** Set this to **Transport Menu**.

    - **Select Menu.** Make sure this is set to Transport Menu.

    - **Position.** Select Position-7.

4. Click Save & Close and then click View Site. You should see your new menu on the left-hand side of the site as in Figure 6.18.

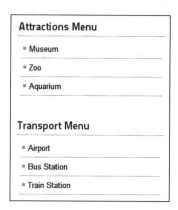

Figure 6.18   The completed Transport Menu

Festivals Menu

Step 1: Categorize:

1. Go to Menus, then Menu Manager.

2. Click New and enter **Festivals Menu** into each field. Then click Save & Close.

Step 2: Add:

1. Go to Menus, then Main Menu.

2. Check the boxes next to your Independence Day, Mothers Day and New Years links and use the area at the bottom of the page to move them to the Festivals menu.

Step 3: Show:

1. Go to Extensions, Module Manager.

2. Click New in the top-right corner and click Menu inside the pop-up.

3. Set Title and Select Menu to read Festivals Menu and set Position to Position-7.

4. Click Save & Close and then click View Site. You should see your new menu on the left-hand side of the site as in Figure 6.19.

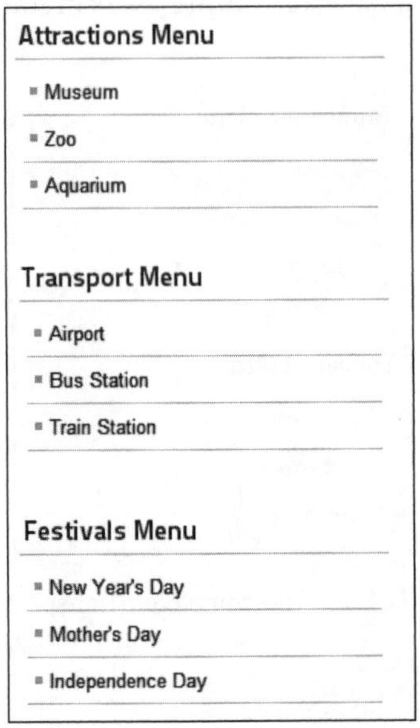

Figure 6.19   The completed Festivals Menu

About Joomlaville Menu

This time there are no instructions, but hopefully now you're feeling more confident.

Again, don't worry if you can't remember all the steps; full instructions are online at http://www.joomlaexplained.com/Chapter6.

Here are your tasks:

1. **Categorize:** Create an About Joomlaville Menu.

2. **Add:** Move the City Overview, City Location, and City History links into the About Joomlaville Menu.

3. **Show:** Create and publish a module showing the About Joomlaville Menu.

Figure 6.20 is what your article should look like at the end.

Figure 6.20   Finished About Joomlaville menu

Congratulations! You now have four menus on your site, each containing a logically organized group of links.

So far we've only been linking to individual articles, but it's possible to do more with Joomla. It's possible to link to whole groups of articles at once. Let's take a look at how we take advantage of those more advanced layout options using menus.

More Advanced Layout Options Using Menus

Many times you do just want to link to one article. However, there will also be times when you want to have multiple articles on one page. For example, think of your favorite news or blog site. How is it laid out?

Most likely, it has 5, 10, or even 15 stories on the front page. Also it probably doesn't show the whole text of the article. Most likely it shows the first part of the article and then includes a Read More link as we saw in a previous chapter.

Using menus, we can get a layout in Joomla that's just like your favorite news or blog site. Using menus we can also show a list of all our article categories or all the articles inside one category. This section shows what those layouts would look like.

First, a blog layout is shown in Figure 6.21.

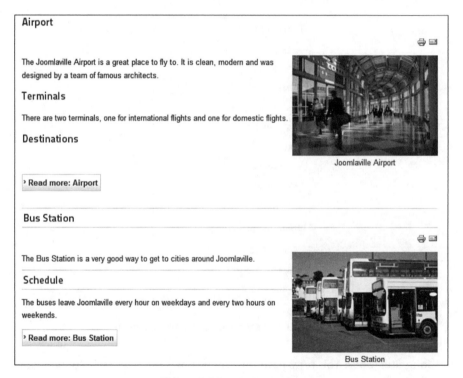

Airport

The Joomlaville Airport is a great place to fly to. It is clean, modern and was designed by a team of famous architects.

Terminals

There are two terminals, one for international flights and one for domestic flights.

Destinations

Joomlaville Airport

> Read more: Airport

Bus Station

The Bus Station is a very good way to get to cities around Joomlaville.

Schedule

The buses leave Joomlaville every hour on weekdays and every two hours on weekends.

> Read more: Bus Station

Bus Station

Figure 6.21   A blog layout

Second, a list of all our article categories is shown in Figure 6.22.

Figure 6.22   A layout showing a list of all our article categories

Third, a list of all the articles inside one category is shown in Figure 6.23.

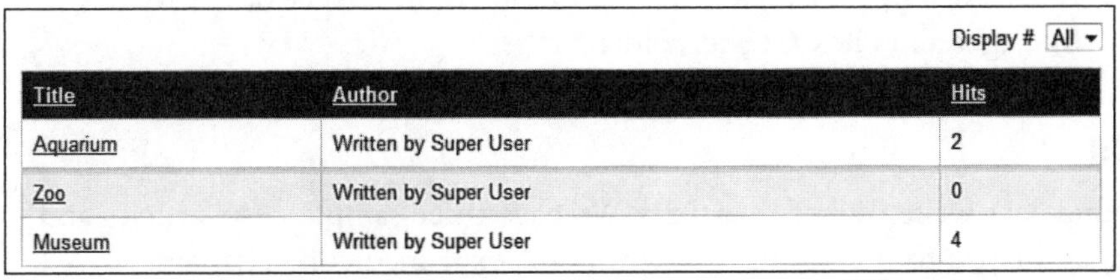

Title	Author	Display # All ▾ Hits
Aquarium	Written by Super User	2
Zoo	Written by Super User	0
Museum	Written by Super User	4

Figure 6.23   A layout showing all the articles in one category

In the next section, we show you how to use all these different layouts. In doing so, we also wrap up everything we've learned in the last three chapters.

We also add a news area to our site so that we can report on the latest events in Joomlaville. In doing this, we put it all together: the Joomla workflow, Joomla content, and Joomla menus.

Putting It All Together in a Blog Layout

First let's show you how the blog layout works. This is a great layout for fresh and topical information. To test it, we create an area of our site called News. It's an area where you can write about latest happenings in the city.

We use Joomla's CASh workflow:

1. Categorize
2. Add
3. Show

Categorize

First, let's create the category for our blog:

1. Go to Content, then Category Manager, and click New.
2. Enter **News** into the Title field and click Save & Close.

We're also going to upload images for our news articles, so let's create the folder for them:

1. Go to Content and then Media Manager.
2. Enter **News** into the field at the bottom-right corner of the Media Manager and click Create Folder.

Add

Second, let's write our news articles. We have three sample news articles and images for you to use at http://www.joomlaexplained.com/chapter6.

1. Go to Content, Article Manager, and click New.
2. Make sure you set these four things in the article. Your screen should look like the screen in Figure 6.24:

   - Title.
   - Category: News.
   - Text: Go ahead and use the sample news articles and images from http://www.joomlaexplained.com/Chapter6.
   - Read More link: Place this in the middle of the text. The Read More link is needed so we can take full advantage of the blog layout.

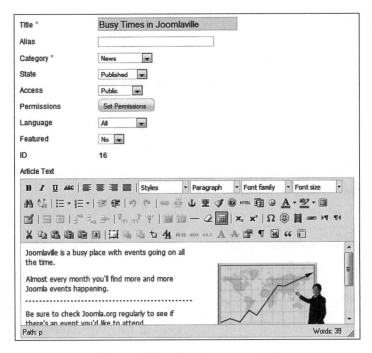

Figure 6.24   Creating a new article

3. Repeat these steps so that you have at least three articles in your News category.

Show

Go and make a menu for our news:

1. Go to Menus, Main Menu, and click New.

2. Set these three settings for your new link as in Figure 6.25:

   - Click Select next to Menu Item Type and choose Category Blog.

   - Enter **Joomlaville News** into the Title field.

   - Choose Joomlaville News from the Choose a Category drop-down.

Figure 6.25   Creating a menu link to your news

3. Click Save & Close and then View Site. Find the Main Menu on the left-hand side and click News. You should see the layout shown in Figure 6.26.

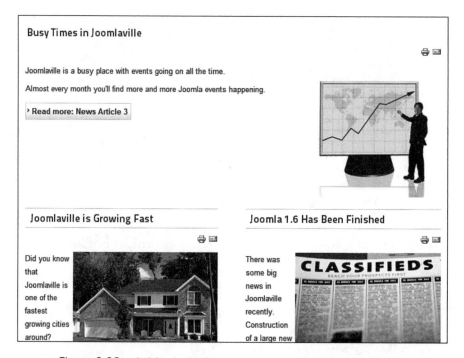

Figure 6.26   Articles in the News category presented in a blog layout

Selecting the Options

Just as with our articles, we can change the options for this layout, and we can do this in two places:

- Individually for just this blog layout: On the right-hand side of the menu link. For example, Go to Menus in the drop-down menu, then Main Menu, click on News, and click on Blog Layout options on the right-hand side.

- Globally for all blog layouts: Go to Content in the drop-down menu, then Article Manager, then Options, and click on Blog/Featured Layouts.

If possible, it's always best to change the options globally because you only have one place to control the whole site. To see the options for a blog layout, click Content, Article Manager, Options and then click the Blog/Featured Layouts tab, which is shown in Figure 6.27.

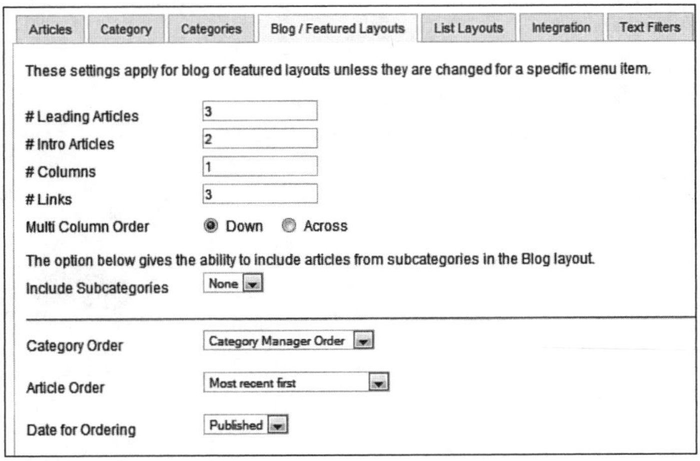

Figure 6.27   Blog layout options

Here are what the options shown in Figure 6.27 mean:

- **Leading Articles.** These articles have the full width of the page layout, regardless of whether the page is divided into columns.

- **Intro Articles.** These articles adjust to the number of columns in the layout. So if there are two columns, these will take up 50% of the layout. If there are three columns, they will take up about 33% of the layout.

- **Columns.** This is the number of columns the blog is divided into. Honestly, any more than two gets very crowded.

- **Links.** You won't see any information about these articles except for a link at the bottom of the page.

Your page will be laid out with Leading Articles at the top, followed by Intro Articles, and then Links at the bottom. To see how this works, go ahead and change your options to the following settings:

- Leading Articles: 3
- Intro Articles: 2
- Columns: 1
- Links: 3

Now when you visit your News menu link it looks like Figure 6.28.

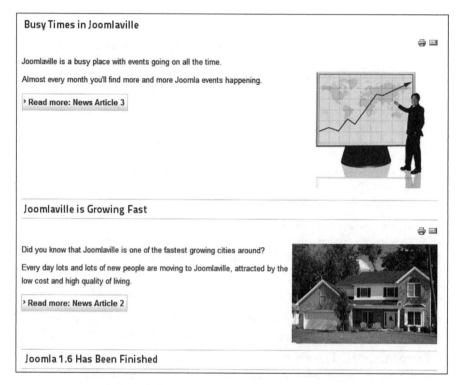

Figure 6.28   Changed options for the blog layout

Putting It All Together in a List Layout

Now let's show you how the list layout works. This is more appropriate for information that doesn't change often. To test it, we create an area of our site called Parks for information about where residents can go to relax and have fun.

As always, we're going to use Joomla's CASh workflow:

1. Categorize
2. Add
3. Show

Categorize

First, let's create the category for our parks:

1. Go to Content, Category Manager, and click New.
2. Enter **Parks** into the Title field and click Save & Close.

We're also going to upload images for our parks, so let's create the folder for them:

1. Go to Content, Media Manager.
2. Enter **Parks** into the field at the bottom-right corner of the Media Manager and click Create Folder.

Add

Second, let's write our Parks articles. We have three sample Parks articles for you to use at http://www.joomlaexplained.com/chapter6.

1. Go to Content, Article Manager, and click New.
2. Make sure you set these three things in the article:
   - **Title.** Lake Park, City Park, and Wood Park might be good example titles.
   - **Category.** Parks.
   - **Text.** Go ahead and use the sample news articles and images from http://www.joomlaexplained.com/chapter6.
3. Repeat these steps so that you have at least three articles in your Parks category.

Show

Let's make a menu for our parks:

1. Go to Menus, Main Menu, and click New.

2. Set these three settings for your new link:

   - Click Select next to Menu Item Type and choose Category List.
   - Enter **Parks** into the Title field.
   - Choose Parks from the Choose a Category drop-down.

3. Click Save & Close and then click View Site. Find the Main Menu on the left-hand side and click Parks. You should see the layout in Figure 6.29.

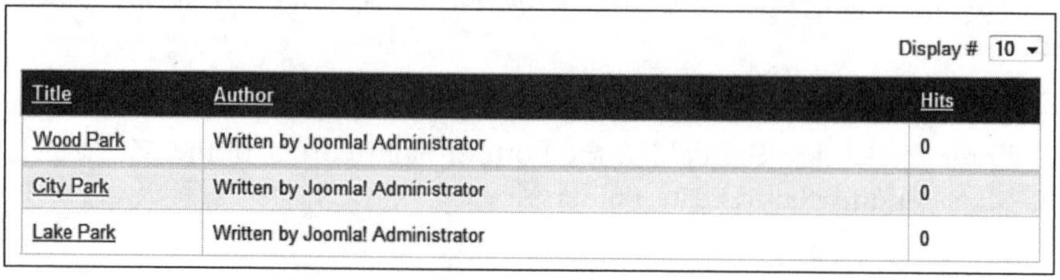

Title	Author	Hits
Wood Park	Written by Joomla! Administrator	0
City Park	Written by Joomla! Administrator	0
Lake Park	Written by Joomla! Administrator	0

Display # [10 ▾]

Figure 6.29   Articles in the Parks category presented in
a category list layout

Selecting the Options

Just as with our articles and our blog layout, we can change the options for the list layout, and we can do this in two places:

- Individually for just this list layout: On the right-hand side of the menu link. For example, Go to Menus in the drop-down menu, then Main Menu, click on Parks, and click on the List Layout options on the right-hand side.

- Globally for all list layouts: Go to Content in the drop-down menu, then Article Manager, Options, and click on List Layout.

If possible, it's always best to change the options globally because you only have one place to control the whole site. To see the options for a list layout, click Content, Article Manager, Options, and then click the List Layouts tab as in Figure 6.30.

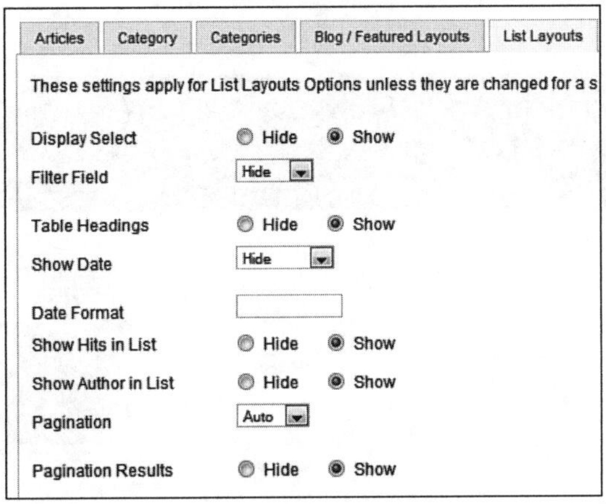

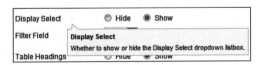

Figure 6.30   List Layout options

This time around, I won't explain what every option does, but instead let me show you how to find out for yourself. Hover your mouse over the text for every option, and you'll find a yellow information box with an explanation. For example, Figure 6.31 shows how you can find out the purpose of the Display Select option.

Figure 6.31   Examining List Layout options

Congratulations! You now have a good understanding of how menus work in Joomla. Your Joomla site should look like Figure 6.32. Don't worry if it's not an exact copy. As long as you're comfortable with the categorize/add/show workflow for menus that we've practiced here, you're ready move on to the next chapter.

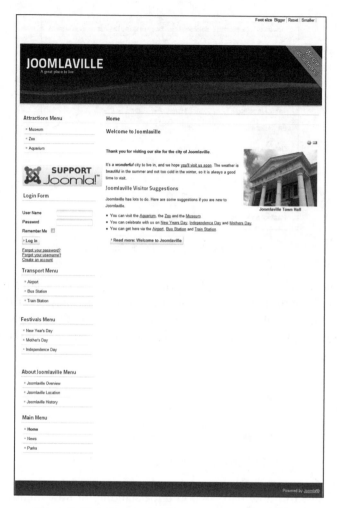

Figure 6.32   Your Joomla site at the end of Chapter 6

What's Next?

Each time you were creating menu links in this chapter, you saw a screen like Figure 6.33. You undoubtedly noticed that you could link to many more things beyond just articles. In fact, you can link to Contacts, Newsfeeds, Search, Weblinks, the User Manager, and much more.

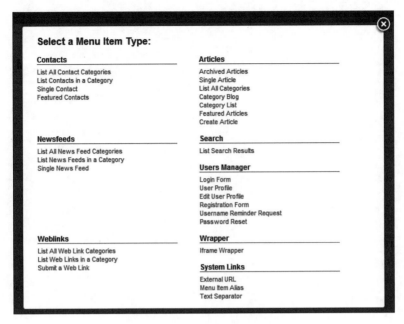

Figure 6.33   Menu link options

In the next chapter, we show what all those extra features are and how they can enhance your Joomla site. These extra features are all called Components. Turn the page, and let's see how Components work.

7

Joomla! Components Explained

If you want to add an exciting extra feature to your site, there's a good chance it's a component. Do you want to show an advertising banner? That's a component. Want a contact form? That's a component, too. How about an events calendar or a discussion forum? Both components.

Joomla arrives with seven default components such as advertising banners and contact forms. In this chapter we show you how they work.

In Chapter 11, "Adding Joomla Extensions Explained," we show you how to find and add extra components such as events calendars and discussion forums.

Things You Can Do After Reading This Chapter

- Understand the seven default Joomla components:
    - **Banners.** Shows advertising banners.
    - **Contacts.** Creates contact forms.
    - **Messaging.** Sends private messages to other site administrators.
    - **News feeds.** Shows news from other Web sites.
    - **Search.** Allows people to search your site.
    - **Web links.** Creates a directory of links to other sites.
    - **Redirect.** Tracks when people try to visit pages that don't exist on your site and allows you to redirect them to the correct page.

Banners Component

The Banners component has two main tasks:

- Shows advertising banners
- Collects all the data about those banners, such as the number of times each one has been shown and the number of times each one has been clicked on

Banners uses the CASh workflow of Categorize, Add, Show. Let's use that workflow to add an advertising banner onto our site.

Setting Up an Advertising Banner

Let's walk you through the process of setting up an advertising banner. Here's how we do it.

Categorize

Just as with our articles, our banners are organized into categories. So we need to create a category for them:

1. Go to Components in the main drop-down menu, then click on Banners, and then Categories.

2. Click New. The Banner categories will each be used for different areas of the site, so naming them according to their position (Leaderboard, Left Column, Right Column) is a good idea.

Let's create a banner for the left-hand side of our site, so enter **Left Column** into the Title field as in Figure 7.1. Click Save & Close when you're finished.

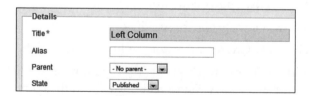

Figure 7.1   Create a Joomla Banner category

With Banners there's also a second method of organization—by advertising client. Why is this useful? You might want to sell banner space to several different clients and have an easy way to track all their banners. If you want to do this, the process of setting up a client is exactly the same as for a category.

Add

Now let's create the banner that visitors will see.

1. Go to Components in the main drop-down menu, and then click on Banners.

2. Click New, and you see the banner setup page. I recommend you fill in five fields as you create your first banner:

   - **Name.** Give the banner a descriptive title. In this case, enter **Left Column Joomla.org Banner**.

   - **Category.** Choose the Left Column category you created earlier.

   - **Image.** Click Select, and you see a pop-up. This takes you to the banners folder in Media Manager. You can upload a new advertising banner here or even browse to other folders. In this case, click on the image called white.jpg, make sure the image location is entered at the bottom of the page, and then click Insert.

   - **Alternative Text.** This is the descriptive text that appears if the image doesn't show. Enter **Joomla.org Banner**.

   - **Click URL.** This is the Web address you will send people to when they click the banner. Let's put **http://www.joomla.org** in here.

When all five fields are filled in, your screen should look like Figure 7.2.

Name *	Left Column Joomla.org Banner
Alias	
Category *	Left Column
Type	⦿ Image ○ Custom
State	Published
Image	images/banners/white.png Select Clear
Width	
Height	
Alternative Text	Joomla.org Banner
Click URL	http://joomla.org

Figure 7.2   Add a Joomla banner

Show

Now we just need to tell Joomla where to show the banner:

1. Go to Extensions, then Module Manager, and click New.

2. You see a pop-up screen where you can decide which type of module to create. Click Banners.

3. You see a screen like Figure 7.3. There are four key options to choose:

   - **Title.** Give the module a logical name such as Left Column Banner.

   - **Show Title.** Hide.

   - **Position.** Select Position-7, which is where all of our other modules such as Main Menu, Attractions Menu, and Transport Menu and are located.

   - **Category.** Choose the Left Column category you created earlier.

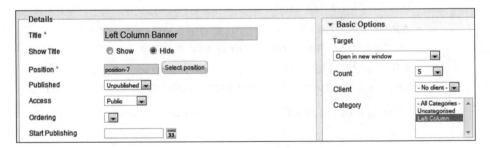

Figure 7.3   Creating a Banner module

4. Click Save & Close, and you're finished. Click View Site, and you can see your banner in the left column as in Figure 7.4. Go ahead and click on the banner a few times to test that it works. It should hopefully send you to http://joomla.org.

Banner Options

By default, Joomla collects only basic data about how often the banner is shown (Impressions) or how often it's clicked on (Clicks). You can find that information by going to Components, then Banners, and looking in the Impressions and Clicks columns as in Figure 7.5.

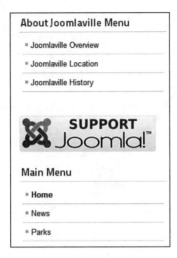

Figure 7.4   Showing a banner

Name ≛	Published	Sticky	Client	Category	Ordering	Impressions	Clicks
Left Column Joomla.org Banner (Alias: left-column-joomlaorg-banner)	✓	○		Left Column	1	3 of Unlimited	0 - 0.00%

Figure 7.5   Impressions and clicks recorded for a banner

However, if that data is important for your site, you might need more accurate details and information on the impressions and clicks. It isn't good enough to replace any professional advertising systems, but it works well for the average user's needs. Here's how you can start recording that more detailed data:

1. Go to Components, then Banners, and click on your banner name: Left Column Joomla.org Banner.

2. You see the same screen you saw earlier in this process, and this is where we can enable tracking. Depending on your needs, set Track Impressions and/or Track Clicks to Yes as in Figure 7.6.

3. Click Save & Close and then go to the Tracks link.

4. Every day the impressions and clicks will be recorded here. You can sort and organize them according to category, client, or date. If you want to immediately see how this works, visit a few pages on the front of your site and come back to this page. The screen you see will be like Figure 7.7.

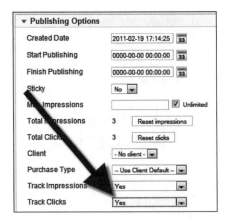

Figure 7.6   Setting up a banner to track impressions and clicks

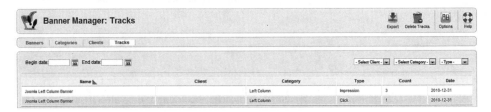

Figure 7.7   Tracking banner impressions and clicks

Contacts Component

The Contacts component has one main task: It allows visitors to contact you. You probably guessed that already.

Contacts allows you to easily set up Contact Us forms. If you just want one contact form for the whole site, that's easily done. You can also set up a whole directory of contact forms for different people or different departments. Contact forms look like Figure 7.8.

The CASh workflow applies to contacts just as much as for content, menus, and banners. We're going to Categorize, Add, and then Show.

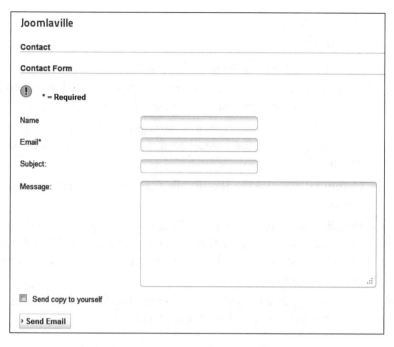

Figure 7.8   Default Joomla Contact component

Categorize

Just as with our articles and banners, our contacts are organized into categories:

1. Go to Components, Contacts, and then Categories.

2. Click New and enter a general name for our category, such as **Joomlaville Contacts**. Your screen looks like Figure 7.9. Click Save & Close to finish.

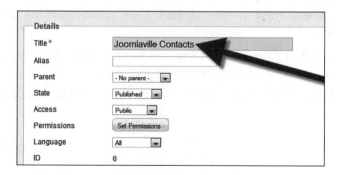

Figure 7.9   Creating a Joomla Contact category

Add

To create the contact form, follow these steps:

1. Go to Components and then click on Contacts.

2. Click New, and you see the contact form creation page. I recommend you fill in at least three fields as you create your first contact form:

   - **Name.** Give the contact form a descriptive title. For example, as we're making a general contact form for the city, enter **Joomlaville Mayor**.

   - **Category.** Choose the Joomlaville Contacts category you created earlier.

   - **Email.** Click the Contact Details tab on the right-hand side of the page and enter your e-mail address into the Email field. This e-mail won't be made public, but whenever anyone uses the contact form, an e-mail gets sent to this address.

3. When all three fields are filled in, your screen should look like Figure 7.10. Click Save & Close to complete this contact form.

Figure 7.10   Add a Joomla contact form

We're also going to make a small option change. This is a design change because I personally think another layout is easier to read than the default Contacts layout:

1. In the Contact Manager, click Options in the top-right corner, and you see the global options you can choose for the contact forms.

2. As in Figure 7.11, set the Display Format option to Plain and click Save.

Figure 7.11   Global options for Joomla's contact forms

Show

Now that we have our contact form ready, the final step is to make it publicly visible via a menu link:

1. In the Administrator area, go to Menus and then Main Menu.

2. Click New, and you see the menu link setup page. I recommend you set these three fields:

   - **Menu Item Type.** Choose Single Contact.
   - **Menu Title.** Joomlaville Mayor.
   - **Select Contact.** Choose Joomlaville Mayor.

   When you're finished, you see a screen like Figure 7.12.

Figure 7.12   Adding a new Joomla contact menu link

3. Click Save & Close and then View Site. You should be able to see your new menu link in the Main Menu. When you click on it, you see your new contact form as in Figure 7.13.

Options

As we saw during the creation of that first contact form, there are many options we can set for contact forms. Go to Extensions, then Contacts, and open up the contact form you just created.

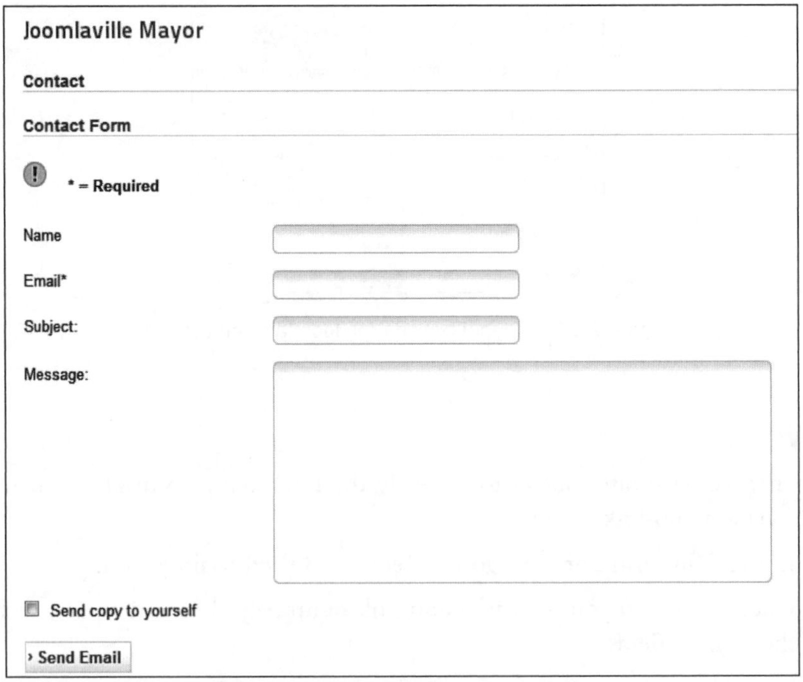

Figure 7.13   A new Joomla contact form

On the right-hand side of the page you see several sliding tabs. Click on Contact Details as we did before, and you can enter more than just an e-mail address. As Figure 7.14 shows, you can also include an address, phone numbers, a Web site address, and more.

Click on the Display Options sliding tab that you can see in Figure 7.14 on the right-hand side of the page. You'll find it under Publishing Options and Contact Details.

Here there are a wide range of display options you can set. As always, you can do this individually for this one contact form or globally for all contact forms on the site:

- **Individually.** Inside a contact form, click on the Display Options sliding tab.

- **Globally.** Go to Extensions, Contacts, and then click on the Options button.

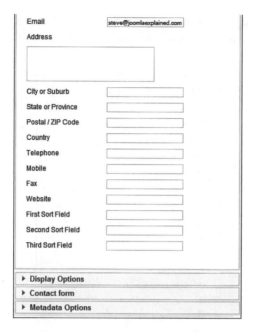

Figure 7.14   Contact form details

Messaging Component

The Joomla Messaging component is by far the simplest component: It allows you to send private messages to other members of your site.

In fact it's even simpler than that because it only allows you to send private messages to people who are logged in to the Administrator area of your site.

This component is so simple that it doesn't use the CASh workflow. To send a private message to other users, we actually need another user who can access this administrator area. Here's how to add another user:

1. Under the Users drop-down, click on User Manager.

2. Click on the Demo User name. This is a dummy account that was set up when you installed your Joomla site. There are three settings you need to change as in Figure 7.15:

   - **Password.** Give this user a password that's difficult to guess. Be sure not to use the same password that you created for your own account.

   - **Block this User.** No.

- **Assigned User Groups.** Check the box next to Administrator. This allows the user to access the administrator area of your site.

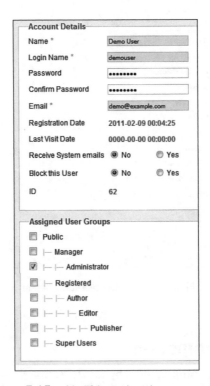

Figure 7.15   Modifying a Joomla user account

Now we can go ahead and try the Messaging component. Here's how we do it:

1. Go to Messaging under the Components drop-down and then click New.

2. Click Select User and click on the Demo User name.

3. Set a title for the subject and enter the message. Your screen should look like Figure 7.16.

4. Click Send to finish and send the message.

5. Click Log Out in the very top-right corner of the screen.

6. Log in as the Demo User using the account details you just changed.

7. Up in the top-right corner you see a new notification that you have a new message as in Figure 7.17.

Figure 7.16   Sending a private message

Figure 7.17   Receiving a private message

8. Either click that link or go to Extensions, Messaging, and then click on Read Private Messages.

9. You see a screen as shown in Figure 7.18. This is your private messaging inbox, and all your messages will be stored here.

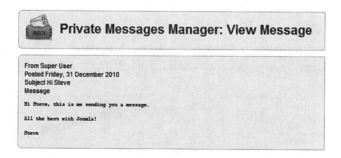

Figure 7.18   Your private messaging inbox

10. Click the title of your new private message, and you see the message itself as in Figure 7.19.

11. If you don't mind talking to yourself, click Reply in the top-right corner, and you can respond with a new private message.

From Joomla! Administrator
Posted Saturday, 19 February 2011
Subject Welcome
Message

Hi

Welcome to the Joomlaville site.

Happy to have you on board!

Steve

Figure 7.19   Your private message

News Feeds Component

The News Feeds component allows you to automatically show news from other Web sites.

News Feeds use a technology called RSS or Real Simple Syndication to pull in the feeds from other sites.

Let's walk you through the process of setting up feeds on our site. We use the normal Joomla workflow.

Categorize

Just as with our articles, banners, and contacts, our News Feeds are organized into categories:

1. Go to Components, Newsfeeds, and then Categories.

2. Click New and enter a general title for our category such as **News from Other Sites**. Your screen looks like Figure 7.20.

Figure 7.20   Creating a News Feeds category

Add

First, we need to find the feeds that we're going to import. The normal way to do this is to browse to the sites you're interested in and look for a little RSS icon. The common design for an RSS icon is a square image with a dot in the bottom-left corner and two waves coming out of it toward the top-right corner. If you're not sure what RSS feed icons look like, I've posted some examples at http://joomlaexplained.com/chapter7.

When looking for RSS feeds on other sites, you may need to hunt around a little as different sites put the feed in different places. Some put their RSS icons in the browser bar, some in the sidebar, and some in the site footer.

1. Go to Components, Newsfeeds, and then Feeds.

2. Click New and you see the News Feeds creation page. I recommend you fill in at least three fields as you create your first contact form:

    - **Name.** Give the contact form a descriptive title. In this example we're going to list the latest Joomla extensions, so a logical title might be **Latest Joomla Extensions**. Sometimes this Joomla stuff is hard, isn't it?

    - **Link.** Enter **http://feeds.joomla.org/JoomlaExtensions**.

    - **Category.** Choose the News from Other Sites category you created earlier.

Before you click Save & Close, make sure your page looks like Figure 7.21.

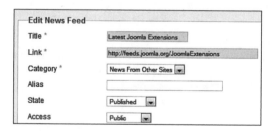

Figure 7.21   Creating a news feed

Show

All we need now is to make a menu link to our news feed:

1. In the Administrator area, go to Menus and then Main Menu.

2. Click New and you see the menu link setup page. I recommend you fill in three fields:

- **Menu Item Type.** Choose Single News Feed.
- **Menu Title.** Enter **Latest Joomla Extensions**.
- **Feed.** Latest Joomla Extensions.

When you're finished, you see a screen like Figure 7.22.

Figure 7.22   Creating a menu link to a news feed

3. Click Save & Close and then View Site. You should see your new menu link in the Main Menu. When you click on it, you see your feed as in Figure 7.23.

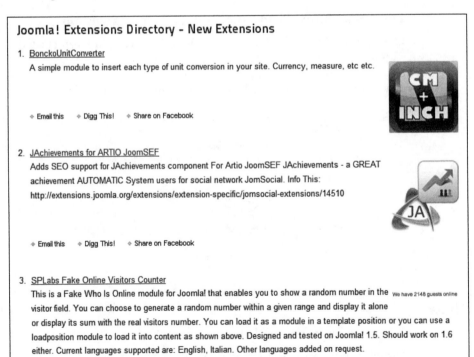

Figure 7.23   Viewing a news feed on the visitor area of your site

Redirect Component

The Redirect component records broken links that people try to visit on your site and allows you to safely redirect them to a working page.

Redirect is as simple as the Messaging component: It requires no workflows, no configuration, and no installation. It's already up and running for you.

Go to Components and then click on Redirect. After your site has been running for a while, you'll start to see this screen fill up as shown in Figure 7.24. The Expired URL column shows the broken links that people have tried to use.

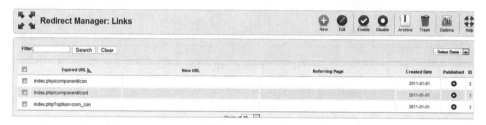

Figure 7.24   Redirect results

Why would there be broken URLs on your site? There are two likely reasons:

- **Mistyped URL.** Someone may have mistyped the URL to one of your pages—it may even have been you. If this is the case, the location of the broken URL shows in the Referring Page column so you know where to go to fix the link.

- **Old URL.** If you moved your site to Joomla from another type of Web site, it's possible that your URLs have changed. People may still be trying to visit those old URLs.

It doesn't really matter which of these two reasons is causing the problem because the Redirect component is here to fix it for you. It automatically redirects any broken URL to a working URL of your choice.

Our site is new, so you don't have any broken URLs yet, but we can still see how it works:

1. Click Components, Redirects, and then click New.

2. I recommend you fill in all three fields as shown in Figure 7.25:

   - **Source URL.** Enter the URL of a page that doesn't exist. For example, you could enter something like http://joomlaexplained.com/ Chater7, which is almost a valid URL but has had a couple of characters removed.

- **Destination URL.** Enter the URL of the page you want people to be redirected to. For example, if http://joomlaexplained.com/chapr7 is the broken URL, you probably want to enter **http://joomlaex-plained.com/chapter7**.
- **State.** Set this to Enabled.

Figure 7.25   Redirecting a broken URL

3. After you have your Source URL and Destination URLs entered, you can test to see whether it's working. Click Visit Site and enter the Source URL into the address bar of your browser. That broken URL should automatically redirect to the Destination URL. In this example, I could type in http://joomlaexplained.com/chater7 and be automatically redirected to http://joomlaexplained.com/chapter7.

Search Component

The Search component allows people to search for keywords on your site.

It's as simple to use as the Messaging and Redirect components, but it's far more important.

Of all the components introduced in this chapter, this is the only one almost guaranteed to be used on every Joomla site.

Here's how we set it up:

1. Go to Extensions and then Module Manager.

2. Click New and choose Search.

3. You see the search module setup page. I recommend you fill in two fields:

- **Title.** Give the module a useful name. We're not trying to make you think too hard here, so why not try Search Box?
- **Position.** Choose Position-0.

4. Click Save & Close and then click Visit Site. Your search box should be up in the top-right corner of your screen as in Figure 7.26.

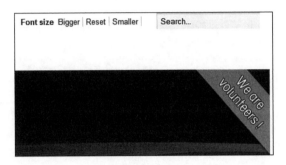

Figure 7.26   Search box

5. Type Joomlaville into the search box and press Enter or Return on your keyboard. You see search results returned as in Figure 7.27.

#	Search Phrase	Hits ⇌	Results
1	joomlaville	2	8
2	joomlaville sports	1	5
3	where is Joomlaville	1	14
4	Why the silly name?	1	5

Figure 7.27   Search results for the keyword Joomlaville

If you want, you can also make a menu link to this search form so that people can search and find results all on the same page. Here's how we do that:

1. Go to Main Menu under the Menus drop-down and click New.

2. There are two fields you need to set:

   - **Menu Item Type.** List Search Results.
   - **Menu Title:** Search This Site.

After you've created that menu link, go to the visitor area of the site, click Search This Site under Main Menu, and you see a screen like Figure 7.28. You can use this form to search the site. By default, Joomla searches for content that contains all the words you type in, but you can change this by checking the boxes next to Any Words or Exact Phrase.

Figure 7.28   The Search component on your site

Options

There aren't many options you can choose for the Search component, but one is particularly useful. This option allows you to track all the searches that people have made on your site. Those search results give you a good idea about what is popular or even what is hard to find on your site. Here's how to set it up:

1. In your Administrator area, go to Components in the main drop-down menu, then click Search.

2. Click Options and set Gather Search Statistics to Yes.

Now whenever someone uses your site's search, it is recorded here. I've used the search box several extra times to show you how it works in Figure 7.29.

If you click Show Search Results just under the Options button, Joomla even shows you how many results were returned for that search term. Over time this list can become large and affect the performance of your site, so that's why it's not enabled by default.

#	Search Phrase	Hits ≜
1	Joomlaville	1
2	Joomlaville Parks	1
3	joomlaville airport	2

Figure 7.29   Recorded search results

Web Links Component

The Web Links component is a directory of links to other sites. It's most commonly used for a Resources or Useful Links area of your site.

Web links is organized in an identical way to the News Feeds component, the only exception being that you're adding Web site URLs rather than RSS URLs.

Let's walk through the process of setting up Web links on our site, using the CASh workflow.

Categorize

Just as with our articles, banners, contacts, and news feeds, our Web links are organized into categories:

1. Go to Components, Weblinks, and then Categories.

2. Click New. Enter the name **Joomla.org Links** for your category. Your screen looks like Figure 7.30.

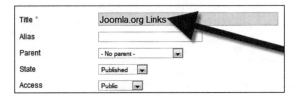

Figure 7.30   Creating a Web Links category

Add

Now let's add some URLs into our newly created category:

1. Go to Components, Weblinks, and then Weblinks again.

2. Click New, and you see the Web links creation page. I recommend you fill in at least three fields as you create your first Web link. The example we use is the main Joomla Web site:

   - **Title.** Main Joomla Website.

   - **URL.** Enter **http://www.joomla.org**.

   - **Category.** Joomla.org Links.

Before you click Save & Close, make sure your page looks like Figure 7.31.

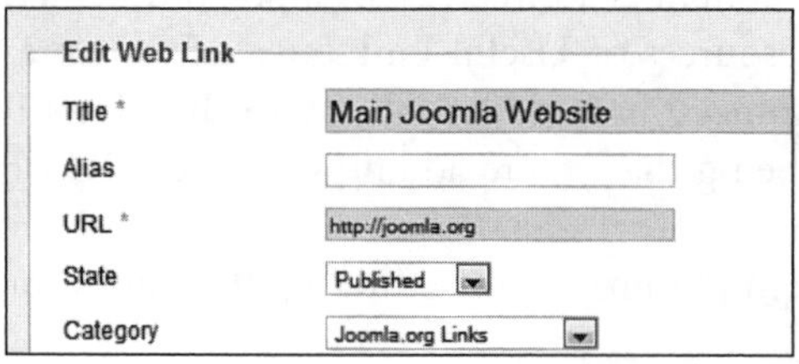

Figure 7.31 Creating a Web link

Go ahead and repeat the process, adding these links to the same category:

- **Title.** Joomla Support Forum URL: http://forum.joomla.org
- **Title.** Joomla Extensions Directory URL: http://extensions.joomla.org
- **Title.** Joomla Documentation URL: http://docs.joomla.org

When you're finished your Web links page looks like Figure 7.32.

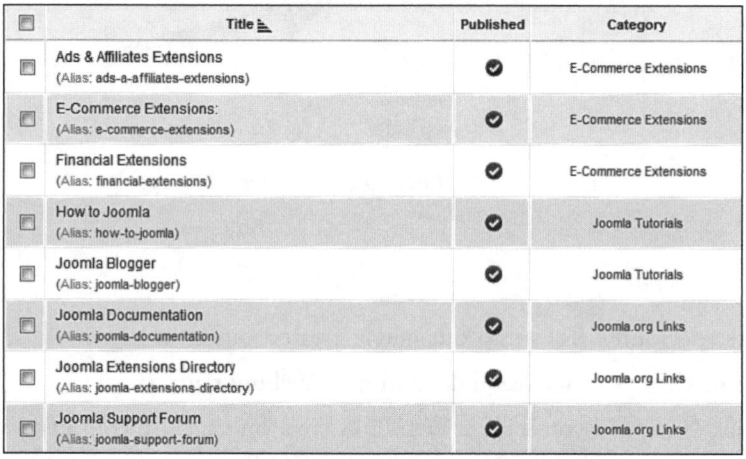

	Title	Published	Category
	Ads & Affiliates Extensions (Alias: ads-a-affiliates-extensions)	✔	E-Commerce Extensions
	E-Commerce Extensions: (Alias: e-commerce-extensions)	✔	E-Commerce Extensions
	Financial Extensions (Alias: financial-extensions)	✔	E-Commerce Extensions
	How to Joomla (Alias: how-to-joomla)	✔	Joomla Tutorials
	Joomla Blogger (Alias: joomla-blogger)	✔	Joomla Tutorials
	Joomla Documentation (Alias: joomla-documentation)	✔	Joomla.org Links
	Joomla Extensions Directory (Alias: joomla-extensions-directory)	✔	Joomla.org Links
	Joomla Support Forum (Alias: joomla-support-forum)	✔	Joomla.org Links

Figure 7.32 Four Web links

Show

All we need to do now is make a menu link to our useful links:

1. In your Administrator area, go to Menus and then Main Menu.
2. Click New, and you see the menu link setup page. I recommend you fill in three fields:

- **Menu Item Type.** Choose List Web Links in a Category.
- **Menu Title.** Enter **Joomla.org Links**.
- **Category.** Choose Joomla.org Links.

When you're finished, you see a screen like Figure 7.33.

Figure 7.33   Creating a menu link to Weblinks

3. Click Save & Close and then View Site. You should see your new menu
   link in the Main Menu. When you click on it, you see your Web links as in
   Figure 7.34. Click on them to be taken to the appropriate URL.

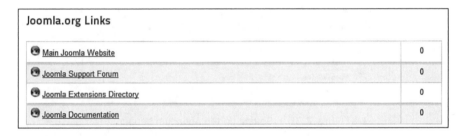

Figure 7.34   Web links live on your site

Practicing Components

Banners

To practice banners, we're going to set up two banners. First, let's set up a banner
advertising the Joomlaville Aquarium. We place it on the left of our site's footer.

Categorize

1. Go to Components, Banners, and then Categories, and click New.
2. Enter **Footer Left** for the Title field.

Add

1. To create the banner, go to Components, Banners, and then Banners again,
   and click New.

2. Enter these four fields. Your screen looks like Figure 7.35.

- **Name. Aquarium Footer Banner**.

- **Category.** Footer Left.

- **Image.** Upload and choose the Aquarium banner that you can download from http://joomlaexplained.com/Chapter7.

- **Click URL.** Enter **/aquarium**. (It's worth clicking on your Attractions menu to verify that this is the URL of the Aquarium page. Yours may be a little different, for example, /index.php/ aquarium. Check Chapter 15 for more on Joomla's URLs.)

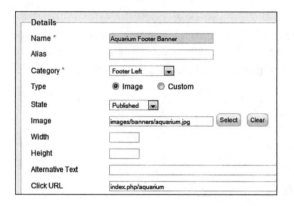

Figure 7.35   Setting up the Aquarium banner

Show

Now we just need to tell Joomla where to show the banner.

1. Go to Extensions, then Module Manager, and click New.

2. Choose Banners and enter these four fields. Your screen looks like Figure 7.36:

- **Title. Footer Left Banner**

- **Show Title.** Hide

- **Position.** Position-9

- **Category.** Footer Left

Figure 7.36   Setting up the Aquarium banner

3. Click Save & Close and then View Site. You should be able to see your banner as in Figure 7.37.

Figure 7.37   Showing an Aquarium banner on your site

Now, see if you can do the same thing but with a banner for the Joomlaville Zoo:

1. Download the banner from http://joomlaexplained.com/chapter7.

2. Go through the Categorize, Add, Show workflow and add the banner to the position-10 module area.

When you're finished, the banner should appear as in Figure 7.38. If you get stuck at any point, you can find the workflow for this module at http://joomla-explained.com/chapter7.

Figure 7.38   Showing a Zoo banner on your site

If you're ready to really challenge yourself, let's see if we can create a rotating pattern for our banners. We add a new banner for the Museum to the footer position that currently has the Zoo banner. Every time you visit a new page, you'll see either the Museum or the Zoo banner.

1. Download the Joomlaville Museum banner from http://joomlaexplained. com/chapter7.

2. Create an entry for it in the Banners component and place it in the Footer Right category.

3. Inside the Footer Aquarium Banner module, there are two options you need to change to make sure that only one banner shows every time the page loads:

   - Count
   - Randomize

If you're stuck, the answer is on http://joomlaexplained.com/chapter7.

Contacts

To practice Contacts, we set up two contact forms starting with a form for Joomlaville's Park Keeper. Here are steps to help you with this task.

Categorize

1. Go to Components, Contacts, and then Categories. Check that Joomlaville Contacts is in place—hopefully it is, and we can move on to adding a new contact.

Add

1. Go to Components, Contacts, and then Contacts again and click New.

2. Enter these three fields. It should look like Figure 7.39.

   - **Name. Joomlaville Park Keeper**.

   - **Category.** Joomlaville Contacts.

   - **Email.** Enter an e-mail address in here, even if it's the same as before. This field is under the Contact Details tab on the right-hand side.

Figure 7.39   Creating a Joomlaville Park Keeper contact form

Show

1. Go to Menus then Main Menu and click New.

2. Enter these three fields:

   - **Menu Item Type:** Choose Single Contact.

   - **Menu Title.** Enter **Contact Joomlaville's Park Keeper**.

   - **Select Contact.** Choose Joomlaville Park Keeper.

3. When you're finished, save the menu link, visit the front of the site, and click the Contact Joomlaville's Park Keeper menu link. You should see a screen like Figure 7.40.

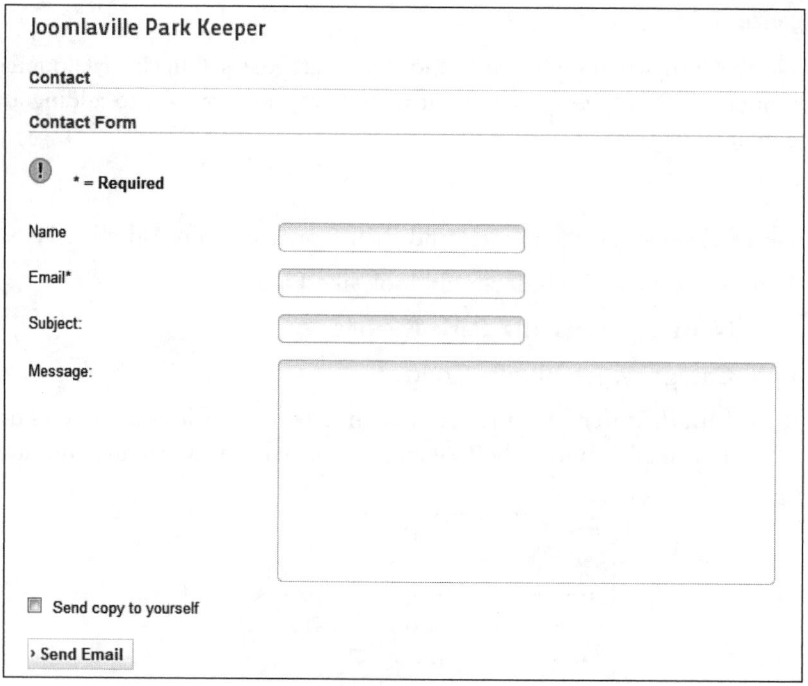

Figure 7.40   A new Joomlaville Park Keeper Contact menu link

Now, see if you can do the same thing but with a contact form for the Joomlaville Webmaster:

1. **Categorize.** Already done for you with the Joomlaville Contacts category.

2. **Add.** Create a contact called Joomlaville Webmaster.

3. **Show.** Create a menu link to the Joomlaville Webmaster contact form.

If you get stuck at any point, you can find the workflow for this contact form at http://joomlaexplained.com/chapter7.

Let's try another more challenging task. Let's see if we can add interesting information to the Joomlaville Webmaster contact form. Open the form and fill in these fields:

- **Contact Details/Image.** There's an image on http://joomlaexplained.com/chapter7.

- **Address.** Make up a fake address for him in Joomlaville.

- **Web site.** http://joomla.org.

- **Show Links.** Show.

- **Display Options/Link A Label.** Twitter.
- **Display Options/Link A URL.** http://www.twitter.com/joomla.
- **Display Options/Link B Label.** Facebook.
- **Display Options/Link B URL.** http://www.facebook/joomla.
- **Display Options/Link C Label.** YouTube.
- **Display Options/Link C URL.** http://www.youtube.com/user/joomla.

Now when you save the contact forms with those options, it should look like Figure 7.41.

Figure 7.41   The Joomlaville Webmaster contact form with more details

News Feeds

To practice working with the Newsfeeds component, we pull in two more useful sources of Joomla information. First, let's get the updated news from sites that write about Joomla. Here are steps to help you with this task.

Categorize

1. Go to Components, News Feeds, and then Categories. Check that News from Other Sites is in place—hopefully it is, and we can move on to adding a new feed.

Add

1. Go to Components, News Feeds, and then Feeds and click New.
2. Enter these three fields. Your screen should look like Figure 7.42.

   - **Name. Joomla News Sites**
   - **Link.** http://feeds.joomla.org/JoomlaConnect
   - **Category.** News From Other Sites

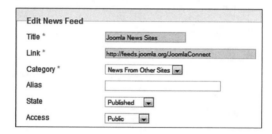

Figure 7.42   Creating a new Joomla news feed

Show

1. Go to Menus, then Main Menu, and click New.
2. Enter these three fields. Your screen should look like Figure 7.43:

   - **Menu Item Type.** Choose Single News Feed
   - **Menu Title. Joomla News Sites**
   - **Feed.** Joomla News Sites

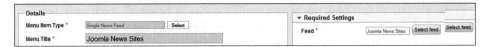

Figure 7.43   Adding a news feed for Joomla News Sites

3. When you're finished, save the menu link, visit the front of the site, and click the Joomla News Sites menu link. You should see a screen like Figure 7.44.

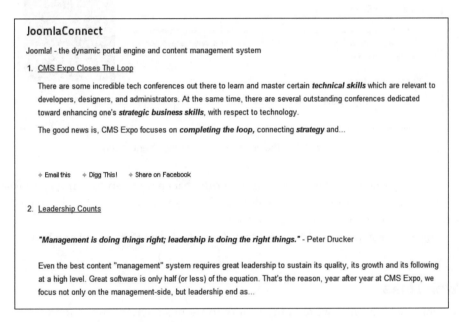

Figure 7.44   Joomla News Sites news feed

Now see if you can do the same thing but with a feed for major Joomla announcements:

1. Categorize: Already done for you with the News from Other Sites category.

2. Add: Create a feed called Joomla Announcements and use this URL: http://www.joomla.org/announcements.feed?type=rss.

3. Show: Create a menu link to the Joomla Announcements feed.

When you're finished, the feed should look as in Figure 7.45. If you get stuck at any point, you can find the workflow for setting up this news feed at http://joomlaexplained.com/chapter7.

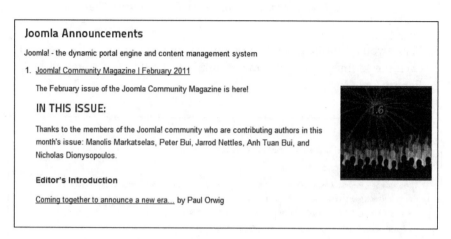

Joomla Announcements

Joomla! - the dynamic portal engine and content management system

1. Joomla! Community Magazine | February 2011

The February issue of the Joomla Community Magazine is here!

IN THIS ISSUE:

Thanks to the members of the Joomla! community who are contributing authors in this month's issue: Manolis Markatselas, Peter Bui, Jarrod Nettles, Anh Tuan Bui, and Nicholas Dionysopoulos.

Editor's Introduction

Coming together to announce a new era... by Paul Orwig

Figure 7.45   The Joomlaville Announcements feed

Let's try one more task that's a little more challenging. Go to http://joomla-explained.com and look for the RSS feed. See if you can create a feed entry for that site and also a menu link to the feed.

Again, if you're stuck, look on http://joomlaexplained.com/chapter7 for help.

Web Links

To practice Web links, we're going to link to more sources of useful Joomla information. First, let's get some links to sites with Joomla tutorials. Here are steps to help you with this task.

Categorize

1. Go Components, Web links, then Categories and click New.

2. Create a category called Joomla Tutorials.

Add

1. Go to Components, Web Links, and then Web Links again.

2. Set up Web links for the following URLs. Each one should look like Figure 7.46, which used OSTraining Tutorials as an example.

- **Title.** OSTraining Tutorials: http://ostraining.com/blog/joomla
- **Title.** How to Joomla: http://howtojoomla.net
- **Title.** Joomla Blogger: http://joomlablogger.net

3. Go online and see if you can find other good Joomla tutorial sites to list here.

Figure 7.46   Creating a new Joomla Tutorial Web link

Show

1. Go to Menus, Main Menu, and then click New.
2. Enter these three fields. Your screen should look like Figure 7.47.
   - **Menu Item Type.** Choose List Web Links in a Category
   - **Menu Title. Joomla Tutorials**
   - **Category.** Joomla Tutorials

Figure 7.47   Creating a new category of Web links

3. Go to the visitor area of your site and click the Joomla Tutorials menu link. You should see a screen like Figure 7.48.

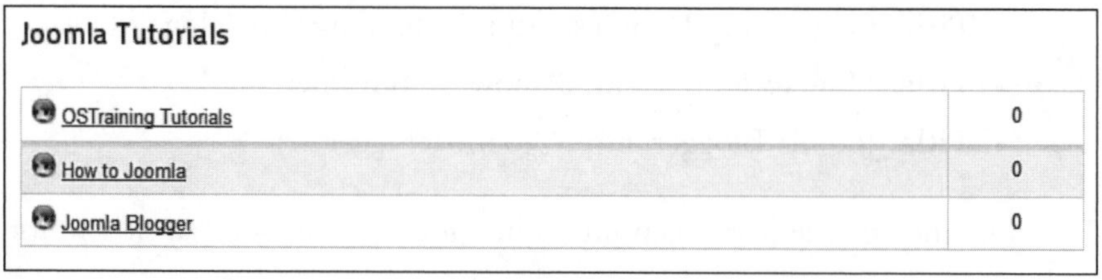

Joomla Tutorials	
🌐 OSTraining Tutorials	0
🌐 How to Joomla	0
🌐 Joomla Blogger	0

Figure 7.48   Viewing a new category of Web links

Now see if you can do the same thing but with links to various types of Joomla Extensions:

1. Categorize: Create a category called Media Extensions.

2. Add: Set up Web links for these URLs:

   - **Title.** Photo Gallery Extensions: http://extensions.joomla.org/extensions/photos-a-images

   - **Title.** Multimedia Extensions: http://extensions.joomla.org/extensions/multimedia

   - **Title.** Social Extensions: http://extensions.joomla.org/extensions/social-web

3. Show: Create a menu link to Joomla Media Extensions category.

When you're finished, the Web links should appear as in Figure 7.49. If you get stuck at any point, you can find the workflow for setting up this Web link at http://joomlaexplained.com/chapter7.

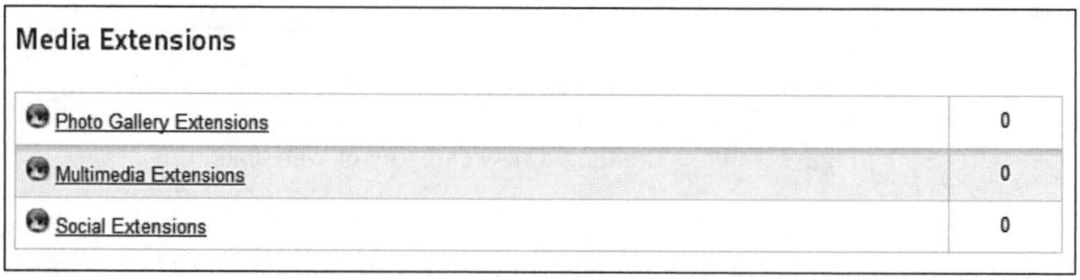

Media Extensions	
🌐 Photo Gallery Extensions	0
🌐 Multimedia Extensions	0
🌐 Social Extensions	0

Figure 7.49   The Media Extensions Web links category

Hopefully you were expecting a challenge here by now! Here's your advanced task for Web links. When you're finished, you should be able to see a result that looks like Figure 7.50.

1. Categorize: Create a category called E-Commerce Extensions.

2. Add: Go to http://extensions.joomla.org and look down the left-hand side of the page. Find the URLs for these categories and enter them into your site as Web links:

   - Ads & Affiliates

   - E-Commerce

   - Financial

3. Show: Create a menu link to Joomla E-Commerce Extensions category.

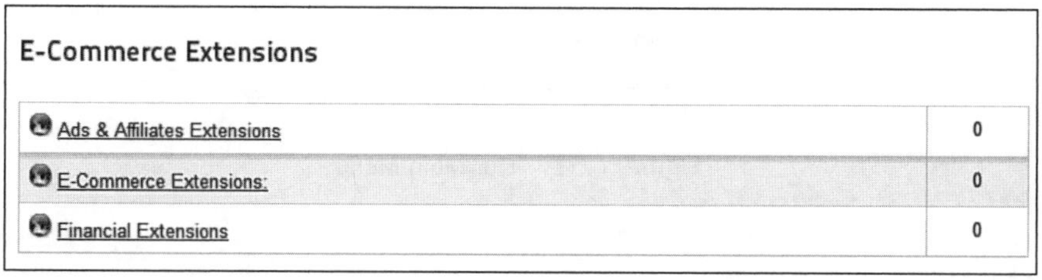

E-Commerce Extensions	
🌐 Ads & Affiliates Extensions	0
🌐 E-Commerce Extensions:	0
🌐 Financial Extensions	0

Figure 7.50   The E-Commerce Extensions Web links category

If you're stuck look on http://joomlaexplained.com/chapter7 for help.

Cleaning Up the Menu Links

Our Main Menu is shown in Figure 7.51, and it now looks a bit of mess with too many links. Let's see if we can tidy them up and introduce you to a new menu feature in the process.

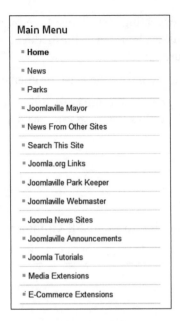

Figure 7.51   Our Main Menu

Contacts

First, we tidy up our contact forms. We make a link to all our contacts and then have individual contact links become submenu links. Here's how we do it:

1. Go to Menus, Main Menu, and then click New.

2. Enter these three fields. Your screen should look like Figure 7.52:

   - **Menu Item Type.** List Contacts in a Category

   - **Menu Title. Joomlaville Contacts**

   - **Select a Category.** Joomlaville Contacts

Figure 7.52   Creating a menu link to all your Contact forms

Now here's the new menu feature:

1. Open up one of the menu links to a contact form that you've already made. One example is the menu link called Joomlaville Mayor.

2. In the Parent Item drop-down, choose Joomlaville Contacts as in Figure 7.53.

Menu Item Type *	Single Contact	Select
Menu Title *	Joomlaville Mayor	
Alias	joomlaville-mayor	
Note		
Link	index.php?option=com_contact&view=contact	
State	Published	
Access	Public	
Menu Location *	Main Menu	
Parent Item	- Joomlaville Contacts	
Target Window	Menu Item Root	
	- Home	
Default Page	- News	
	- Parks	
	- News From Other Sites	
Language	- Search This Site	
	- Joomlaville Links	
Template Style	- Joomlaville Park Keeper	
	- Joomlaville Webmaster	
ID	- Joomla News Sites	
	- Joomlaville Announcements	
	- Joomla Tutorials	
	- Media Extensions	
	- E-Commerce Extensions	
	- Joomlaville Contacts	

Figure 7.53   Making the Joomlaville Mayor link into a submenu link

3. Repeat that for the Joomlaville Park Keeper and Joomlaville Webmaster links

When you're finished, your Main Menu screen should now look like Figure 7.54.

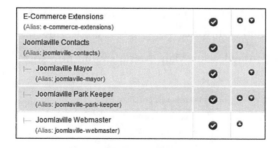

Figure 7.54   The Joomlaville Contacts links—neatly organized.

4. Go to the visitor area of your site and click on Joomlaville Contacts under Main Menu. You see that other contact links are hidden, but they become visible after you've clicked, as in Figure 7.55.

Figure 7.55   The Joomlaville Contacts links converted into submenu links

News Feeds

Now, let's tidy up our news feeds. We make a link to all our news feeds and then have individual news feed links become submenu links. Here's how we do it:

1. Go to Menus, Main Menu, and then click New.

2. Enter these three fields and then save that link:

   - **Menu Item Type.** List News Feeds in a Category
   - **Menu Title. News from Other Sites**
   - **Select a Category.** News from Other Sites

And now for our new submenu feature:

1. Open up one of the news feed links you've already made such as Joomla News Sites.

2. In the Parent drop-down, choose News from Other Sites and click Save.

3. Repeat that for the Latest Joomla Extensions, Joomla Announcements, and JoomlaExplained.com feeds.

When you're finished, your Main Menu should now look like Figure 7.56.

Figure 7.56   Your news feed menu links, neatly organized into submenu links

Web Links

Here (I promise!) is the final challenge for you in this chapter. Let's repeat that submenu process one more time for our Web links:

1. Make a new menu link to the List All Web links Categories type and name it **Joomlaville Web links**.

2. Place the Joomla.org Links, Joomla Tutorials, Media Extensions, and E-Commerce Extensions links as submenus underneath that new menu link.

When you're finished, your Main Menu should now look like Figure 7.57.

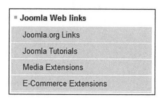

Figure 7.57   Your Web links menu links,
neatly organized into submenu links

Now that we've finished Chapter 7, your Main Menu should look like Figure 7.58. Hopefully you'll agree that it is much more organized than before.

```
Main Menu

  ▪ Home

  ▪ News

  ▪ Parks

  ▪ Search This Site

  ▪ Joomlaville Contacts

  ▪ News from Other Sites

  ▪ Joomla Web links
```

Figure 7.58   Your complete Main Menu at the end of Chapter 7

Also, now that we've finished Chapter 7, your whole Joomla Web site should look similar to Figure 7.59.

Don't worry if your Main Menu or the whole site is not 100% the same as Figure 7.59.

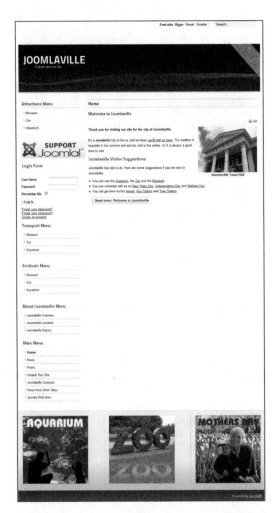

Figure 7.59   Your complete Joomla site at the end of Chapter 7

The goal here is to not perfectly re-create this site about Joomlaville. The goal is for you to understand the concepts and the processes. If you now feel comfortable creating banners, contact forms, search boxes, Web links, and more, that's great: You're ready to move on to the next chapter.

What's Next?

In this chapter we introduced components, which add exciting extra features to your Joomla site. Components are just one of several types of extensions that you can use to improve your Joomla site.

In Chapter 8, "Joomla Modules Explained," you learn about another type of extension: modules.

Modules allow us to show small, but important, blocks of information to our visitors. Turn the page, and let's see how useful they can be.

8

Joomla! Modules Explained

Modules make life easier for our site's visitors. They are small blocks that allow visitors to quickly find information, links, or features. Because they're small, they're often found around the outside of your site's page.

Things You Can Do After Reading This Chapter

- Understand modules
- Create modules

There are also four ways in which you can control modules. In this chapter, you learn how to

- Change the position of modules
- Change the order modules appear in
- Change menu links modules appear on
- Change when modules appear

Understanding Modules

Modules normally go around the left, right, top, and bottom of your site. The default Joomla template has more than a dozen different places where you can place them. If we turn on one option, we can see them on the front of our site:

1. Go to Extensions, Template Manager, and then Options, and you see the screen shown in Figure 8.1.
2. Set Preview Module Positions to Enable and click Save & Close.

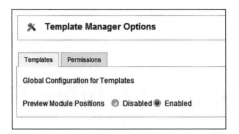

Figure 8.1   Turning on the option to see template positions

3. Now click Templates in the horizontal toolbar, and you see all the installed templates. Scroll down and click Preview next to Beez_20 as shown in Figure 8.2.

Figure 8.2   Finding the link to see module positions in Beez_20

4. You see the template we've been looking at throughout the book, but you also now see the various module positions it contains as shown in Figure 8.3.

Because it's not always easy to see the module positions on the site, we've created a clearer image of the positions in Figure 8.4.

Figure 8.3 Module positions in Beez, the default Joomla template

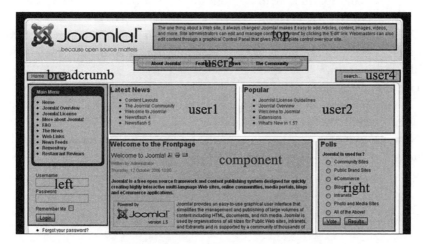

Figure 8.4 Module positions in rhuk_milkyway, the default template
in the previous version of Joomla

In most cases, the designer of a template provides a map of the different modules for you. Figure 8.5 is an example from a company called Joomlashack.com, which sells Joomla templates. The template has the positions shown in Figure 8.5.

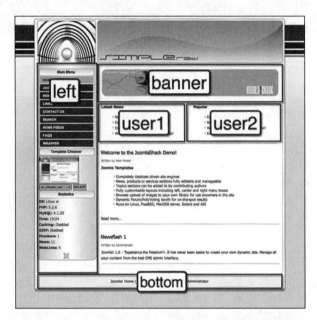

Figure 8.5   Example from Joomlashack.com of module positions in a template

Here's another example with 20 positions from a company called YooTheme.com (see Figure 8.6).

The examples used so far are straightforward, but some designers get flexible with their layouts. Figure 8.7 is another example from a company called JoomlaBamboo.com.

Hopefully whenever you download a template, there will be a grid showing all the module positions, just like Figure 8.7. However, if there isn't, you can always go to the Template Manager and click on Preview.

Now, let's put that new knowledge into action and place modules into those positions.

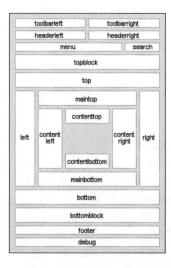

Figure 8.6   Example from YooTheme.com of module positions in a template

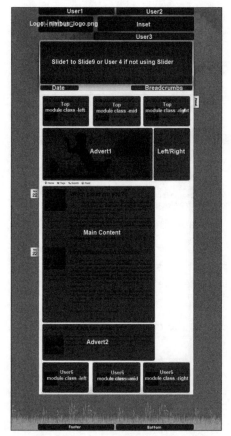

Figure 8.7   Example from JoomlaBamboo.com of module positions in a template

Creating New Modules

Modules are often the last part of Joomla's CASh workflow:

- Categorize
- Add
- Show—this is the purpose of module

This is good news! It means that creating new modules is often easy.

For example, we add a module showing the latest articles on our site. This will be useful to visitors because they won't have to go searching around to find out what's new. Making this module is easy because in previous chapters we already created the categories and added the articles. All that's left is to Show.

Let's go and create that new module to show our visitors the latest articles.

1. Go to Extensions, Module Manager, and then click New in the top-right corner.

2. You see a pop-up screen like the one in Figure 8.8. Click on Latest News.

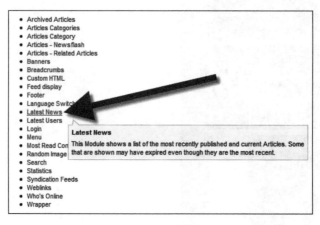

Figure 8.8   Choosing to create a Latest News module

3. You now see a screen like Figure 8.9. This is the type of screen you will always see when creating or editing a module.

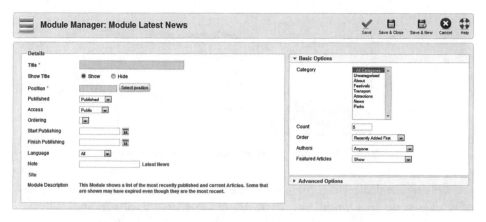

Figure 8.9   The module creation and editing screen

4. Enter these three settings for your new module as in Figure 8.10.

   - **Title. Latest Joomlaville Articles**
   - **Position.** position-6
   - **Category.** Highlight all the categories

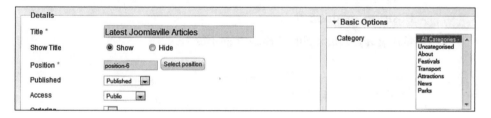

Figure 8.10   Choosing the settings for your
Latest Joomlaville Articles article

5. Click Save & Close to record your changes and then click View Site. You see your new module on your front page, as in Figure 8.11.

Figure 8.11   Your new Latest Joomlaville Articles module

Let's repeat that process one more time as it's something you might do a lot of while setting up a Joomla site. We're going to set up a similar module. The only difference this time is that it will show the most popular Joomlaville articles (the ones that have been visited the most often) rather than the latest articles. Here's how we do it:

1. Go to Extensions, Module Manager, and then click New in the top-right corner.

2. You see a pop-up screen. Click on Most Read Content.

3. Enter these three settings for your new module as in Figure 8.12.

   - **Title. Popular Joomlaville Articles**

   - **Position.** position-6

   - **Category.** Highlight all the categories

Figure 8.12   Choosing the settings for your Most Read Content module

4. Click Save & Close to record your changes, and then click View Site. You see your new module on your front page, as in Figure 8.13. It is under the Latest Joomlaville Articles module you made earlier.

Figure 8.13   The Most Read Content module visible on your site

Hopefully you agree the process was straightforward. We can now leave these modules, and they'll update automatically. For example, every time we add a new article, you see it appear under Latest Joomlaville Articles.

However, as we add more modules we might end up with many of them in one single position. For example, we now have two modules in position-6 and seven modules in position-7. You can see the modules in position-7 in Figure 8.14. What happens if we want to reorder them? Main Menu has fallen a long way down the list, almost to the bottom. It would be great if we could reorder the modules so Main Menu is higher up the page again. Read on to see how.

Figure 8.14   Modules on your Joomla site

Changing the Order of Modules

Now you know how to create Joomla modules and place them in different positions on your site. However, what happens when you have multiple modules in one position? For example, you might decide that Most Popular Joomla

Explained Articles should be on top and Latest Joomla Explained Articles should be underneath. In addition to changing the position of modules, you can also change the order of them. Let's see how to do that:

1. Go to Extensions, Module Manager, and you see a list of all your modules as shown in Figure 8.15. Currently, they're all sorted according to position.

Figure 8.15   Joomla modules sorted by position

2. We can change the sorting of the modules simply by clicking on the Ordering title as shown in Figure 8.16, and sort the modules using that criteria.

3. Check the list carefully. Small blue up and down arrows have appeared next to each module as shown in Figure 8.17. You can click those to move the modules up and down. You can see how that works by clicking on the blue up arrow next to Main Menu.

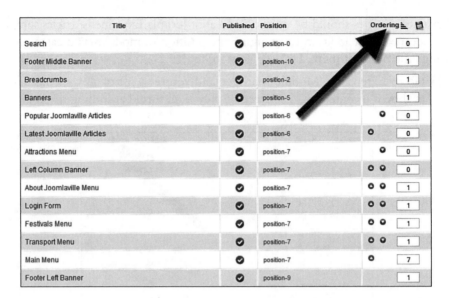

Title	Published	Position	Ordering ≛ 📋	
Search	✓	position-0		0
Footer Middle Banner	✓	position-10		1
Breadcrumbs	✓	position-2		1
Banners	◉	position-5		1
Popular Joomlaville Articles	✓	position-6	○	0
Latest Joomlaville Articles	✓	position-6	○	0
Attractions Menu	✓	position-7	○	0
Left Column Banner	✓	position-7	○ ○	0
About Joomlaville Menu	✓	position-7	○ ○	1
Login Form	✓	position-7	○ ○	1
Festivals Menu	✓	position-7	○ ○	1
Transport Menu	✓	position-7	○ ○	1
Main Menu	✓	position-7	○	7
Footer Left Banner	✓	position-9		1

Figure 8.16   Joomla modules sorted by order

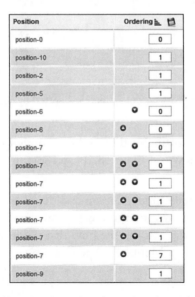

Position	Ordering ≛ 📋	
position-0		0
position-10		1
position-2		1
position-5		1
position-6	○	0
position-6	○	0
position-7	○	0
position-7	○ ○	0
position-7	○ ○	1
position-7	○ ○	1
position-7	○ ○	1
position-7	○	7
position-9		1

Figure 8.17   Changing the order of your Joomla modules using arrows

There's also a quicker way to move a module up several positions. The modules are ordered by numbers, which are shown in Figure 8.18. To guarantee that Main Menu moves to the top, do the following:

1. Place your cursor in the Ordering box next to Main Menu and enter a very low number such as –10.

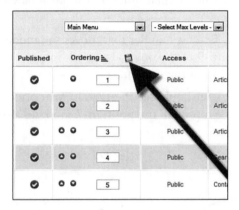

Figure 8.18   Changing the order of your Joomla modules using numbers

2. Click the small save icon at the top of the column.

3. After that's done, you should see Main Menu at the top of all the position-7 modules as in Figure 8.19.

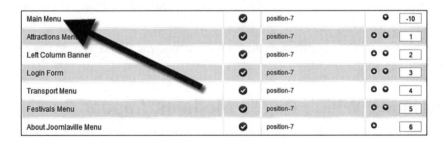

Figure 8.19   Main Menu at the top of the modules in position-7

Let's repeat the process one more time. For example, you might decide that you want more people to register and log in to your site. You can increase the chances of them doing this by moving the Login Forum up the page to make it more visible:

1. Inside Extensions and Module Manager, find the Login Form module. You can use either of these two methods:

   - **Method 1.** Click several times on the small blue up arrow next to Login Form.

   - **Method 2.** Enter a number that moves the module higher: Any number from -9 to 0 would be a good option. Then click the Save icon at the top of the column.

2. After that's done, you should see the Login Form placed just under the Main Menu at the top of all the position-7 modules as in Figure 8.20.

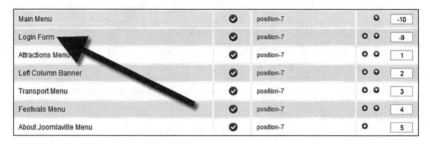

Figure 8.20   Login Form placed just under Main Menu

3. Click View Site, and you should see your modules have changed position as in Figure 8.21.

You're ready for your next challenge—how to show different modules on different pages.

Changing Which Pages Modules Appear On

It is possible to have different modules appear when you click different menu links. Why would you want to do this? For example, if people visit your Joomlaville News category, you can show them your latest news articles, and if people visit your Parks category, you can show them a module with a list of the Joomlaville parks. If all modules appeared on all pages, things would quickly become messy!

Figure 8.21   Congratulations. You've successfully
reordered your Joomla modules.

Let's use the example of Parks. We will make a module that automatically updates with a list of all the parks in our city. Here's how we do it:

1. Go to Extensions, Module Manager, and then click on New.

2. Choose Articles Category as the module type. This shows a list of all the articles in one category.

3. Enter these three settings for your new module as shown in Figure 8.22.

- **Title. Joomlaville Parks**
- **Position.** position-6
- **Filtering Options, then Category.** Parks

Figure 8.22   Creating an Article Categories module with a list of Parks

4. If we leave things as they are, this module appears on every page. We can change this by going to the bottom of the page, where we control which menu links this module appears on.

Scroll down to the Menu Assignment box. The first thing to do is remove the option for this module to appear on every page. Click the Module Assignment drop-down and choose Only on the Pages Selected as in Figure 8.23.

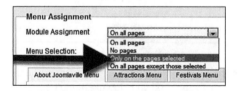

Figure 8.23   Menu Assignment for Joomla modules

5. Because we want most items unchecked, click Toggle Selection on the right-hand side as in Figure 8.24. That reverses all the current selections: making them all unchecked.

Figure 8.24   Unchecking the options for where the module will appear

6. Now click the Main Menu tab and check the box next to Parks as in Figure 8.25.

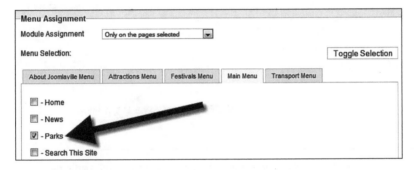

Figure 8.25   Choosing for the module to appear on the Parks page

7. Click Save & Close, then Visit Site and click Parks in your Main Menu. Your new List of Joomlaville Parks module should appear on this page and no others as in Figure 8.26.

Let's do that one more time to practice how it works. Let's add a welcome banner to our site's front page. To do this, we use what we learned about the Banners component in an earlier chapter and combine it with what we learned about modules in this chapter.

Categorize

We set up a category for our banner:

1. Go to Components, Banners, then Categories and click New.

2. Enter **Frontpage Header** in the Title field and click Save.

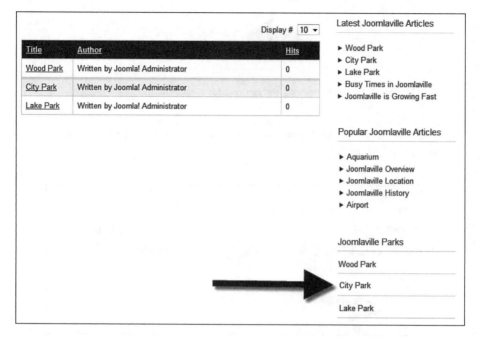

Figure 8.26   Your Joomlaville Parks module only on the Parks page

Add

Add a banner:

1. Click the horizontal Banners tab inside the Banners component and click New.

2. Enter these settings:

   - **Name. Welcome Frontpage Banner**
   - **Category.** Frontpage Header
   - **Image.** Download the Welcome image from http://joomlaex-plained.com/chapter8 to use as the image here.

3. Click Save & Close to finish adding your banner.

Show

1. Go to Extensions, Module Manager and then click on New.

2. Choose Banners as the module type.

3. Enter these five settings for your new module. Your settings should look like Figure 8.27.

- **Title. Frontpage Header Banner**
- **Show Title.** Hide
- **Position.** position-12
- **Category.** Frontpage Header
- **Module Assignment.** Under Module Assignment, choose Only on the Pages Selected. Then click Toggle Selection to uncheck all the menu links. Finally, click the Main Menu tab and check the Home box only.

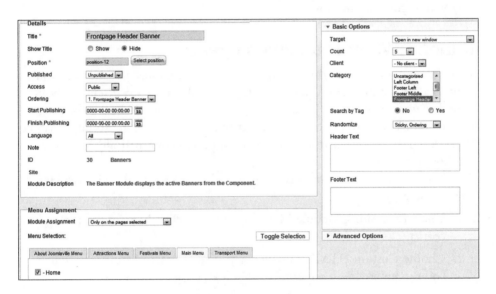

Figure 8.27   Creating a front page banner module

4. Click Save & Close, then click Visit Site, and your new banner should only appear on the front page as in Figure 8.28.

So far we've discussed *where* modules appear, and we've chosen what position, what order, and what pages they appear on:

- **Position.** position-6, position-7, position-12
- **Order.** First, second, third inside their module position
- **Pages.** Which menu links you click to make them appear.

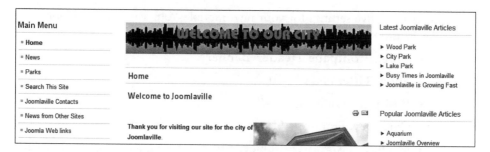

Figure 8.28   Your front page banner showing in a module

It's also possible to control *when* modules appear. Let's show you how and why you might want do this:

Change When Modules Appear

This is the only feature in this chapter that is new in Joomla 1.6. Imagine you want to advertise the New Year's party in Joomlaville. The advertisement looks great, but what happens on January 1? The advertisement will be out-of-date, and you won't want to get out of bed first thing in the morning to unpublish it. What you need is a way for the module to unpublish automatically. We show you how to do that now.

This setting is perhaps the easiest of all we've covered in this chapter. Here's how to use it:

1. Go to Extensions, Module Manager, and then click New in the top-right corner.

2. Choose Custom HTML: This allows you to create a module into which you can enter almost anything at all—text, images, and more.

3. Enter these three settings for your new module. Your module screen should look like Figure 8.29.

    - **Title. Joomlaville New Year's Party!**

    - **Position.** position-6

    - **Text.** You're invited to celebrate with us in Joomlaville on New Years Day! Everyone is welcome to have fun with us in the town center. (Use the Article button below the text to insert a link to the New Year's article you've written. You can change the link text if you like).

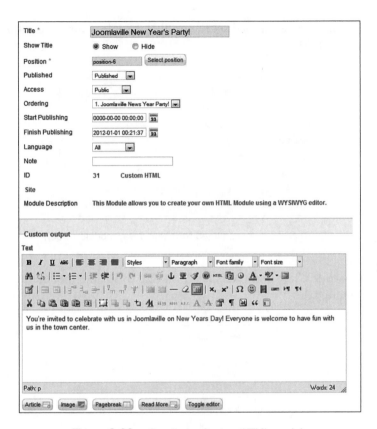

Figure 8.29   Creating a Custom HTML module

4. Now we can set the date on which this module will unpublish. Click on the small calendar icon next to the Finish Publishing field and you see a calendar like the one in Figure 8.30. Choose the date you want the module to stop publishing on your site: I'm going to choose January 1.

Figure 8.30   Picking the unpublish date for a module

By the time you're finished setting up this module, your screen should look like Figure 8.31.

Figure 8.31   A completed New Year's Day module screen

5. Click Save & Close and then click Visit Site to see the module in action (see Figure 8.32).

Figure 8.32   Your Joomla New Year's Party module live on the site

At the beginning of this chapter, I explained there are four ways you can control the modules on your site:

- Position
- Order
- Menu links
- Time and Date

Now that we've seen examples of all four, let's go ahead and practice them.

Practice

First, let's create a banner to advertise a special Mother's Day offer. Follow along with me and set it up.

Categorize

1. Go to Components, Banners, and then Categories and click New.
2. Enter **Footer Right** in the Title field and click Save & Close.

Add

1. Click the horizontal Banners tab inside the Banners component and click New.
2. Enter these settings:

   - **Name. Mother's Day Footer Banner**
   - **Category.** Footer Right Banner
   - **Image.** Upload and select the Mother's Day banner from http://joomlaexplained.com/chapter8
   - **Click URL.** mothers-day

Show

1. Go to Extensions, Module Manager, and then click on New.
2. Choose Banners as the module type.

3. There are several settings to choose from; however, I've outlined the following four questions you need to answer for modules. After you've entered them correctly, your screen should look like Figure 8.33.

- **Position.** Choose position-11.

- **Order.** There's only one module in this area, so no need to choose.

- **Menu links.** This banner will appear on all pages, so again there's no need to choose.

- **Time and Date.** Choose for the module to finish publishing on the day after Mother's Day in your country.

Figure 8.33   Creating a Mother's Day banner module

4. Click Save & Close and then Visit Site, and your new banner should appear as in Figure 8.34.

Figure 8.34   Your Mother's Day banner showing in a module

Now let's practice each of the ways in which we can control modules. I'm going to give you the tasks in the following sections. See if you can complete them using what you learned in the chapter so far. If you get stuck, instructions for each step are at http://www.joomlaexplained.com/chapter8.

Position

Move the Login Form to position-6. When you're done it should look like Figure 8.35.

Figure 8.35   The Login Form placed in position-6

Order

Move the Joomlaville New Year's Party! module to the top of the position-6 column. When you're done, it should look like Figure 8.36.

Menu Links

Move the Left Column Banner module so that it appears only when people click on Joomla Web links under Main Menu. To see the module more easily, it might also be useful to place it in position-12. When you're done, it should look like Figure 8.37.

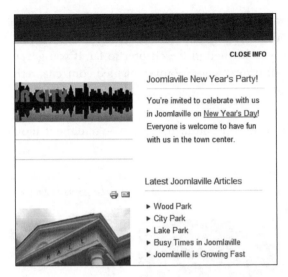

Figure 8.36   The Joomlaville New Year's Party! placed at the top
of the position-6 column

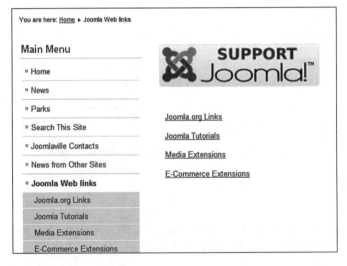

Figure 8.37   The Left Column Banner placed in position-12
on the Joomla Web links page

Time and Date

Create a new Custom HTML module. Here are some fields for you to enter:

- **Title.** Welcome to Our New Site

- **Position.** position-6

- **Finish Publishing.** Make sure that you choose a date that is only a few weeks in the future. After all, you can't continue to welcome people to your new Web site for too long.

- **Text.** Enter some text welcoming people to your new Web site. For example, you could write "Welcome to our new website. If you find any bugs, please contact the Joomla webmaster" and use the link button in the editor to link the Joomla Webmaster text to his contact form.

When you've published your module it should look like Figure 8.38.

Figure 8.38   The Login Form placed in position-7

Wonderful. You have practiced and you understand the four ways that you can control modules on your Joomla site. In this chapter and in previous chapters, you also saw examples of some default Joomla modules such as:

- Articles Categories
- Banners
- Custom HTML
- Latest news

- Login
- Menu
- Most Read Content
- Search

By the end of Chapter 8, your site should look similar to Figure 8.39. Again don't worry if your site doesn't look exactly like Figure 8.39. So long as you understand the four ways you can control a module on your site, you're ready to move on to the next chapter.

Figure 8.39   Your Joomla site at the end of Chapter 8

What's Next?

You've now worked with two types of Joomla extensions. You saw components that add large extra features such as advertising banners and contact forms. You also saw modules that add small blocks of information around the outside of our site.

We're now going to look at plug-ins, which are the smallest extensions of all. They are Joomla's tiny helpers. Each one has a small task that it completes such as allowing your visitors to vote on articles or including social bookmarking links in articles.

Turn the page and find out more about them.

9

Joomla! Plug-ins Explained

Plug-ins are tiny but useful additions to your site. Each plug-in does one simple thing. For example, one plug-in allows your visitors to vote on articles you've written. Another plug-in stops any e-mail address on the site from being collected by spammers.

Things You Can Do After Reading This Chapter

- Understand plug-ins
- Enable and use plug-ins

The Plug-in Manager

Plug-ins are the easiest thing we're going to do in this book! Why? Because at the beginner level you don't need to do much more than understand them and use them. Most of them are so simple that they just need to be turned on or off.

Go to Extensions, Plug-in Manager, and you see a page like the one shown in Figure 9.1.

There are 35 default plug-ins here. Because they are so small, they even have their own categories. We introduce you to plug-ins by using these categories.

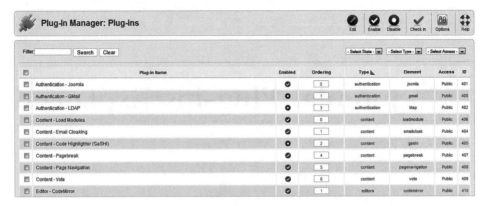

Figure 9.1   The Plug-in Manager

Authentication Plug-ins

Authentication is a posh word for "login." These plug-ins give you a variety of ways to log in to your Joomla site. To see them clearly, click on the Select Type drop-down in the top-right as shown in Figure 9.2 and choose Authentication.

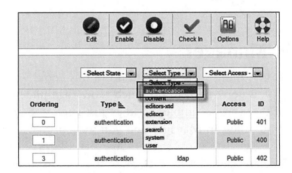

Figure 9.2   Choosing to view only one type of plug-in

When you've done that, you see three plug-ins as in Figure 9.3.

The Joomla plug-in allows you to log in using your account on this Joomla site. For obvious reasons, please don't disable this particular plug-in. You won't be able to log in again if you do.

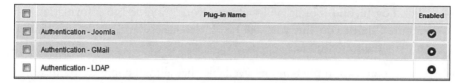

Figure 9.3   Authentication plug-ins shown in the Plug-in Manager

There are two disabled plug-ins here: GMail and LDAP. If you enable these plug-ins, here's what they'll do:

- **GMail.** If you enable this plug-in, people will be able to log in with their Google.com account details. They won't have permanent accounts, but they will be able to browse around and act as if they were normal users.

- **LDAP.** This plug-in is much geekier. LDAP is a popular form of user database often used on corporate networks. If you have a list of users in the LDAP format, you can enter the database details here, and Joomla allows those users to log in, again on a temporary basis.

If you have a Google account, it's easy to test the authentication of the GMail plug-in. Here's how to do it:

1. Click on the red circle next to the Authentication – GMail plug-in. It should change to a green check mark.

2. Go to the visitor area of your site and find the login module.

3. Enter your Google e-mail address and password as in Figure 9.4.

Figure 9.4   Testing the GMail plug-in

4. Click Log In, and Joomla will welcome you as a user. No information will be stored about you, but you will be able to access areas of the site that are only for registered users.

Extra authentication plug-ins are available that allow people to log in using their accounts on other popular platforms such as Twitter, Facebook, and OpenID. In Chapter 11, "Adding Joomla Extensions Explained," we show you how to add those to your site.

Content Plug-ins

Content plug-ins are those that directly affect your articles. These are probably the plug-ins that you will use most often.

Let's see the default content plug-ins. To do that, click on the Select Type drop-down in the top-right and choose Content. You'll see seven plug-ins as in Figure 9.5.

	Plug-in Name	Enabled
☐	Content - Joomla	✔
☐	Content - Load Modules	✔
☐	Content - Email Cloaking	✔
☐	Content - Code Highlighter (GeSHi)	◉
☐	Content - Pagebreak	✔
☐	Content - Page Navigation	✔
☐	Content - Vote	✔

Figure 9.5   Content plug-ins shown in the Plug-in Manager

Here's what those seven content plug-ins do:

- **Joomla.** This plug-in performs some maintenance tasks for your articles, such as e-mailing you if a new one is added.

- **Load Modules.** This plug-in allows you to place modules inside your articles. Why would you want do this? Let's take the example of the search box. We can place that inside an article to make it easy for people to find. Here's how we do it:

    1. Go the Article Manager and open the Welcome to Joomlaville article.

    2. Enter a heading and some intro text to explain what the search box is for. For example, you could write: **"Looking for Something Specific in Joomlaville"** as a heading.

3. Place this into your article after the end of the text: {loadposition top}. That will load all the modules that are currently in the top position. Your article should look like Figure 9.6.

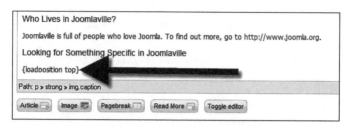

Figure 9.6   Using the Load Module plug-in to place
a module inside an article

4. Save the article and go to the visitors area of your site. Your article should now include a working search module as in Figure 9.7.

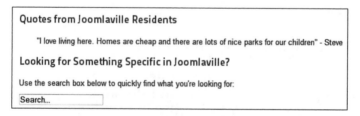

Figure 9.7   A search box inside an article

- **Email Cloaking.** This plug-in automatically hides e-mail addresses on your site from spammers. If you place your e-mail address in an article, it still looks like a normal e-mail address. In fact, it still acts like a normal e-mail address: If people click on it, their computers automatically create an e-mail for them to send to you. The difference is, if this plug-in is enabled, anyone trying to copy your e-mail gets a bunch of unreadable code. If you want to see how this works, do this:

1. Go to the Welcome to Joomlaville article and write a heading such as **"Can't Find What You're Looking For?"** and write a sentence that gives people your e-mail address for more help. Save the article and look for it in the visitor area of your site. My heading sentence is shown in Figure 9.8.

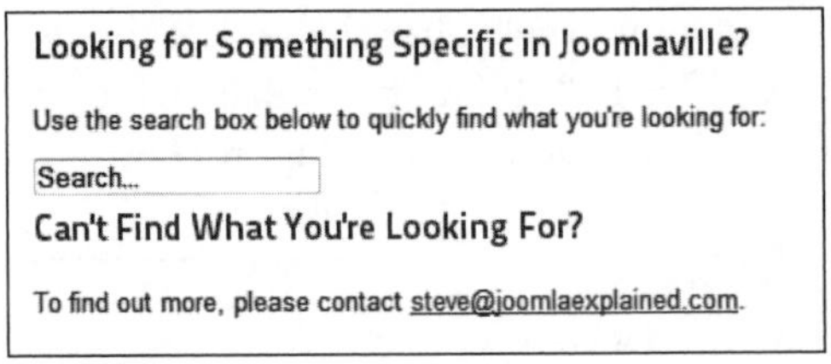

Looking for Something Specific in Joomlaville?

Use the search box below to quickly find what you're looking for:

| Search... |

Can't Find What You're Looking For?

To find out more, please contact steve@joomlaexplained.com.

Figure 9.8   An e-mail address inside an article

2. Right-click on the screen where you see the e-mail address. You should see a link with a label such as Source or View Source. Click on this link, and you see the code that is used for your site.

3. Search the code you see for the text you just wrote into the article. One common way to do this is to click the Control and F buttons on your keyboard. When you find the text, you'll see the code in Figure 9.9. The e-mail address has disappeared, and it can't be found by spammers. The e-mail address will only be made visible to your visitors.

```
<p>To find out more, please contact
<script type='text/javascript'>
<!--
var prefix = '&#109;a' + 'i&#108;' + '&#116;o';
var path = 'hr' + 'ef' + '=';
var addy32305 = 'st&#101;v&#101;' + '&#64;';
addy32305 = addy32305 + 'j&#111;&#111;ml&#97;&#101;
var addy_text32305 = 'st&#101;v&#101;' + '&#64;' +
document.write('<a ' + path + '\'' + prefix + ':' +
document.write(addy_text32305);
document.write('<\/a>');
//-->\n </script><script type='text/javascript'>
```

Figure 9.9   The code used to hide e-mail addresses
from spammers in a Joomla article

- **Code Highlighter (GeSHi).** Did I mention that the LDAP plug-in was geeky? This Code Highlighter plug-in is even geekier. It allows you to display rather than use code inside articles. This is useful if you have a site about code and want to show examples. Normally if you try to display any type of code inside a Joomla article, it's likely to look messy. The GeSHi plug-in allows you to display the code neatly. For information about how this plug-in works, visit http://qbnz.com/highlighter/.

- **Pagebreak.** Remember back in Chapter 5, "Joomla Content Editing Explained," when we were editing articles? You used the Pagebreak button to split one single article into several pages. That's what this plug-in does. Figure 9.10 is a reminder of what it does.

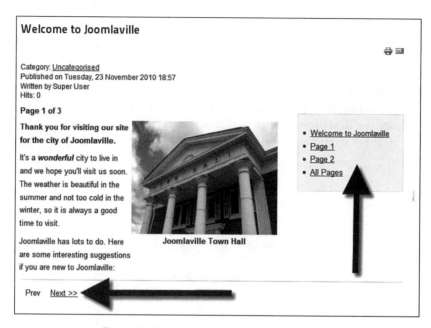

Figure 9.10   A pagebreak in a Joomla article

- **Page Navigation.** If you have too many articles for one single blog or list page, this plug-in creates multiple pages and links to them. You can see an example in Figure 9.11.

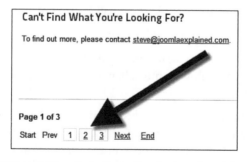

Figure 9.11   Page Navigation for Joomla articles.

- **Vote.** This plug-in does exactly what its name suggests: It allows people to vote on your articles. Here's how you can see it in action:

  1. Go to the Article Manager, click Options, and set Show Voting to Show on the first page you see.

  2. Go to the articles in the visitors area of your site, and you can vote on each one using a 1 to 5 rating as in Figure 9.12.

It's not very sophisticated voting. For example, it won't prevent determined people from voting multiple times. Nevertheless, it's a fun extra feature that you can turn on. Just don't forget to turn this off for certain articles using the Options area: For example, you don't want people voting on your staff member profiles!

Figure 9.12   Voting on Joomla articles

Editors and Editors-XTD Plug-ins

Content plug-ins affect how your articles look in the visitors area of your site. Editors and Editors-XTD plug-ins affect how your articles look when you're editing an article:

- Editors plug-ins provide the whole editor area at the top of your articles.

- Editors-XTD plug-ins provide the small buttons at the bottom of your articles.

You can see them both in action in Figure 9.13.

The Editors plug-ins allow you to change the editor area for your articles. By default there are three options:

- **TinyMCE.** This is the default editor that you've been looking at throughout the book and appears in Figure 9.13. If you go to the Plug-in Manager and click on the TinyMCE name, you see one option that is very useful: Functionality. By default, this is set to Advanced. However, there is also a Simple option that moves the editor to the bottom of your articles and only provides the most important editing features. It looks like the screen in Figure 9.14. This Simple option might be appropriate for nontechnical users. If you choose the Simple option for TinyMCE, the editor will look like Figure 9.14 inside your articles.

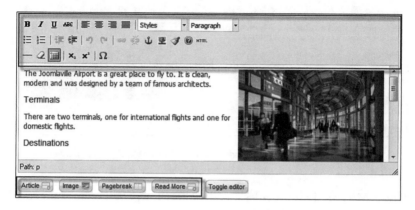

Figure 9.13   Editors and Editors-XTD plug-ins

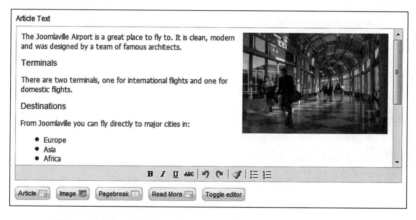

Figure 9.14   The Simple version of the TinyMCE editor plug-in

On the other hand, if you set the Functionality option in the TinyMCE plug-in to Extended, you get many more features. The Extended version looks like the screen shown in Figure 9.15 and might be appropriate for advanced users. The Extended option allows you to insert tables into your articles and take advantage of many more added features.

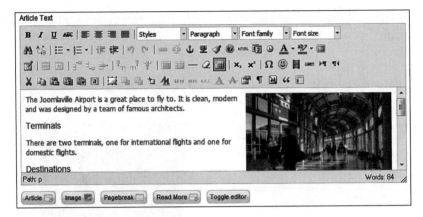

Figure 9.15   The Extended version of the TinyMCE editor plug-in

- **Code Mirror.** This provides a code editor for people who want to edit the article code directly. It looks like Figure 9.16.

```
Article Text

1   <p><img class="caption" src="images/transport/airport.jpg" border="0" alt="
2   <h2>Terminals</h2>
3   <p>There are two terminals, one for international flights and one for domes
4   <h2>Destinations</h2>
5   <p> </p>
6   <hr id="system-readmore" />
7   <p>From Joomlaville you can fly directly to major cities in:</p>
8   <p> </p>
9   <ul>
10  <li> Europe</li>
11  <li>Asia</li>
12  <li>Africa</li>
13  <li>North and South America.</li>
14  </ul>
15
```

Figure 9.16   The Code Mirror editor

- **None.** This is exactly what it sounds like. There will be no editor area, just the article text presented plainly on the page as in Figure 9.17.

You can change the editor used on the site in two ways:

- **For everyone.** Go to the Site menu, then Global Configuration, and change the Default Editor option.
- **For just one user.** Go to the Users link in the drop-down menu, click on User Manager, click on the name of the user, and change the Editor option.

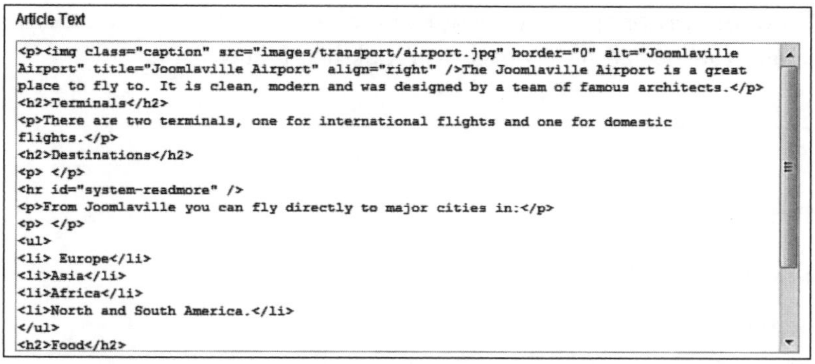

```
Article Text

<p><img class="caption" src="images/transport/airport.jpg" border="0" alt="Joomlaville
Airport" title="Joomlaville Airport" align="right" />The Joomlaville Airport is a great
place to fly to. It is clean, modern and was designed by a team of famous architects.</p>
<h2>Terminals</h2>
<p>There are two terminals, one for international flights and one for domestic
flights.</p>
<h2>Destinations</h2>
<p> </p>
<hr id="system-readmore" />
<p>From Joomlaville you can fly directly to major cities in:</p>
<p> </p>
<ul>
<li> Europe</li>
<li>Asia</li>
<li>Africa</li>
<li>North and South America.</li>
</ul>
<h2>Food</h2>
```

Figure 9.17   No editor

You're unlikely to add many extra Editor-XTD buttons for one good reason: There's not much more room. However, the ones that are there are useful, and you'll likely use the Article, Image, and Read More buttons frequently.

Search Plug-ins

Search plug-ins are vital to make the search feature on your site work. Let's show you just how vital they are:

1. Go to Extensions in the drop-down menu and then choose Plug-in Manager.

2. Click on the Select Type drop-down in the top-right and choose Search.

3. We're going to disable all these plug-ins, so click the green check marks next to each one so that they turn into red circles as shown in Figure 9.18.

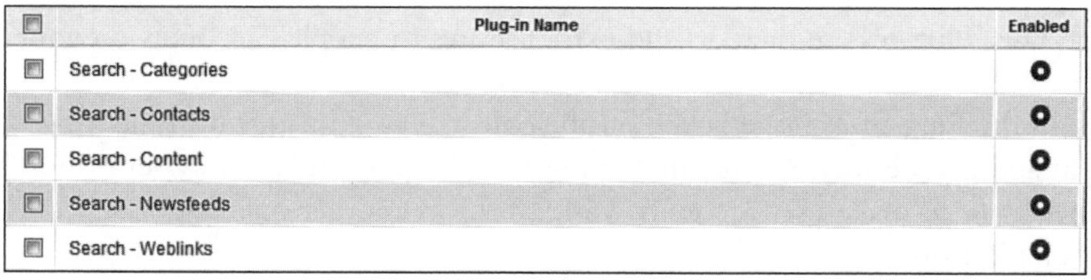

	Plug-in Name	Enabled
	Search - Categories	O
	Search - Contacts	O
	Search - Content	O
	Search - Newsfeeds	O
	Search - Weblinks	O

Figure 9.18   Disabling the search plug-ins

4. Go to the visitor area of your site and try a search. You won't get any results. Your search results page will look like Figure 9.19.

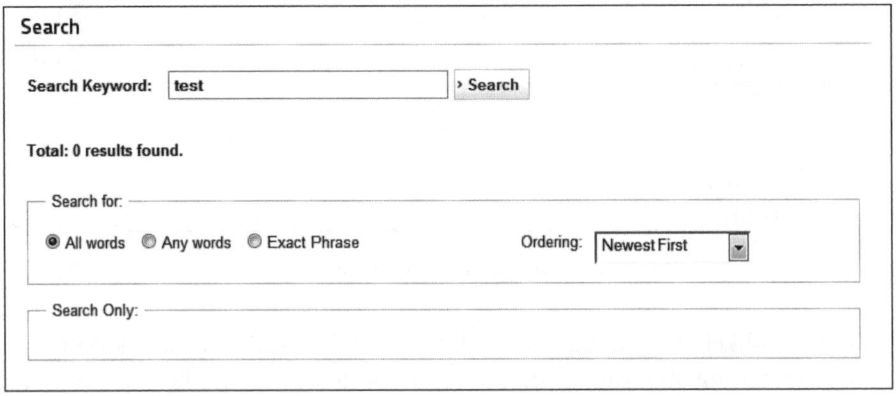

Search

Search Keyword: [test   ] › Search

Total: 0 results found.

Search for:
◉ All words ○ Any words ○ Exact Phrase   Ordering: [Newest First ▼]

Search Only:
[   ]

Figure 9.19   Using the Search form with the search plug-ins disabled

Each of the five default plug-ins is indexing a different part of our site. Without them we won't be able to search for categories, contacts, content, newsfeeds, or Weblinks.

In Chapter 11, we show you how to install extra features such as calendars, photo galleries, and shopping carts. Each one of these components requires a plug-in if you want your users to search for their content.

So if you want your site to be useful, be sure to go back to the Plug-in Manager and enable these search plug-ins again.

User Plug-ins

The User Plug-ins are there to add extra features to people's accounts on your site.

In the Plug-in Manager, click on the Select Type drop-down in the top-right and choose user. You see three plug-ins. The plug-in labeled User – Joomla! is necessary to make user accounts work, so this is another one that you shouldn't disable!

The other two plug-ins are worth looking at:

- **Profile.** By default, your site users are only asked for their names, user-names, e-mail addresses, and passwords. If you want to collect more information from them, use this plug-in. Click on the title of the plug-in, and you see a screen like Figure 9.20.

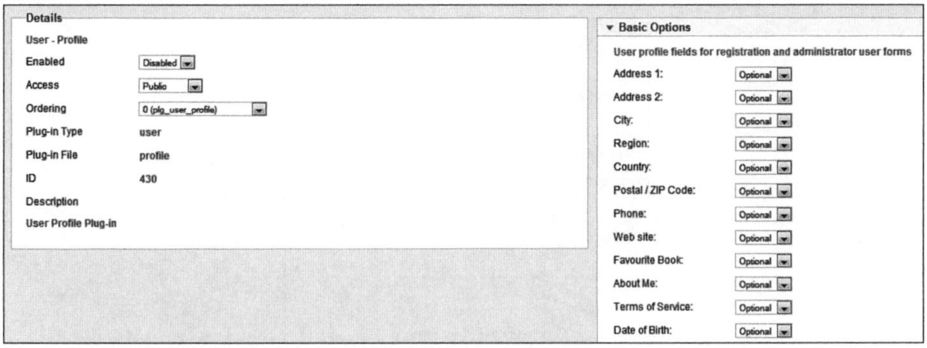

Figure 9.20 The User Profile plug-in in the administrator area

1. Under the Basic Options screen, go ahead and decide what information people will be asked for when they register and whether it's required or optional.

2. Enable the plug-in via the Enabled option, click Save & Close, and go to the visitors area of your site.

3. Find the Login Form module and click Create an account. You see a screen like Figure 9.21. The normal Name, Username, Password, and Email Address fields appear, but underneath you see all the extra fields that you selected,

- **Contact Creator.** This plug-in automatically creates a contact form for everyone who has a user account. Enable this plug-in, and whenever someone registers, they automatically get a listing inside the Contacts component. This could be used as a nice social feature if you have people registering on your site.

Figure 9.21   The User Profile plug-in: adding extra fields to your site's
registration form

Extension, System, and Other Plug-in Types

There are only two default plug-in types that we haven't covered here: extension
and system. You're unlikely to need to modify either of these beyond installing
and enabling them, which is a process we cover in the next chapter.

- **Extension plug-ins.** These are a tool used by developers to install and
  manage their extensions.

- **System plug-ins.** These help your site operate smoothly. They can almost
  all be enabled and disabled from inside the Global Configuration screen. It's
  easier to manage them from there.

- **Other plug-in types.** Some extensions may create whole new plug-in
  types for themselves. Large extensions such as shopping carts and social
  networks are particularly likely to do this. However, you simply are asked
  to install and enable them.

Finally, Figure 9.22 shows how your site looks at the end of Chapter 9. For the first time, there have been no major changes. That's because, as you've seen, plug-ins really don't change your site's overall appearance much. They might modify small options on articles or add interesting features to individual articles, but often their effect is not easily visible on the site.

Figure 9.22   Your Joomla site at the end of Chapter 9

What's Next?

You now understand how to manage extra features on your site. You know about components, modules, and also plug-ins.

The one really important thing we haven't covered yet is how to make your site look really good. That's what we cover in the next chapter.

We show you how to make your site look plain or colorful, playful or corporate, light or dark. We look at templates that control the design and layout of Joomla sites.

Let's turn the page and find out more about them.

10

Joomla! Templates Explained

Templates control the design and layout of our site.

- If you want a pink and green site, look for a pink and green template.
- If you want a site with a large header banner, look for a template with room for it.
- If you want to build a business site, look for a template with a corporate look and feel.
- If you want to build a personal blog, look for a template that reflects your personality.

Joomla arrives with three default templates for your site's visitors, and in this chapter we show you how they work. In Chapter 11, "Adding Joomla Extensions Explained," we show you how to find and add extra templates that have more features and a wider variety of designs.

Things You Can Do After Reading This Chapter

- Understand templates
- Change templates
- Change template options
- Use different designs and layouts on different pages

Understanding Templates

Templates are what attract many people to Joomla. You can use an amazing variety of designs and possibilities. With just a few clicks of your mouse you can completely redesign your site.

Figure 10.1 shows a minimal design called Simple Shop from a company called JoomlaBamboo.com. This template barely uses any images at all and only has a left and center column.

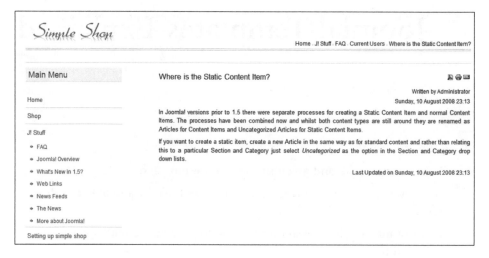

Figure 10.1   Simple Shop template from JoomlaBamboo.com

With a mouse click you can change to another template. You might choose a more colourful design like JA Events, shown in Figure 10.2. This is from a company called Joomlart.com and is designed for people holding events. It features many colorful images and even moving elements.

Click the mouse again, and you can redesign your site again. Figure 10.3 is Dominion from a company called Rockettheme.com, and it's very different from both of the previous templates. It features dark colors and a large slideshow in the header.

No matter what type of site you want to build, you can find a template to meet your needs.

Before we show you how they work, here is one important thing to know about templates: They do not change your content in any way.

Figure 10.2   JA Events template from JoomlArt.com

Figure 10.3   Dominion template from Rockettheme.com

Templates do not change your content. They may move it, hide it, or show it in a different color, but they do not harm your content. To show you what that means, let's compare one article in different templates. Figures 10.4, 10.5, and 10.6 show an article called The Joomla Community, which is displayed in the three templates we've just seen.

Figure 10.4 shows the The Joomla Community article in the Simple Shop template from JoomlaBamboo.com.

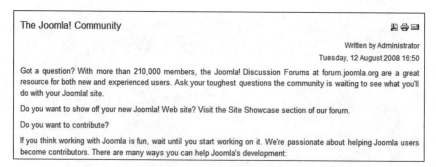

Figure 10.4   The Joomla Community article in the Simple
Shop template from JoomlaBamboo.com

Figure 10.5 shows the The Joomla Community article in the JA Events template from JoomlArt.com.

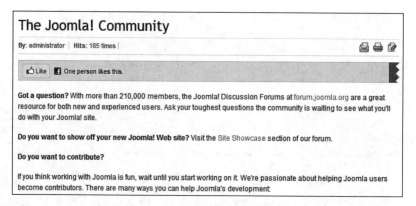

Figure 10.5   The Joomla Community article in the
JA Events template from JoomlArt.com

Figure 10.6 shows the The Joomla Community article in the Dominion template from Rockettheme.com.

The color, layout, font, spacing, and almost everything about the display of the article changes. The only thing that doesn't change is the content.

If you change your template, your articles stay the same. If you change your template, your components stay the same. They may look different, but their content will not change. If you publish a template that you don't like, you can just revert back to the previous template, and everything will be back to the way it was before.

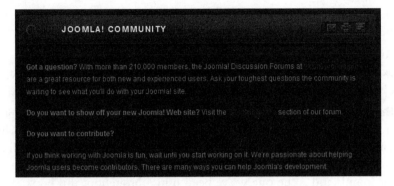

Figure 10.6   The Joomla Community article in the
Dominion template from Rockettheme.com

Changing Templates

By default, five templates are installed on your Joomla site. To see them, go to Extensions and then Template Manager. You see a screen like the one Figure 10.7.

There are two things to really pay attention to here:

- **The Location column.** This tells you whether the template is designing the visitors area (Site) or the private administrator area (Administrator). We work with the three Site templates that control what your visitors see.

- **The Default column.** This tells you which templates are currently being used.

Style	Location	Template ⬆	Default	Assigned	ID
Atomic - Default	Site	atomic	☆		3
Beez5 - Default-Fruit Shop	Site	beez5	☆		6
Beez2 - Default	Site	beez_20	★		4
Bluestork - Default	Administrator	bluestork	★		2
Hathor - Default	Administrator	hathor	☆		5

Figure 10.7   The Joomla Template Manager

There are two Administrator templates: Bluestork and Hathor. They are only for the Administrator area and can't be used for your site's visitors. Bluestork is the design for the administrator area that you're looking at right now. Hathor is a design that makes it easier for people with visual or physical requirements to run a Joomla site.

There are three visitor templates that you can use to design your site. Here's a brief description of the three visitor templates before we see them live:

- **Atomic.** A plain white template. It is designed to be a framework for experienced designers to build on and create their own designs quickly and easily. As a Joomla beginner, you're unlikely to use this on a live site.

- **Beez5 and Beez2.** As you might guess from the names, these templates are related. They have the same layout and features. Although Beez5 has some substantial code differences to help advanced users, the only difference that you'll see is a slight color variation. Beez2 is the default template for Joomla and is the one we've been using throughout this book.

Because the two versions of Beez are so similar, they'll make a good first example for changing templates. Here's how we change the design of our Joomla site:

1. In the Default column, click on the star in the Beez5 row as shown in Figure 10.8.

	Style	Location	Template ≞	Default
☐	Atomic - Default	Site	atomic	☆
☐	Beez5 - Default-Fruit Shop	Site	beez5	☆
☐	Beez2 - Default	Site	beez_20	★
☐	Bluestork - Default	Administrator	bluestork	★
☐	Hathor - Default	Administrator	hathor	☆

Figure 10.8   Changing your Joomla template

2. That's it. The golden star has moved to the Beez5 row, and you've changed your Joomla template. To see it live on your site, click View Site and see the new design as in Figure 10.9.

Everything is similar to how it looked before. The only major differences are the colors and the header image. All your modules are still there and in the same place.

That's not always going to be true. Some templates have radically different designs and layouts. To take just one example, let's change the template to Atomic:

1. In Extensions and Template Manager, look for the Default column and click on the star in the Atomic row. The gold star should move up to Atomic.

2. Click View Site, and you see that much has changed as in Figure 10.10.

Figure 10.9   The Beez5 template on your site

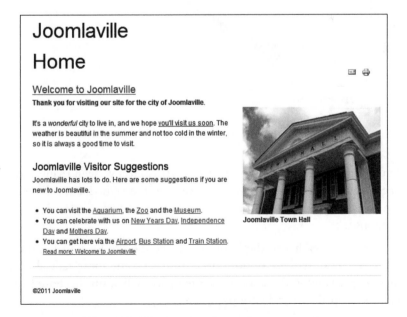

Figure 10.10   The Atomic template on your site

As you can see, Atomic comes with a radically different design and layout. In Chapter 11 we show you how to find and install your own templates. So if you want a minimal design, a colorful design, a dark design, or something completely different, we will now show you how to get it on your site.

Changing Template Options

We can redesign our site by changing the template. Often it's also possible to redesign our site and still keep the same template. Most templates come with design options.

Let's use Beez2 as an example and make it into the default template again:

1. In Extensions and Template Manager, look for the Default column and click on the star in the Beez2 row. The gold star should move down to Beez2.

2. Click on the Beez2 – Default name as in Figure 10.11.

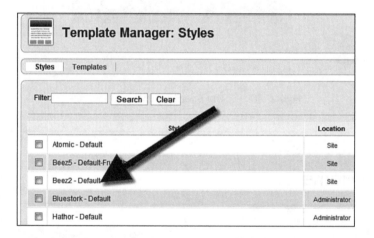

Figure 10.11   Click to see a template's options

3. You see a screen like the one in Figure 10.12. You've seen many Joomla pages by now, and the options are always on the right-hand side. Templates are no different. Look on the right-hand side, and you see an Advanced Options tab.

4. We were here earlier in the book to change the site logo, name, and slogan. However, let's use these options now to make some more radical changes including changing the color of the template. Click on the Template Colour drop-down and choose Nature.

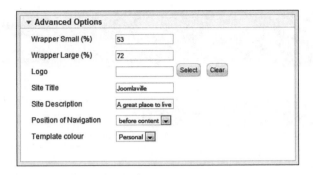

Figure 10.12   Beez2 template options

5. Click Save and then View Site. Your site should now be green and look like Figure 10.13.

Figure 10.13   Beez2 template with the Nature color option

The Beez2 options can also change the layout for you. Here's how:

1. Bring up the Beez2 options and look for the Position of Navigation drop-down. Change Before Content to After Content.

2. Click Save and then View Site. Your main menus should have moved to the right and look like Figure 10.14.

Figure 10.14   Beez2 template with the after content option for menus

Each template has different options. Some allow you to change the design. Some allow you to change the layout. Some have no options at all.

3. Click Close and leave the Beez2 screen. Click on the Atomic – Default link, and you see a screen like Figure 10.15. The right-hand side of the screen is blank. Atomic has no options that you change.

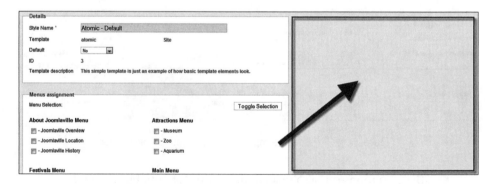

Figure 10.15   Options for the Atomic template

Although some templates have no options, others come with very advanced options. Figure 10.16 is the Solar Sentinel template from Rockettheme.com.

With this template, it's possible to pick any color you like for the template, directly from the template options.

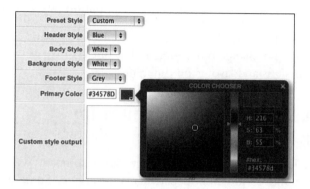

Figure 10.16   SolarSentinel template options for design

Some templates also give you options to completely change the site layout. Figure 10.17 shows a Rockettheme.com template that allows you to change the number of module positions inside ten different regions of your site.

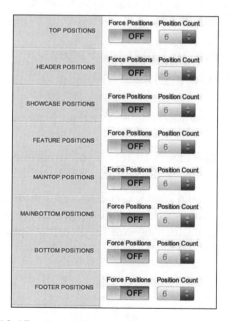

Figure 10.17   Rockettheme.com template options for layout

So if we want to change our site's design or layout, we have two options:

- We can change the template.
- If our existing template has the appropriate options, we can change those.

Joomla allows the flexibility to change our site's design and layout whenever we want. We can also change our design and layout *wherever* we want. We can have different designs and layouts on different pages.

Different Designs and Layouts for Different Pages

Not every site looks the same on every page. Some company Web sites have different color schemes for different departments or services. Some Web sites need different layouts on the home page than on the inside pages.

Joomla allows us to meet this need in two ways:

- Different templates on different pages
- Different styles of the same template on different pages

Let's go ahead and look at both those options. First, we see how to have different templates on different pages.

Different Templates on Different Pages

To show you how different templates can work on different pages, let's put the Beez5 template on the Zoo page. Here's how we do it:

1. Go to Extensions and then choose Template Manager and click on Beez5 - Default–Fruit Shop.

2. You see a screen like Figure 10.18. All you need to do is look for the Menus Assignment area at the bottom and check the box next to Zoo.

3. Click Save & Close and then View Site. Click on the Zoo link in the Attractions menu. You see that the Zoo page looks like Figure 10.19 and is now the only page on the site with the Beez5 template. Every other page has the regular blue Beez2 design.

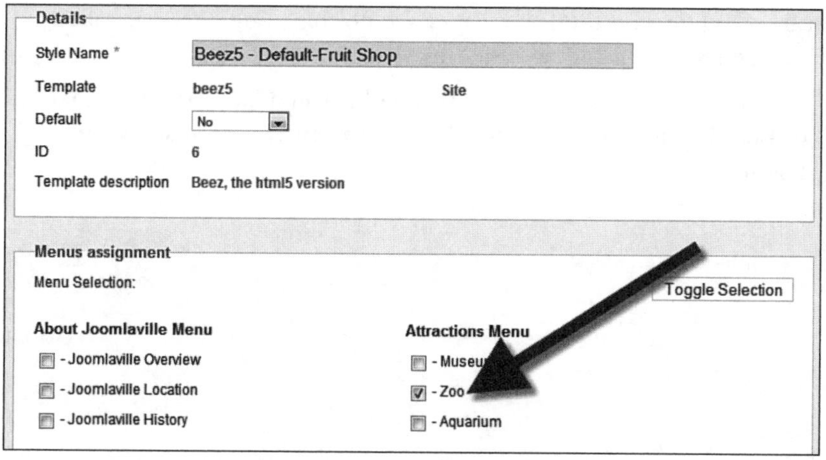

Figure 10.18   Choosing menu links for Beez5 to appear on

Figure 10.19   The Zoo article with the Beez5 template

Different Template Styles on Different Pages

Rather than replace the whole template on particular pages, we can also make changes to the template options and show those on different pages. For example, we can have the normal blue Beez2 option on most pages, but we can have the green Beez2 option on the Parks pages. We do this using a feature called Template Styles, which is new in Joomla 1.6.

1. Go to Extensions and then Template Manager. Check the box next to Beez2 and click Duplicate in the top-right corner as shown in Figure 10.20.

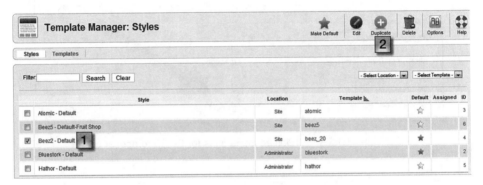

Figure 10.20   Creating a new template style

2. You'll see that an extra template style has been added: Beez2 – Default (2) as in Figure 10.21.

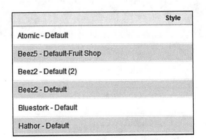

Figure 10.21   A new Beez2 template style

3. Click on that name, and you can choose options for this new style of Beez2. Here are my recommendations for a style for the News page. Enter them as shown in Figure 10.22:

- **Style Name.** Beez2 – News

- **Template Color.** Personal

- **Menus Assignment.** Only check the News box

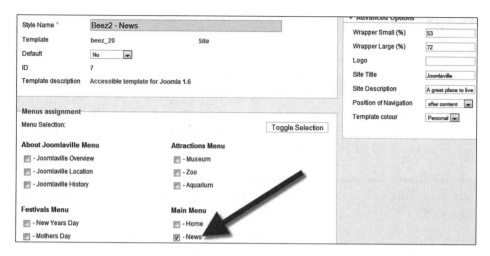

Figure 10.22   Creating the options for a new template style

4. Click Save & Close and then View Site. Click on News link in the Main Menu. You see that the News page looks like Figure 10.23 and is now the only page on the site with the Beez News style. Every other page has the regular default Beez style.

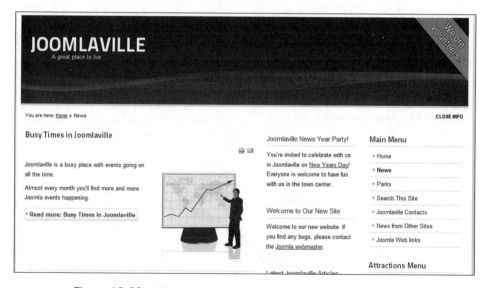

Figure 10.23   The new Beez – News template style live on your site

Practice

This practice area is really short for two reasons:

- We have many more chances to practice with templates in the next chapter when we start finding and installing exciting new templates.

- If you use too many templates and template styles on your site, things can get confusing. My recommendation when you're getting started is to use a maximum of three or four.

We already have three templates on our site, so let's practice by adding just one more. Your task is to create a new template style only for the home page of your site:

1. Create a new template style by duplicating Beez2 and call it Beez2 – Frontpage.

2. Choose the following options as shown in Figure 10.24:

   - **Logo.** Click Clear

   - **Position of Navigation.** Before content

   - **Template Color.** Personal

   - **Menus Assignment.** Only choose Home under Main Menu

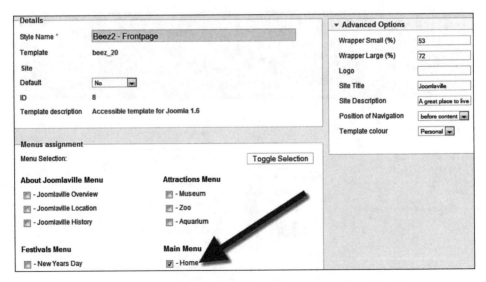

Figure 10.24   Creating the new Beez2 – Frontpage template style

When you finish creating that new template style, go to your home page, which should look like Figure 10.25.

Figure 10.25   The new Beez2 – Frontpage template style
live on your site's front page

Figure 10.25 also shows you how your site should look at the end of Chapter 10. As before, it's not a problem if your site looks a little different. If you understand how to change templates, change template options, and also create new template styles, you're ready to go on to the next chapter.

What's Next?

Back in Chapter 2, "Joomla Installations Explained," you installed Joomla. In every chapter since then, you've learned more and more about the features included with that first installation. You've seen how to add content and menus. You've also seen how to use components, modules, plug-ins, and templates.

However, so far you've only seen Joomla's default features. What if you want to add extra features with a new component, a new module, a new plug-in, or even a new template? Turn the page to see how to add extensions to your Joomla site.

11

Adding Joomla! Extensions Explained

It's time to move beyond the default extensions. We've shown you the components, modules, plug-ins, and templates that you see when you install Joomla. In this chapter, we show you how to find extensions that meet the unique needs of your site.

Things You Can Do After Reading This Chapter

- Research components, modules, and plug-ins
- Install components, modules, and plug-ins
- Research and install templates

Research Components, Modules, and Plug-ins

So far in this book we've looked at the default components, modules, and plug-ins:

- **Components.** There were seven including Banners, Contacts, Messaging, Newsfeeds, Redirect, Search, and Weblinks.
- **Modules.** There were more than 20. We didn't look at every default module, but we did practice with Search, Custom HTML, Latest News, Most Read Content, and more.
- **Plug-ins.** There were more than 30, and we looked at some of them that allowed us to vote on articles, search our site, automatically create contacts, and more.

Those default extensions are great for beginners. They serve as useful examples that you can use when learning Joomla. When it comes to building real sites you'll probably have more advanced needs. You may already be thinking about photo galleries, videos, shopping carts, social networking, and other features you'd like on your Joomla site.

There's one place to find all these features and more: http://extensions. joomla.org. This site is known as the Joomla Extensions Directory (JED) and lists absolutely everything that you might want to add to your Joomla site. It is the key place to evaluate all the components, modules, and plug-ins you might want on your site. The JED is constantly being updated, improved, and looked after. Joomla users are constantly testing and providing feedback on the extensions. There are also JED administrators who are experienced Joomla people who monitor the extensions for problems. I wouldn't recommend going anywhere else to look for extensions. The following sections explain how we use the JED to find and evaluate extensions.

Find the Right Category

Let's start our search by heading over to the JED and taking a look. If you visit http://extensions.joomla.org, you'll see a page like the one in Figure 11.1.

Figure 11.1   The Joomla Extensions Directory

There are two ways to find what you're looking for here, and they are both marked in Figure 11.2. You can either use the search box at the top of the page or the Categories list on the left.

Figure 11.2   Ways to search on the Joomla Extensions Directory

If you know what you're looking for and want to drill down quickly, then the Search box is a good option. When you're seeing the JED for the first time, the Categories list is good place to start. It allows you to browse if you're not sure exactly what you're looking for. For example, let's see if we can find a good way to show photos for our site. Take a look down the list of categories and find a category that matches what you're looking for, as in Figure 11.3.

If you click on Photos & Images, you see a whole range of further categories to choose from as in Figure 11.4. We're looking for a photo gallery, so go ahead and click on the category called Photo Gallery. The page is located at http://extensions.joomla.org/extensions/photos-a-images/photo-gallery.

You will not suffer from a lack of choice. As I write this there are nearly 7,000 extensions on the JED, and by the time you read this the number will likely be much higher. There are more than 400 extensions in the Photos & Images category alone. It will take you some time to learn how to browse through the JED and find what you're looking for. Fortunately, the JED is laid out to help you—if you know what you're looking for.

Figure 11.3   The Categories list on the Joomla Extensions Directory

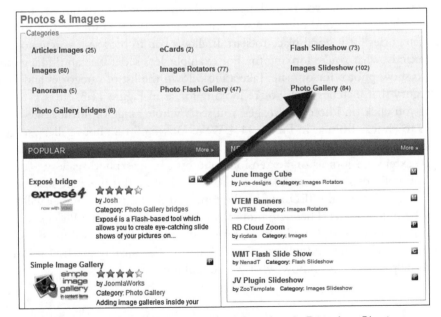

Figure 11.4   The Photo & Images category: Joomla Extensions Directory

So what should you be looking for? Here on the main category page are some important things that will help you find the right extension.

Rating

The extensions are ordered by feedback from people like you. Joomla users are allowed to vote on extensions and leave their comments. The extensions that have the most positive feedback rise to the top. So, if we see 80 extensions in the Photo Gallery category, the quickest way to sort is by looking at the top. In Figure 11.5 you can see that the first photo galleries all have a score of more than four out of five stars.

If you scroll to the bottom of the page and click Next, you see that there are several more pages of Photo Gallery extensions. The difference with these pages is that the extensions here may only have two or three stars out of five. Some extensions on these pages might not work well, but it's possible that some extensions have not been used often enough to get an accurate rating.

Figure 11.5   The Photo Gallery category on the JED

It's worth noting how many votes each extension has. An extension with five stars but only one vote might not be that good. An extension with no votes might be a hidden gem that is simply new or undiscovered.

Compatibility

Remember that there are several different versions of Joomla. Every extension has small icons showing which version of Joomla it works with.

Joomla 1.0 has a red icon, Joomla 1.5 has a green icon, and Joomla 1.6 has a blue icon. Although the colors aren't visible, you can see the icons in Figure 11.6.

| 1.0 NATIVE | 1.5 NATIVE | 1.6 NATIVE |

Figure 11.6   Compatibility icons in the JED

We're looking for the blue icon. If an extension isn't marked with that blue icon, then it's unlikely to work with our version of Joomla.

Commercial or Non-Commercial

About 75% of the extensions on the JED are completely free to use. The other 25% of the extensions are commercial, and you have to pay to download them. They generally cost from $5 up to $150 for the most advanced. You can see a commercial or non-commercial label on each extension (see Figure 11.7).

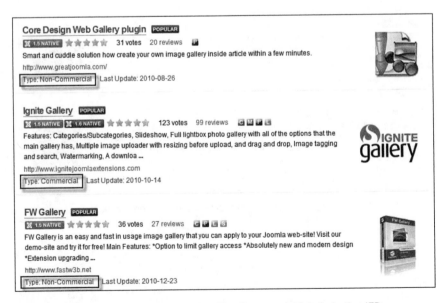

Figure 11.7   Commercial or Non-Commercial labels in the JED

Commercial extension developers make money by selling their extensions. They have a variety of business models:

- Some charge for the extension. Often paying for the extension gives you access to download it and any updates for a certain period of time such as six months or a year.

- Some provide the main part of the extension for free and charge for extra features.

- Some give the extension away for free and charge for support.

Non-commercial extension developers often make money by doing work for clients who need Joomla help. Even non-commercial extension developers have business models: After all, everyone needs to pay the bills and keep their lights on.

- Some use the extension as a form of advertising to help them attract business. For example, someone might download a photo gallery, realize that they need an extra feature, and then hire the developer of the photo gallery to code that feature.

- Some do work for clients and then get their permission to release the code to the Joomla community afterward.

- Some rely on donations. If you use a non-commercial extension and see a donation button on the developer's site, it's good practice to send them some money.

Regardless of whether you use a commercial or non-commercial extension from the JED, they all have two things in common:

- You can use them on as many sites as you want.

- The code is completely open. If you know how, you can change anything and everything about how they work.

Different Types of Extensions

It's perfectly possible for one extra feature to require more than one kind of extension. Something can require a component, a module, and a plug-in.

For example, a photo gallery might have the following extensions:

- A component to sort, organize, and display the photos in the center of the site

- A module to show the five most popular photos in the side-column of the site

- A plug-in to allow visitors to search the photo gallery

Figure 11.8 shows a photo gallery called XGallery that uses all three of those types of extensions.

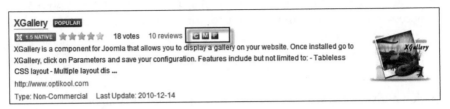

Figure 11.8   Extension type labels shown in the JED

All in all, six labels are used for extensions. Four are very common, and we address them in this book:

- **C: Component.**
- **M: Module.**
- **P: Plug-in.**
- **L: Language.** This means the extension has a language translation that can be installed.

Two more types are much rarer and are of more use to advanced Joomla users:

- **S: Special.** This means the extension has software that can be installed that is unique to it and isn't a component, module, plug-in, or language.
- **T: Tool.** This means it has software that can't be installed from Joomla.

Figure 11.9 shows what all the labels look like.

Figure 11.9   Extension type labels used in the JED

So, simply by looking at the Photo Gallery category we can work out four important pieces of information about everything we see. Here are two examples.

JPhoto is shown in Figure 11.10:

- **Rating.** Four out of five stars, but not many people have voted yet.
- **Compatibility.** Works with Joomla 1.5 only.

- **Commercial or Non-Commercial.** Commercial.
- **Extension Types.** Component, Module, and Plug-in.

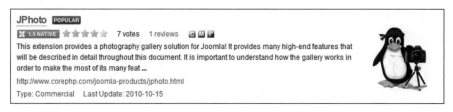

Figure 11.10   JPhoto shown in the Photo Gallery category

The Simple Image Gallery Module is shown in Figure 11.11:

- **Rating.** Four out of five stars, with 15 people voting
- **Compatibility.** Works with Joomla 1.5 and Joomla 1.6
- **Commercial or Non-Commercial.** Non-Commercial
- **Extension Types.** Module (the name of this extension might have given that away!)

Figure 11.11   Simple Image Gallery Module
shown in the Photo Gallery category

In fact, the Simple Image Gallery Module sounds like a good candidate for us to explore further. It works on Joomla 1.6, it has reasonably good feedback, and it's free to download. Let's evaluate it further.

Evaluate an Individual Extension

To find the Simple Image Gallery Module, either browse the Photo Gallery category until you find it or type **Simple Image Gallery Module** into the search box at the top of the site. Here's the URL of the page: http://extensions.joomla. org/extensions/photos-a-images/photo-gallery/13173.

When you're on the Simple Image Gallery Module page it should look like Figure 11.12.

Figure 11.12   Simple Image Gallery Module shown in the JED

In Figure 11.13 I highlighted two interesting areas that we didn't see on the full category listing:

- **Important links.** You may see links to the extension's demo, download site, documentation, and support areas. Not all extensions will have all four, but many will. If it doesn't have a demo, documentation, or any support links, proceed with caution.

- **Reviews.** This is the feedback of people just like you. Some will praise the extension, others will point out its flaws, but these reviews are always worth reading.

Figure 11.13   Links and reviews for the Simple Image Gallery Module

First, let's click on the demo link to see if this looks like a good photo gallery. The demo should look like Figure 11.14.

That looks pretty good. So there's one more thing to check—the reviews. You can see them on the extension's listing page and in Figure 11.15. They're all really positive, saying things like:

- "Highly recommended for all users."

- "Nice Module and very simple."

- "This is by far one of the quickest modules I've downloaded for my Joomla site without having problems or difficulty figuring it out."

- "Nice One. It looks very simple, yet elegant."

Believe me, not all the reviews on all the extensions are this positive!

Figure 11.14   A demo of the Simple Image Gallery Module

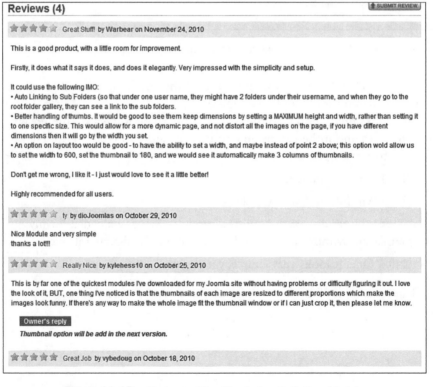

Figure 11.15   Reviews of the Simple Image Gallery Module

Overall, we checked six things about this extension, and they all look good:

- **Rating.** Four out of five stars, with 15 people voting
- **Compatibility.** Works with Joomla 1.5 and Joomla 1.6
- **Commercial or Non-Commercial.** Non-Commercial
- **Extension Types.** Module
- **Important Links.** Demo looks good
- **Reviews.** Very positive

That's how we find and evaluate an extension. You could repeat the same process on any other kind of extension you want on your site, and we practice this more later in the chapter.

For now it's time to download, install, and test this extension we've found.

Install Components, Modules, and Plug-ins

Here's the process we use for downloading and installing an extension. Some extensions may require a slightly different process (such as opening your wallet in 25% of cases!), but they are all similar.

Install a Module

The first example we use is installing a module:

1. Click on the download button. Each extension we find on the JED has a download link. Figure 11.16 shows where it is for the Simple Image Gallery Module.

Figure 11.16   Download link for the Simple Image Gallery Module

2. Go to the download area. Often this is on the developer's Web site. Figure 11.17 shows where it is for this extension.

Figure 11.17   Download the Simple Image Gallery Module

3. Choose which version to download. Because this module works with Joomla 1.5 and 1.6, we need to choose the right version. Click on the 1.6 download as in Figure 11.18.

4. The module downloads to your computer. Most likely it will go to your Downloads folder as shown in Figure 11.19, but the most important thing is that you know where it goes! The module is a compressed file and has a name like: mod_sp_simple_gallery_j16.zip. This is a well-named file because the mod_ reminds us that it's a module, and the j16 reminds us that it is built for Joomla 1.6. You don't need to uncompress this file unless the instructions specifically tell you to.

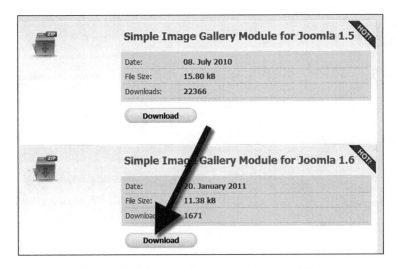

Figure 11.18   Download the 1.6 version of the
Simple Image Gallery Module

Figure 11.19   The compressed file of the Simple Image Gallery Module

5. Now let's upload it to the Joomla site. Log in to the administrator area of your site and go to Extensions, and then Extension Manager. You see a screen like Figure 11.20. This is where we upload all the extensions we need for our Joomla site: components, modules, plug-ins, templates, and languages are all installed from here. Let's see how it works:

6. Click the Browse button and search for the mod_sp_simple_gallery_j16.zip file that you downloaded; then click the Upload & Install button. Figure 11.20 shows you how this works.

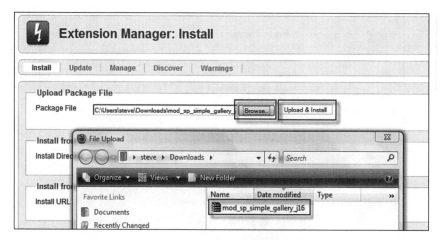

Figure 11.20   Browsing for the Simple Image Gallery Module file

7. You should see a message saying "module successfully installed" and also a description of the module.

Joomla automatically knows the right place to put this extension. If it were a component, it would now appear under the Components drop-down menu. If it were a template, it would appear in the Template Manager, and if it were a plug-in it would appear in the Plugin Manager. Given that it's a module, you can probably guess where we can now find the Simple Image Gallery Module—that's right, in the Module Manager. If you go there, you should see the new module on this page as in Figure 11.21.

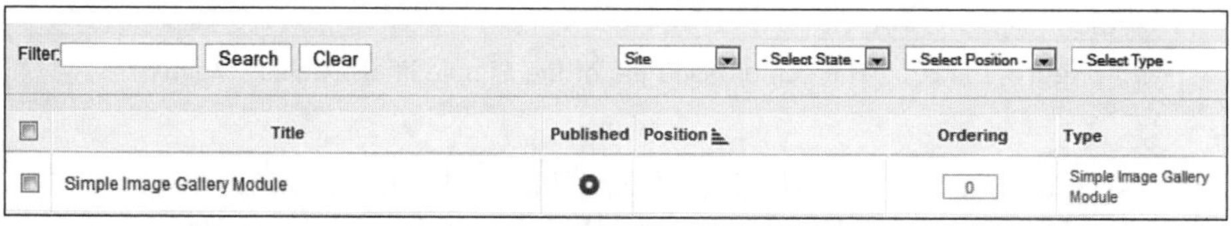

	Title	Published	Position ≜	Ordering	Type
☐	Simple Image Gallery Module	⭘		0	Simple Image Gallery Module

Figure 11.21   The Simple Image Gallery Module successfully installed

Now we can use it just like any other module we've used so far in this book. Here's how we'd enable it on our site:

1. Click on the Simple Image Gallery Module name and choose these settings:

    ▪ **Title.** Joomlaville Photos

    ▪ **Position.** Position-8

- **Published.** Published

- **Module Assignment.** On all pages

2. Save the module and visit the home page of your site. You should see the module appear as in Figure 11.22.

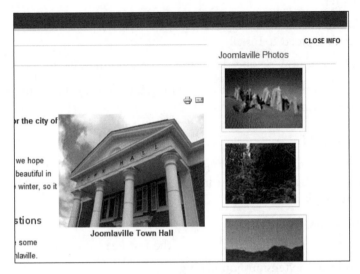

Figure 11.22   The Simple Image Gallery Module enabled on your site

Congratulations! You've successfully installed your first extension.

If you want, you can go back and change the options for the module. It will take any folder in your Media Manager and turn it into a photo gallery. You just need to enter the folder name and location into the Gallery Path option. Me? I'm lazy and I'm going to pretend that these photos are of the beautiful Joomlaville!

We do have other things to try, such as installing a plug-in and a component. In a moment, we walk you through how we install them. However, first let's recap what we just did so that we understand the workflow for installing an extension:

1. **Research.** Go to http://extensions.joomla.org and look for the extension using the search box or Category links. Then evaluate the extension using the following criteria:

   - Rating

   - Compatibility

   - Commercial or Non-Commercial

- Extension Types
- Important Links
- Reviews

2. **Download.** Click the download link to get the extension file onto our computer.

3. **Upload.** Go to the Extension Manager, click Browse, find the extension, and click Upload & Install.

4. **Use.** We can now go ahead and use the extension as we would normally.

That's the workflow. Now let's go and use the same workflow to add a plug-in and a component to our site.

Install a Plug-in

The example we use when installing a plug-in is social networking. Let's see if we can find, install, and use a plug-in that allows people to share our articles on sites like Facebook and Twitter.

Step 1: Research

Our first step is to find plug-ins that have the features we need.

1. Go to http://extensions.joomla.org.

2. Look down the Categories list, and there's a category called Social Web that looks promising. Click on that link.

3. Inside the Social Web category there's a category called Social Bookmarking. Click on that link. You now see the full category as in Figure 11.23. The URL of this page is http://extensions.joomla.org/extensions/social-web/social-bookmarking.

Now let's evaluate the plug-ins that we've found. Which ones work with our version of Joomla, have good documentation and support, and have good feedback from other users?

The first thing we need to do is look for the extensions that will work with Joomla 1.6. The extensions are sorted by rating, so let's scroll down until we see the blue 1.6 icon. The first one I find is the ITPSocial Buttons extension seen in Figure 11.24.

Figure 11.23   The Social Bookmarking category on the JED

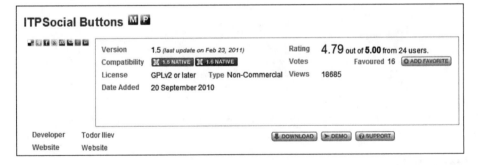

Figure 11.24   The ITPSocial Buttons extension on the JED

Let's use our criteria to evaluate this extension:

- **Rating.** Four and a half out of five stars and a reasonable number of votes.

- **Compatibility.** Joomla 1.5 and 1.6.

- **Commercial or Non-Commercial.** Non-Commercial.

- **Extension Types.** Plug-in.
- **Important Links.** The demo looks good, although there's no support: Hopefully this will be simple enough that we don't need it.
- **Reviews.** They are all positive, and most speak about how easy it is to use.

Step 2: Download

Our second step is to download the files for the plug-in we've chosen:

1. Click the Download link, and you are taken to the developer's site.
2. Click to download the Joomla 1.6 version of the file. The link is high-lighted in Figure 11.25. It downloads a file with a name like plg_itpsocialbuttons_v1.3_J1.6.zip.

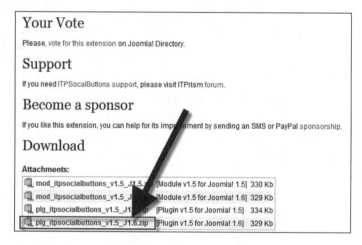

Figure 11.25   Downloading the ITPSocial Buttons extension

Step 3: Upload

Our third step is to upload the plug-in files to our Joomla site.

1. Log in to the administrator area of your site and go to the Extension Manager.
2. Click the Browse button and search for the plg_itpsocialbuttons_v1.3_J1.6.zip file that you downloaded and then click the Upload & Install button.

3. You should see a message saying "plugin successfully installed" and also a description of the module as in Figure 11.26.

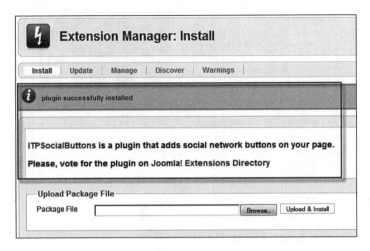

Figure 11.26   Installing the ITPSocial Buttons extension

Step 4: Use

Our fourth and final step is to configure our new plug-in and start using it on our site:

1. Go to the Plug-in Manager and click the red circle in the Enabled column next to Content – ITPSocialButtons.

2. Visit the home page of your site and you should see that social bookmarking links have been added to all your pages, as in Figure 11.27. It won't be on the front page, but it should appear on every other article you've written.

Congratulations—you've successfully installed a plug-in! If you want to, you can tweak the options inside the ITPSocial extensions area in Plugin Manager. Otherwise, we can move on and install a component.

Install a Component

A sitemap is often useful for a site's visitors and for search engines who both use it to find what pages are on your site. Unless it's a particularly large site, the sitemap allows them to quickly see all the pages available.

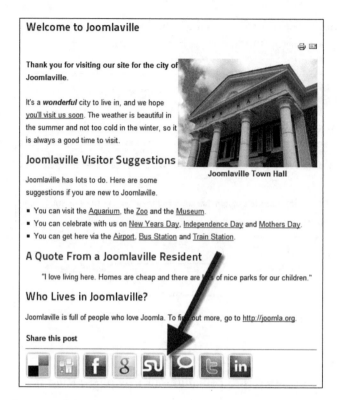

Figure 11.27   The ITPSocial Buttons extension live on your site

Step 1: Research

Our first step is to find components that have the features we need.

1. This time around, it's not immediately clear which category a sitemap would be in, so let's use the Search. Go to http://extensions.joomla.org and click Advanced Search in the top-right corner, next to the search box.

2. Use the search box to narrow down our choices quickly. Fill in these fields as in Figure 11.28 and then click the Search button:

   - **Description.** sitemap
   - **Compatibility.** 1.6 Native
   - **Extension Includes.** Component

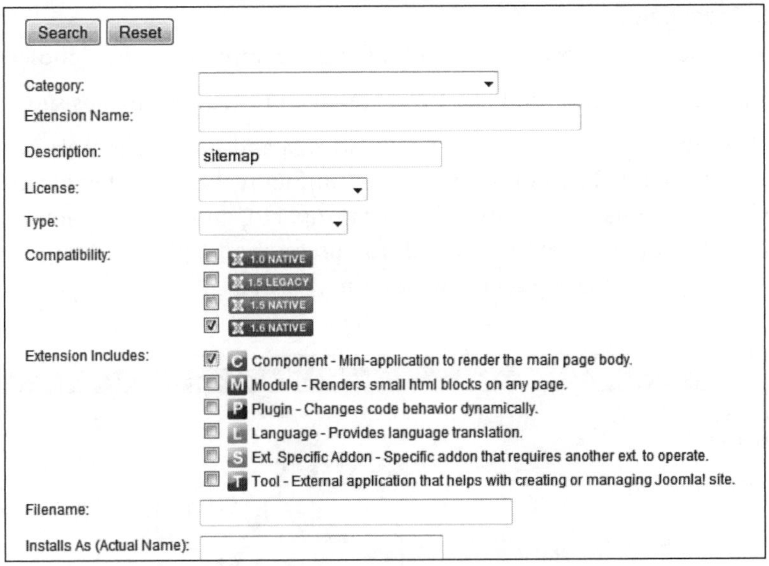

Figure 11.28   The Advanced Search on the Joomla Extensions Directory

Next we evaluate the components that we found. Which ones work with our version of Joomla, have good documentation and support, and have good feedback from other users?

The first result that comes back in this example is called Xmap. Let's use our criteria to evaluate this extension:

- **Rating.** Four and a half out of five stars and a very large number of votes.
- **Compatibility.** Joomla 1.5 and 1.6.
- **Commercial or Non-Commercial.** Non-Commercial.
- **Extension Types.** Component and Plug-in.
- **Important Links.** The demo looks good plus there are links to both support and documentation.
- **Reviews.** They are almost all positive, and most speak about how easy it is to use.

Step 2: Download

Our second step is to download the files for the component we've chosen:

1. Click the Download link, and you are taken to the developer's site.

2. Click through the site to the download area and find the Joomla 1.6 version of the file. The link is highlighted in Figure 11.29. It downloads a file with a name like com_xmap-2.0-beta1.zip. Hopefully you've noticed by now that modules download with the prefix mod_, plug-ins with the prefix plg_, and components with com_.

Release Name	Release Date	Filename	File Size	Download Count
Xmap-2.0-beta2-for-Joomla-1.6	2011-02-25 00:00:00-06	com_xmap-2.0-beta2.zip	120 KB	4143
Xmap-1.2-for-Joomla-1.5	2008-08-01 01:00:00-05	com_xmap-1.2.zip	117 KB	4050
Xmap-1.2.2-for-Joomla-1.5	2009-08-01 01:00:00-05	Xmap1.2.2-UNZIP-First.zip	187 KB	1668
Xmap-1.2.11-for-Jooma-1.5	2011-02-26 00:00:00-06	com_xmap-1.2.11.zip	252 KB	9267
Xmap-1.2.10-for-Jooma-1.5	2011-02-25 00:00:00-06	com_xmap-1.2.10.zip	252 KB	3042

Figure 11.29   Downloading the Xmap extension

Step 3: Upload

Our third step is to upload the component files to our Joomla site:

1. Log in to the administrator area of your site and go to the Extension Manager.

2. Click the Browse button and search for the com_xmap-2.0-beta1.zip file that you downloaded and then click the Upload & Install button.

3. You should see a message saying "component successfully installed" as in Figure 11.30.

Figure 11.30   Successfully installing the Xmap extension

Step 4: Use

Our fourth and final step is to configure our new component and start using it on our site:

1. Go to the Components link under the main drop-down menu, and Sitemap should be an extra option in the menu. Click that link.

2. Click New in the toolbar, and you are taken to the screen you see in Figure 11.31 where you can create a new sitemap. Here are the settings you need:

    - **Title.** Sitemap

    - **State.** Published

    - **Menus.** Check all the menus whose links you want listed in the sitemap

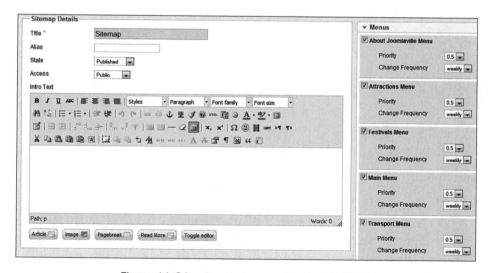

Figure 11.31   Creating a new sitemap with Xmap

3. Click Save & Close; then go to Menus, Main Menu and click New.

4. We're going to make a menu link so that people can see our sitemap. Here are settings to enter:

   ▪ **Menu Item Type.** Choose HTML Site map under the Xmap heading

   ▪ **Menu Title.** Sitemap

   ▪ **Chose a sitemap.** Sitemap

5. Save that menu link, go to the visitors area of your site, and then click the Sitemap link under Main Menu. You should see a list of all the pages you have on your site as in Figure 11.32.

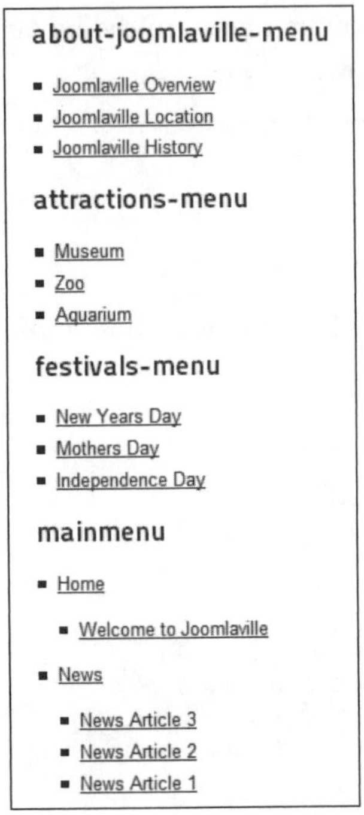

about-joomlaville-menu

▪ Joomlaville Overview
▪ Joomlaville Location
▪ Joomlaville History

attractions-menu

▪ Museum
▪ Zoo
▪ Aquarium

festivals-menu

▪ New Years Day
▪ Mothers Day
▪ Independence Day

mainmenu

▪ Home

   ▪ Welcome to Joomlaville

▪ News

   ▪ News Article 3
   ▪ News Article 2
   ▪ News Article 1

Figure 11.32   A new sitemap with Xmap

That's the process we use for installing components, modules, and plug-ins. Each extension offers different features and options, but the workflow for adding it to your site is the same. The workflow is similar for templates also, and that's what we turn our attention to now.

Find and Install Templates

There are only two major differences between adding a template to a site, compared to adding components, modules, and plug-ins:

- **Price.** Whereas 75% of components, modules, and plug-ins are noncommercial, the opposite is true with templates. The majority of templates are sold by commercial companies. However, competition is strong between these companies, and that keeps prices low. Prices for single templates generally range from $10 up to around $50. Many companies also run template clubs where you can buy a subscription to download all their templates for a limited period of time.

- **Directory.** There is no equivalent of the JED for templates. What that means is the templates generally can't be evaluated so easily. Evaluation is mostly done by viewing a template demo or actually installing and testing the template. Unlike components, modules, and plug-ins, it's harder to find unbiased information, ratings, and reviews to rely on.

I have a list of recommended template designers at http://www.joomla explained.com/templates and a site called http://www.joomla24.com lists all free templates available, but there is no official directory with ratings, reviews, and information. Instead, in the next part of this chapter we give you some guidelines for finding the right template for you.

Find a Free Template

Here are the criteria I recommend beginners use when finding a template. Most of them are the same as for components, modules, and plug-ins:

- **Compatibility.** Does it run on Joomla 1.5 and 1.6?

- **Commercial or Non-Commercial.** Do you want to pay?

- **Documentation.** How well documented is it?

- **Support.** Is there ongoing support for the template?

- **Design.** This is specific only to templates. Does it match the look and the feel that you want for your site? Especially when you're getting started, you have enough to worry about without digging into the code of templates and working hard to make it look the way you want. It's better to start with a template that's as close as possible to the desired end result.

Let's start with http://joomla24.com, which has a list of free templates for Joomla 1.6 and see if we can find a template that will be suitable for a city Web site like the one we're building.

1. Visit http://joomla24.com; click Downloads in the top menu, then Templates for Joomla 1.6, and then General Joomla 1.6 Templates (see Figure 11.33).

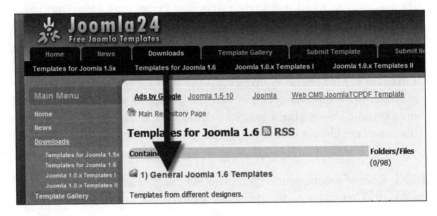

Figure 11.33   Joomla24.com

2. Each template should have a small screenshot beside it so that you know what it looks like. You see immediately that some of them are unsuitable for a city site. Some have designs featuring animals, some have flowers, and some are just too dark. One that stands out as a good prospect is called Phoca Rhein J1.6.

3. Browse through the download area until you find Phoca Rhein J1.6. Click on the link for Phoca Rhein J1.6, and you see a screen like Figure 11.34. Click the download link and, after agreeing to the template's terms and conditions, you download a file with a name like tmpl_phoca_rhein_v1.0.0.zip.

4. Now let's upload it. Go to your Joomla site's administrator area and then go to the Extension Manager.

5. Click Browse, find the tmpl_phoca_rhein_v1.0.0.zip file you just downloaded, and then click Upload & Install. You should see a message saying "template successfully installed."

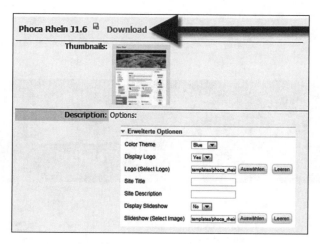

Figure 11.34   Downloading a template from Joomla24.com

6. Go to the Template Manager and scroll down to find phoca_rhein – Default. Click the star in the Default column to make this template enabled on your site.

    However, we currently have a style of Beez applied to the home page. If we want to see this new template on our home page, we need to edit the Beez2-Frontpage and uncheck the Home box under the Menu Assignment area.

    When the template is live, it should look like Figure 11.35.

7. OK, that's good, but there are some things we still need to change. First, let's see if the template has any options or further information for us. Go to the Template Manager and click on the template name: phoca_rhein .You see a screen like Figure 11.36.The options are very similar to Beez2.

8. Go ahead and modify the template options. I'm going to recommend these choices:

    - **Color Theme.** Blue
    - **Display Logo.** No
    - **Logo (Select Logo).** click Clear
    - **Site Title.** Joomlaville
    - **Site Description.** A great place to live
    - **Display Slideshow.** Yes
    - **Slideshow (Select Image).** Click Clear

Figure 11.35   The Phoca Rein template on your site

Figure 11.36   The Phoca Rein template details inside Template Manager

9. Click Save & Close and go to the visitors area, which will now look like
   Figure 11.37.

Figure 11.37   The Phoca Rein template with new option settings

Now that we have our site's name on the template, we also need to change the module positions. Figure 11.38 shows the module positions you will see when you go to the Template Manager in your administrator area. Click the Templates tab and click on Preview next to phoca_rein.

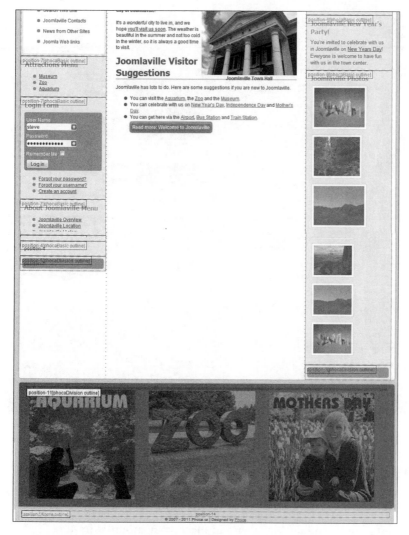

Figure 11.38   Module positions shown on the Phoca Rein template

Because it's hard to read all the module position names, I've created Figure 11.39 which clearly shows all the positions.

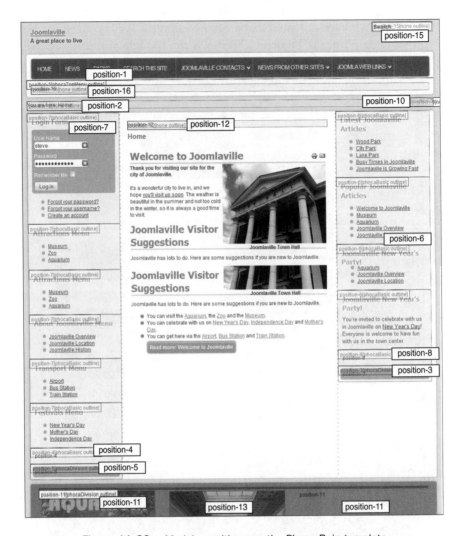

Figure 11.39   Module positions on the Phoca Rein template

The module positions in Phoca Rein are similar to Beez2, but not identical. To make our site look better, we need to move some modules to new positions. Let's see if we can complete the move from Beez to Phoca Rein:

1. Go to your Module Manager and place your modules in these positions

    - **Main Menu:** position-1. Inside this module, set the Show Sub-menu Items option to Yes. This will enable a dropdown menu on the template.

- **Search:** position-15 (set the Show Title option to No)

- **Breadcrumbs:** position-5

- **Latest Joomlaville Article, Popular Joomlaville Articles, New Years Party:** position-6

- **Attractions Menu, Transport Menu, Festival Menu, About Joomlaville Menu, Welcome to Our New Site, Login form:** position-7

- **Joomlaville Photos:** unpublish this module

- **Footer Left Banner:** position-9

- **Footer Middle Banner:** position-10

- **Footer Right Banner:** position-11

2. When you finish moving your modules, your site should look like Figure 11.40.

Congratulations! You've done a great job in getting your template set up!

So, that was our first experience with a free Joomla template. You may have noticed that it wasn't quite as easy as installing the components, modules, and plug-ins.

We had to move all of our modules around and also edit the code to use our own logo.

Fortunately, most sites have a lot of components, modules, and plug-ins and only one template!

Here's the workflow we used to enable and use the Phoca Rhein template:

1. **Research.** Search for and evaluate the template with these criteria:

   - **Compatibility.** Yes, it's ready for Joomla 1.6.

   - **Commercial or Non-Commercial.** Non-Commercial.

   - **Design.** It did give our site the professional look we wanted.

   - **Complexity.** Not too many features, which is good for our needs.

   - **Documentation.** Not much unfortunately.

   - **Support.** None visible.

2. **Download.** Place the file on our desktop.

3. **Upload.** Install the files and make it the default template.

4. **Modules.** Move the modules into new positions.

5. **Modify.** Change the logo and set up any features included.

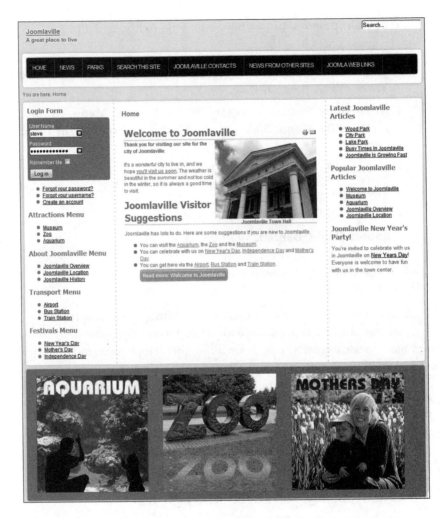

Figure 11.40   The Phoca Rein template with modules in the correct
positions

So this template turned out to meet most of our criteria. The only problems were difficulty in uploading the logo and a lack of documentation.

Fortunately, many templates are more advanced than this example. These more advanced templates may allow us to upload our logos directly from the administrator area, as Beez did. They also allow us a great deal of control over the colors and layout. They may even have great documentation!

Unfortunately, those templates are more likely to be commercial. Let's have a look at the world of commercial templates.

Find a Commercial Template

Most template design companies offer some free templates, but they make their living from the templates they sell.

In Chapter 10, "Joomla Templates Explained," we introduced you to three different designs from three different designers. We saw a minimal template from JoomlaBamboo.com, a colorful template from JoomlArt.com, and a high-concept template from Rockettheme.com.

These are good examples for us to start with.

JoomlaBamboo.com

Visit the main JoomlaBamboo.com Web site, as shown in Figure 11.41.

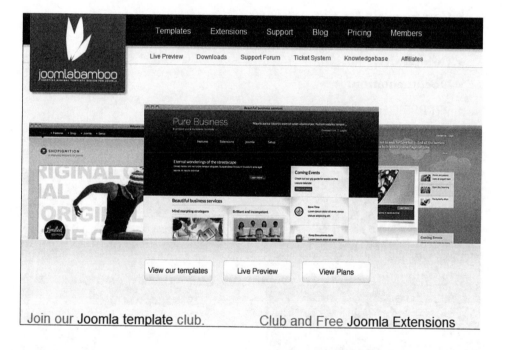

Figure 11.41   The main JoomlaBamboo.com Web site

Remember the criteria we used before? See if you can find out the following information about the templates on JoomlaBamboo.com and write it into the following spaces:

- **Compatibility.** Does it work on 1.6?

- **Commercial.** How much do the templates cost?

- **Design.** Does it match the needs of your site?
- **Complexity.** Does it look easy to set up?
- **Documentation.** Can you see good documentation?
- **Support.** Is there evidence of help if you need it?

JoomlArt.com

Visit the main JoomlArt.com Web site as shown in Figure 11.42.

Let's do the same thing again. See if you can find out the following information about the templates on JoomlArt.com and write it into the following spaces:

- **Compatibility:**
- **Commercial:**
- **Design:**
- **Complexity:**
- **Documentation:**
- **Support:**

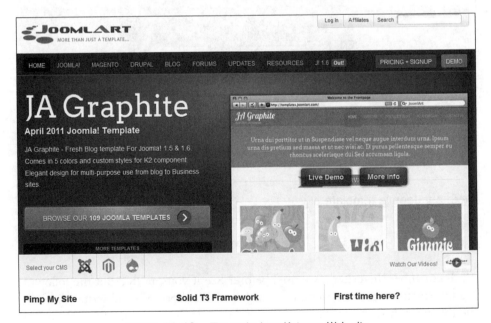

Figure 11.42   The main JoomlArt.com Web site

Rockettheme.com

Finally, visit the main Rockettheme.com Web site, as shown in Figure 11.43.

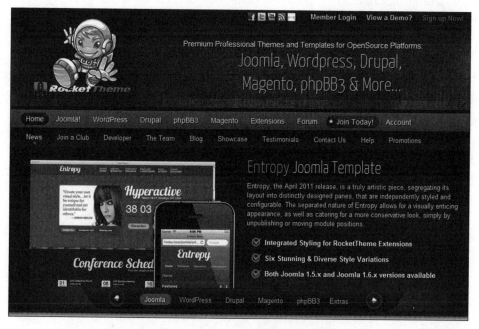

Figure 11.43   The main Rockettheme.com web site

Find out the following information about the templates on Rockettheme.com and write it into the following spaces:

- **Compatibility:**
- **Commercial:**
- **Design:**
- **Complexity:**
- **Documentation:**
- **Support:**

An Overview of Commercial Templates

It's obviously unfair of me to pick just three designers out of the hundreds of template companies. However, as a Joomla beginner you need to start somewhere, and these three give an interesting introduction to the variety of designs you can pick from.

Notice a few things when looking at these sites:

- **Each template company has a very different style.** Most of these companies have 50 or more templates on offer, but each one has a style: colorful or minimal, corporate or fun, busy or plain. Pick the style that meets the needs of your site.

- **Prices.** Most companies sell download access to multiple templates for a fixed period of time. Some companies sell individual templates, but the majority are time-based. You can use the templates forever, but only download them for that fixed period of time.

- **Complexity.** Be warned! Some of these templates can get pretty complicated. Don't imagine that your template will look as good as the demos as soon as you upload them. The demo sites have been set up by experts. Some template companies solve that problem by providing copies of Joomla that come prepackaged with their template and any needed extensions already set up correctly. Instead of downloading Joomla from http://joomla.org, you would download and install their copy of Joomla.

Practice

So far in this chapter we've been through the workflows which have allowed us to find, evaluate, and install components, modules, plug-ins, and templates. Let's practice an example of each one.

Install a Component

Your task to practice adding components is this: Find, install, and use a component so that your visitors can vote on topics of your choice. One suggestion is an extension called AcePolls. Here's a reminder of the workflow to use:

1. **Research.** Go to http://extensions.joomla.org and look for the extension using the search box or Category links. Use the following criteria to find a suitable choice:

   - Rating
   - Compatibility
   - Commercial or Non-Commercial
   - Extension Types
   - Important Links
   - Reviews

2. **Download.** Click the download link to get the extension file onto our computer.

3. **Upload.** Go to the Extension Manager, click Browse, find the extension, and click Upload & Install.

4. **Use.** We can now go ahead and use the extension as we would normally.

If you get stuck, there's a tutorial on http://www.joomlaexplained.com/chapter11 to help you.

Install a Module

Your task to practice adding modules is this: Find and install a module that allows you to count down the days until New Year's Eve. One suggestion is a module called OSTimer.

As before, the workflow we use is this:

1. **Research.**

   - Rating
   - Compatibility
   - Commercial or Non-Commercial
   - Extension Types
   - Important Links
   - Reviews

2. **Download.**

3. **Upload.**

4. **Use.**

If you get stuck, there's a tutorial on http://www.joomlaexplained.com/chapter11 to help you.

Install a Plug-in

Practice adding plug-ins: Find and install a plug-in that allows you to automatically generate metadata for your articles. Two popular forms of metadata are the description that appears in Google's search results and the keywords some search engines use to categorize your site. One suggestion is a plug-in called MetaGenerator.

1. **Research.**
    - Rating
    - Compatibility
    - Commercial or Non-Commercial
    - Extension Types
    - Important Links
    - Reviews

2. **Download.**

3. **Upload.**

4. **Use.**

If you get stuck, there's a tutorial on http://wwwjoomlaexplained.com/chapter11 to help you.

Now that you're at the end of this chapter, your Joomlaville site should look similar to Figure 11.44.

What's Next?

Congratulations! You now have everything you need to build a Joomla site. You've proved that because you now actually have a complete Joomla site.

If you've followed this book through to this point, you can now understand a default Joomla installation and also add extra features and designs to your site. You have completed the entire Joomla site-building workflow:

Step 1: Installation

Step 2: Content

Step 3: Extensions (Components, Modules, and Plug-ins)

Step 4: Templates

Now we're ready to leave our Joomlaville site behind. Hopefully you think it looks pretty good by now. It might have a few mistakes and a few things that could be done better, but that's why we call it practice! If you want to compare your site to the version I built using the same instructions, take a look at http://www.joomlaexplained.com/joomlaville.

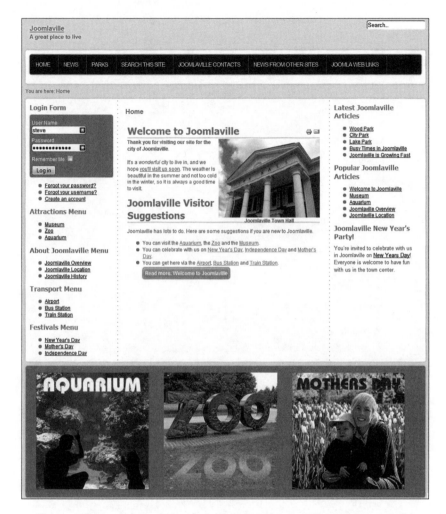

Figure 11.44   Your complete Joomlaville Web site at the end of Chapter 11

How do we improve our skills and build better sites? With more practice! In the next two chapters we build two more sites. Each one is going to take us through the Joomla site-building workflow so that we can really master it and really start to build great sites.

Turn the page, and let's build that first Joomla site to practice the workflow.

12

Putting It All Together: Personal Site

Over the first 11 chapters of this book you learned much about Joomla! You discovered how to add new content, navigation, features, and designs to your Joomla site. You experienced and practiced all fours steps of the Joomla workflow:

Step 1: Installation

Step 2: Content

Step 3: Extensions (Components, Modules, and Plug-ins)

Step 4: Templates

Now it's time to put it all together. We're going to practice everything you've learned. In this chapter, we go through the Joomla workflow and build a personal site for you.

This task brings together everything you've learned and really helps you understand the workflow needed to build a Joomla site. If you get stuck at any point, you can look back at previous chapters for detailed help. I've also built this site online at http://www.joomlaexplained.com/personal so you can see how things should look.

Things You Can Do After Reading This Chapter

- Understand and practice how the whole Joomla workflow fits together.
- Build a personal Web site.

Step 1: Installation

We're going to practice the whole Joomla workflow, and that means we need to start right at the beginning: We install a new Joomla site that we can use for this chapter.

Remember the two installation methods we recommend in Chapter 2:

- **One-click.** Using the automatic installer provided by your hosting company

- **Manual.** Downloading, uploading, and installing the files by yourself

As in Chapter 2, go ahead and choose the method you feel most comfortable with. The only difference between now and Chapter 2 is that we install Joomla into a subfolder called /personal/.

One-Click Installation

Remember that this is an example using the popular hosting software called CPanel, which comes with the one-click installation software called Fantastico. Each hosting company is a little different. We have information for one-click installation with popular hosting companies at http://www.joomlaexplained.com/chapter2/.

1. Log in to your Web hosting account. This is often, but not always, located at http://example.com/cpanel.

2. Find the Fantastico button and click it.

3. Enter the Fantastico Control Panel and click Joomla or Joomla 1.6.

4. Choose to install Joomla by clicking New Installation.

5. Enter your new site details. Choose your own username, password, and e-mail address but make sure to set the following fields:

    - **Install in directory.** Personal
    - **Install Sample Data?** No

6. Confirm your installation details by clicking Finish Installation.

7. Click the links to your site and the administrator area. Bookmark both addresses.

Manual Installation

Manual installation takes longer but gives you a little more control over how your site is set up. This tutorial focuses on installing Joomla using the popular CPanel system, so it does require, your hosting company to have CPanel installed. If your hosting company uses different software, you need to find out how to create a database with them.

Create the Database

Every Joomla site has two halves: the database and the files. First, we create the database we need for this site and also create a user with permission to access that database. Here's how we do it:

1. Log in to your Web hosting account often located at http://example.com/cpanel.

2. Find the button that says MySQL Databases and click it.

3. Find the Create New Database area, enter a name, and click Create Database. Save that information.

4. Find the Add New User area and enter a username and password for your database user. Save that information.

5. Find the Add User to Database area and select both your new database and your new user.

6. Select All Privileges and click Make Changes.

Upload the Joomla Files

Now we need to create the other half of our Joomla site: the files. Here's how we do it:

1. Go to Joomla.org and click the Download Joomla button.

2. Find the Joomla download link for the Full Package and click it.

3. Download the Joomla files to your desktop.

4. Uncompress the .zip files to a folder on your desktop.

5. Log in to your Web server using FTP software such as Filezilla.

6. Move the Joomla folder on your desktop onto your Web server.

7. Open your Web browser and visit the location where you uploaded the files.

8. On Joomla Web Installer Step 1 choose your Language.

9. On Joomla Web Installer Step 2, make sure that Joomla's Pre-Installation Check doesn't produce any red warnings in the top-half of the screen.

10. On Joomla Web Installer Step 3, agree to the Joomla License.

11. On Joomla Web Installer Step 4, enter the database name, username, and password you created earlier.

12. On Joomla Web Installer Step 5: FTP Configuration, leave these options blank.

13. On Joomla Web Installer Step 6: Configuration, enter your Site Name, for example "Steve's Site" and choose a username, e-mail, and password. Make sure you do not click on the option to install sample data.

14. On Joomla Web Installer Step 7: Finish, keeping this screen open in your Web browser.

15. Log in to your Web server using FTP software such as Filezilla and delete the /installation/ folder.

16. Go back to Joomla Web Installer Step 7. Click the links to your site and the administrator area. Bookmark both addresses.

Whether you install Joomla automatically or manually, you should end up with a brand-new site as in Figure 12.1.

Figure 12.1   A newly installed Joomla site

Step 2: Content

Now that our site is ready, we can start to add content. We use the CASh work-flow:

- Categorize
- Add
- Show

Categorize

I suggest we divide our site content into two parts: personal information that won't often change and a blog that will be regularly updated. Here's how the categories could look (see Figure 12.2):

- About Me
- Blog
    - Personal Thoughts
    - Family
    - Job
    - Music
    - Sports

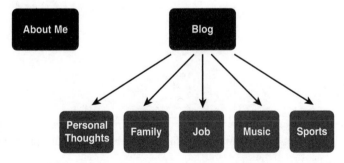

Figure 12.2   New categories for your personal site

Feel free to adjust those categories to meet your needs, but we will be using them for this example:

1. Log in to the administrator area of your new Joomla site and go to the Category Manager.

2. Add the seven categories that we suggested previously. The Category Manager looks like Figure 12.3.

Figure 12.3   Category Manager with new categories
for your personal site

Also to make sure that our site stays as organized as possible, let's go to the Media Manager and use the same structure to make folders for our images. To make life easier and allow us to upload multiple images at once, click Options and set Enable Flash Uploader to No. When finished, the Media Manager looks like Figure 12.4.

Figure 12.4   Media Manager with new folders for your personal site

Add

Now let's write the articles for the site. Go to Article Manager under Content in the main drop-down menu.

Here are some articles that fit well into the categories. Go ahead and either use these examples or some of your own.

Note: Be sure to set Featured to Yes for some or all of the articles. This publishes them to the front page of our site automatically and makes them easier to find for our visitors.

- About Me (Category)
    - Biography (Article)
    - Where I Live (Article)
- Blog (Category)
    - Personal Thoughts (Category)
        - I just got a new computer (Article)
        - I'm going on holiday next week! (Article)
        - Family (Category)
        - My sister just had a baby! (Article)
        - We just went to a family get together (Article)
    - Job (Category)
        - I went to a conference in London (Article)
        - I got a promotion! (Article)
    - Music (Category)
        - Have you heard the new U2 album? (Article)
        - We went to this great concert last week (Article)
    - Sports (Category)
        - I can't wait for the World Cup to start (Article)
        - Who's the best tennis player in the world? (Article)

After you have written those articles, your Article Manager looks like Figure 12.5.

Title ⬆
Biography (Alias: biography)
Have you heard the new U2 album? (Alias: have-you-heard-the-new-u2-album)
I can't wait for the World Cup to start (Alias: i-cant-wait-for-the-world-cup-to-start)
I got a promotion! (Alias: i-got-a-promotion)
I just got a new computer (Alias: i-just-got-a-new-computer)
I went to a conference in London (Alias: i-went-to-a-conference-in-london)
I'm going on holiday next week! (Alias: im-going-on-holiday-next-week)
My sister just had a baby! (Alias: my-sister-just-had-a-baby)
We just went to a family get together (Alias: we-just-went-to-a-family-get-together)
We went to this great concert last week (Alias: we-went-to-this-great-concert-last-week)
Where I Live (Alias: where-i-live)
Who's the best tennis player in the world? (Alias: whos-the-best-tennis-player-in-the-world)

Figure 12.5   Article Manager with new articles for your personal site

Show

First, let's make a link to each of our About Me articles. Here's how we link to each one:

1. Go to Menus then Main Menu and click New.
2. Set these fields:
   - **Menu Item Type.** Single Article
   - **Menu Title.** Enter the name of the article you're linking to
   - **Select Article.** Choose the article you're linking to

Now let's also make a link to our old blog posts. Here's how we do it:

1. Go to Menus then Main Menu and click New.

2. Set these fields:

- **Menu Item Type.** Category Blog
- **Menu Title.** Blog Archives
- **Select Category.** Blog

After you've saved this menu link, your site should look like Figure 12.6.

Figure 12.6   Your Joomla site with articles and menu links

What we should do now is change the options to suit our articles. Here are some examples:

- You might notice that even if you set all of your articles to Featured, only four articles appear on the front page. This can be changed by going to Menus then Main Menu, opening the Home menu link, and changing the numbers under Layout Options. Go ahead and change Leading Articles to 10, and you see up to 10 of your articles set to Featured on the front page.

- We don't really need the author name on every page. Why not? Well, hopefully it's pretty obvious who's writing all the articles. We can turn this setting off by going to Article Manager, clicking on Options, and setting Show Author to Hide. There might be some other options you want to change in here such as setting Show Print Icon, Show Email Icon, and Show Hits to Hide.

Step 3: Components, Modules, and Plug-ins

Now it's time to add some more features to our personal site. Let's utilize some components, modules, and plug-ins to make our site better. We use examples of each. In each case, we first use a default example, and then we head to http://extensions.joomla.org and install another.

Default Component: Contacts

Let's allow people to send an e-mail message to us. We use the Contacts component, and to create the form we use the CASh workflow:

Step 1: Categorize. Go to Components, then Contacts, and then Categories and make sure that at least one category is in place. The Uncategorized category is sufficient because we will only have one single contact form.

Step 2: Add. Go to Components, then Contacts, then Contacts, and click New. Add a contact form for yourself. Fill in at least these details:

- **Name**
- **Email.** Click on Contact Details and add your e-mail address in here. It won't be public on the site, but without it, Joomla won't know where to send the e-mails.
- **Display Format.** To make the contact form easier to see, click Display Options and set Display Format to Plain.

Step 3: Show. Go to Menus then Main Menu and click New. Set these fields:

- **Menu Item Type.** Single Contact
- **Menu Title.** Contact Me
- **Select Category.** Choose the contact form you just created

When you've successfully created your contact form it should look like. Figure 12.7.

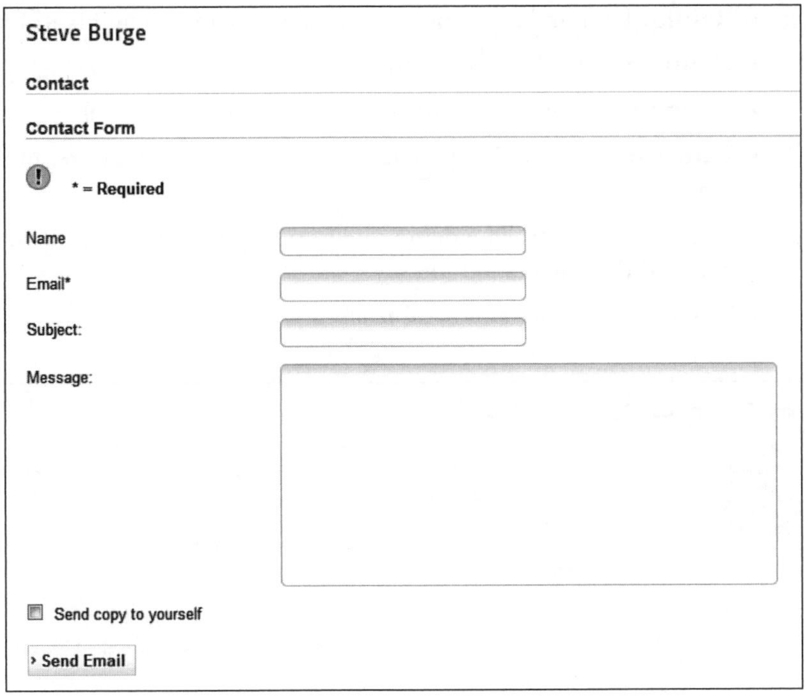

Steve Burge

Contact

Contact Form

⚠ * = Required

Name

Email*

Subject:

Message:

☐ Send copy to yourself

› Send Email

Figure 12.7   A contact form on your personal site

Installed Component: Photo Gallery

Now let's see if we can add a photo gallery to our site. In Chapter 11, we installed a relatively small module for photos. This time, let's look for a larger gallery capable of holding a lot more photos.

Step 1: Research

1. Go to http://extensions.joomla.org and on the left-hand side under the Categories list, click Photos & Images, and then Photo Gallery.

2. Let's look for an extension that matches our criteria. One that stands out is Phoca Gallery. Figure 12.8 shows how it appears on the Joomla Extensions Directory, and here are some ways to evaluate Phoca Gallery according to our criteria:

- **Rating.** Four and a half out of five stars and a huge number of votes.
- **Compatibility.** Joomla 1.5 and 1.6.
- **Commercial or Non-Commercial.** Non-Commercial.
- **Extension Types.** Component, Module, Plug-in, Language, and more!
- **Important Links.** The demo looks good, plus there are both support and documentation links.
- **Reviews.** They are almost all really positive.

Figure 12.8   The Phoca Gallery Extension on http://extensions.joomla.org

Step 2: Download

1. Click the Download link, and you are taken to the developer's site.
2. Click to download the Joomla 1.6 version of the file.

Step 3: Upload

1. Log in to the administrator area of your site and go to the Extension Manager.
2. Click the Browse button and search for the file with a name similar to com_phocagallery_v3.zip file that you downloaded and then click the Upload & Install button.
3. You should see a message saying that Phoca Gallery was successfully installed. You also see a large button saying Install, as in Figure 12.9. Make sure to click on this button to finish the installation.

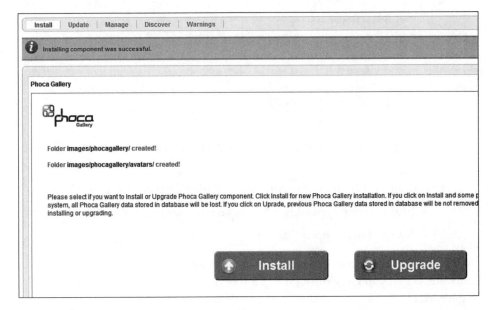

Figure 12.9　Installing the Phoca Gallery extension

Step 4: Use

Go to the Components link in the main drop-down menu, and Phoca Gallery should now be an extra option in the menu. Click that link. Phoca Gallery uses the CASh workflow:

1. **Categorize.** Go to Components, then Phoca Gallery, then Categories, and click New. The only field you need to enter is Title. In this example, my category is called Holiday. Click Save & Close to finish creating the category.

2. **Add.** Go to Components, then Phoca Gallery, then Images, and click New. You see a screen as in Figure 12.10. Fill in at least these details:

   - **Title.** A name for the photos.
   - **Category.** Choose the category you just created.
   - **Filename.** Click Select Filename and upload an image for use in your photo gallery.

   Repeat this process for as many photos as you want to add.

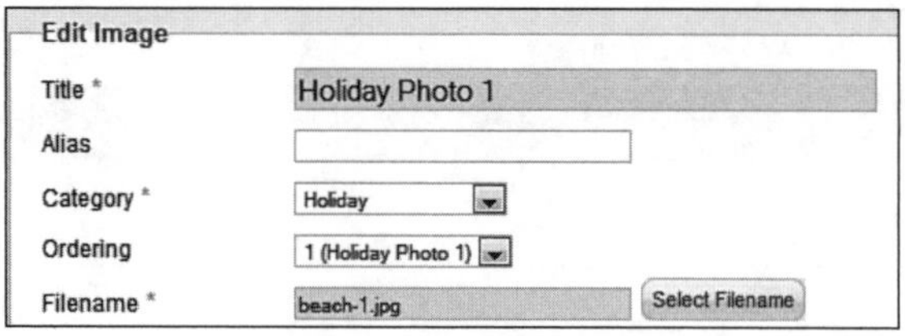

Edit Image

Title *	Holiday Photo 1
Alias	
Category *	Holiday
Ordering	1 (Holiday Photo 1)
Filename *	beach-1.jpg Select Filename

Figure 12.10   Uploading photos to the Phoca Gallery extension

3. **Show.** Go to Menus, then Main Menu and click New. Set these fields:
    - **Menu Item Type.** List of Categories (Categories View)
    - **Menu Title.** Photo Gallery

After you've successfully saved your menu link, go to the visitor area of your site. When you click through to an individual photo, it should look like Figure 12.11.

Figure 12.11   Phoca Gallery showing photos on your personal site

Default Module: Most Read Content

Let's use the default module called Most Read Content to show people what the most popular articles are on our site.

1. Go to Extensions and then Module Manager. Click New and choose Most Read Content.

2. Set these fields as shown in Figure 12.12:

   - **Title. Most Popular Blog Posts**
   - **Position.** position-6
   - **Category.** Choose the Blog category and all the subcategories inside it

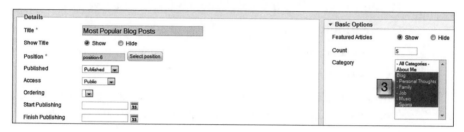

Figure 12.12   Creating a Most Popular Blog Posts module

When you save that module and see it on the visitors area of your site, it should look like Figure 12.13.

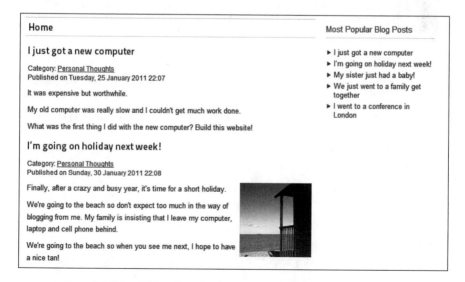

Figure 12.13   A Most Popular Blog Posts module on your personal site

Installed Module: SP Weather

Now it's time to add an extra module to our site. One extra feature that might be useful is adding a weather display so that visitors can see what the weather is like where we live.

Step 1: Research

1. Go to http://extensions.joomla.org and on the left-hand side under the Categories list, click Maps & Weather and then Weather Forecasts.

2. Let's look for an extension that matches our criteria. One that stands out is SP Weather, which is shown in Figure 12.14.

   - **Rating.** Four out of five stars although just from a few users.

   - **Compatibility.** Joomla 1.5 and 1.6.

   - **Commercial or Non-Commercial.** Non-Commercial.

   - **Extension Types.** Module.

   - **Important Links.** The demo is live on the developer's Web site and looks good. Support and documentation links also are available.

   - **Reviews.** They are mostly really positive.

Figure 12.14   The SP Weather Extension on http://extensions.joomla.org

Step 2: Download

1. Click the Download link, and you are taken to the developer's site. Unfortunately at the time of writing, you have to register to download the file.

2. Click to download the Joomla 1.6 version of the file.

Step 3: Upload

1. Log in to the administrator area of your site and go to the Extension Manager.

2. Click the Browse button and search for the file with a name similar to mod_gtranslate16.zip file that you downloaded and then click the Upload & Install button.

3. You should see a message saying "Installing module was successful."

Step 4: Use

1. Go to the Module Manager and open the SP Weather module. Fill in at least these details:

   - **Title. Weather in My City**
   - **Published.** Published
   - **Position.** position-6
   - **City Name.** Enter the name of the city and country you live in
   - **Module Assignment.** On all pages

2. Go to the visitor area of your site, and you see the module in action as in Figure 12.15.

Figure 12.15   The SP Weather module on your site

Default Plug-in: Load Module

This task takes what we just did one step further. We place a dynamic map on the Where I Live page. To do this we combine two skills that we learned in recent chapters: installing a module and using a plug-in. Here's how we use those two skills to show a map inside an article:

Step 1: Research. Go to http://extensions.joomla.org; look for the JGMap module and see if it meets our criteria.

Step 2: Download. Get the JGMap file. Be careful to find the version for 1.6, which will have a name like this: mod_JGMap(1.6).zip.

Step 3: Upload. Install it into your site.

Step 4: Use. Go to the Module Manager and open the module labeled Google Map. Fill in at least these details:

- **Title. Map of Where We Live.**
- **Published.** Published.
- **Position.** position–15.
- **Module Assignment.** On all pages.
- **Search Location.** Type in where you live and hit search. The map adjusts automatically.

That's great for our module, but where does the plug-in come in, and how does it allow you to put a map on your page?

1. Go to the Article Manager and open the Where I Live article.

2. Place this into your article below the other text: {loadposition position–15}. Figure 12.16 shows you how it's done.

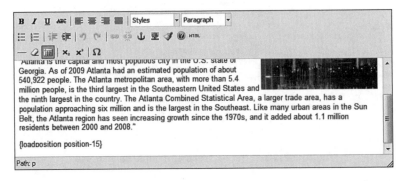

Figure 12.16   Using the Load Module plug-in to place a module inside an article

3. Go to the visitor area of your site, click the menu link to the Where I Live page, and it should look like Figure 12.17.

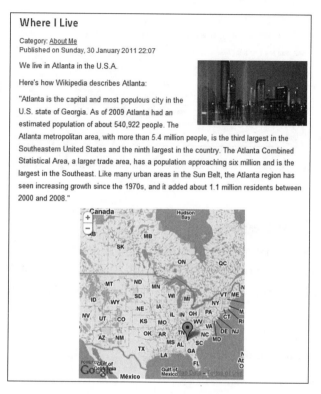

Where I Live

Category: About Me
Published on Sunday, 30 January 2011 22:07

We live in Atlanta in the U.S.A.

Here's how Wikipedia describes Atlanta:

"Atlanta is the capital and most populous city in the U.S. state of Georgia. As of 2009 Atlanta had an estimated population of about 540,922 people. The Atlanta metropolitan area, with more than 5.4 million people, is the third largest in the Southeastern United States and the ninth largest in the country. The Atlanta Combined Statistical Area, a larger trade area, has a population approaching six million and is the largest in the Southeast. Like many urban areas in the Sun Belt, the Atlanta region has seen increasing growth since the 1970s, and it added about 1.1 million residents between 2000 and 2008."

Figure 12.17   The JGMap module inside an article

Installed Plug-in: ITPSocial Buttons

Now we're really going to test your memory and how much you've learned up to this point.

In the previous chapter, we installed the ITPSocial Buttons extension: Your task now is to see if you can install it on this new site also. If you get stuck, the instructions are back in Chapter 11.

When you're finished, your personal site articles should look like Figure 12.18.

Figure 12.18   The ITPSocial Buttons plug-in working on your site

Step 4: Templates

Now we have one final step to finish our personal site: Install a new template. As a reminder, here's the workflow we use to get a new template:

Step 1: Research. Search for and evaluate the template with these criteria:

- Compatibility
- Commercial or Non-Commercial
- Design
- Complexity
- Documentation
- Support

Step 2: Download. Place the file on our desktop.

Step 3: Upload. Install the files and make it the default template.

Step 4: Modules. Move the modules into new positions.

Step 5: Modify. Change the logo and set up any features included.

Let's go through that workflow and get a new template.

Step 1: Research

You can start by looking at the template sites we mentioned earlier by visiting the sites linked to on http://www.joomlaexplained.com/templates or by using a search engine like Google.

One promising template is Adana, which I found by searching at http://www.joomla24.com. You can also use the Joomla24.com search box to find it, plus there's a link to it at http://www.joomlaexplained.com/chapter12. The template is shown in Figure 12.19.

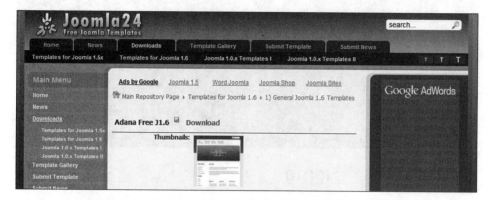

Figure 12.19   The Adana template

I used our criteria to evaluate it:

- **Compatibility.** Works with 1.6.
- **Commercial or Non-Commercial.** Non-Commercial.
- **Design.** Looks simple and straightforward but still stylish.
- **Complexity.** It doesn't appear to have too many features to set up.
- **Documentation.** None visible.
- **Support.** None visible.

Step 2: Download

Download the file from http://www.joomla24.com.

Step 3: Upload

1. Log in to your site and go to the Extension Manager.
2. Click Browse and search for the file with a name like adana-free_j1.6.zip that you just downloaded.
3. Click Upload & Install.

4. Go to the Template Manager and click the empty star next to Adana – Default so that your new template has the gold star beside it.

5. Go to the home page, and your site should look like Figure 12.20.

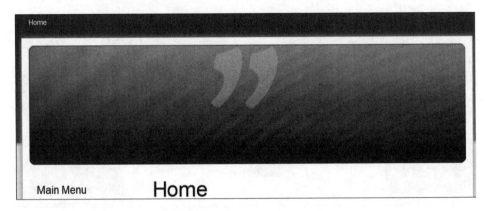

Figure 12.20   The Adana template enabled on your site

Step 4: Modules

To place our modules, we need to find out where the module positions are on this template:

1. Go to the Template Manager, click Options, and set Preview Module Positions to Enabled.

2. In the Template Manager, click the Templates tab, scroll down to Adana, and click Preview. You should see a lot of positions! Figure 12.21 shows some of them.

That's far more positions than we're likely to use! We may end up using only one or two of those positions. Here are some suggestions:

- **Main Menu.** position-1.

- **Weather in My City, Popular Blog Posts.** position-7.

- If you're feeling confident, there's also room for a search module in position-0. Try creating a new search module and placing it there.

Figure 12.21   The Adana template with module positions

When you've moved your modules, the visitor area should look like Figure 12.22.

Figure 12.22   The Adana template enabled on your site
1with your modules

Step 5: Modify

1. Go to the Template Manager and click on Adana – Default.

2. There are quite a few options for this template. Let's start with the Site Details tab, which allows you to change the title, slogan, and copyright used on the site. When you've filled in these details, it should look like Figure 12.23. The title and slogan appear across the top of the site, and the copyright appears at the bottom.

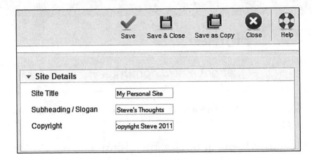

Figure 12.23   Changing Site Details options on the Adana template

More options also are available under the Configuration tab as shown in Figure 12.24. Here you can align the title, upload a new logo, hide the site title, change the font, and even change the color of the template.

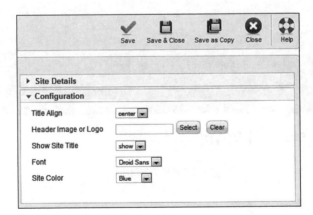

Figure 12.24   Changing Configuration options on the Adana template

When you've finished making your changes, click Save & Close and then Visit Site. You should see your completed Joomla personal site as in Figure 12.25.

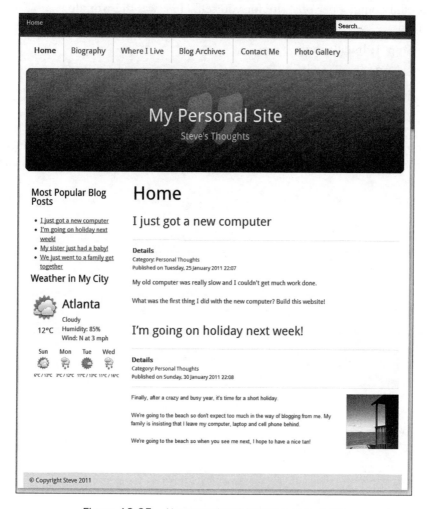

Figure 12.25   Your completed Joomla personal site

What's Next?

Wow—we've just built a complete Joomla site! We used the Joomla workflow to successfully build a personal site for yourself. Here was the workflow we just used:

Step 1: Installation

Step 2: Content

Step 3: Extensions (Components, Modules, and Plug-ins)

Step 4: Templates

Now we're going to build one more site. We try something more advanced: building a professional-looking company Web site. Turn the page and let's build that site.

13

Putting It All Together: Business Site

In Chapter 12, we built a personal Web site by putting together everything you've learned in this book so far. We added new content, navigation, features, and designs to your Joomla! site. In short, we used all fours steps of the Joomla workflow:

Step 1: Installation

Step 2: Content

Step 3: Extensions (Components, Modules, and Plug-ins)

Step 4: Templates

Now it's time to go further again and build a business site. In this chapter, we use the example of a Web design business, but you could use any business that you're familiar with.

As we build the site, we use the same workflow as before, but now you get less guidance. Hopefully you're becoming more confident with Joomla, so we don't provide step-by-step instructions for every task. If you get stuck at any point, you can look back at previous chapters for detailed help. I've also built this site online at http://www.joomlaexplained.com/business so you can see how things should look.

Things You Can Do After Reading This Chapter

- Use the Joomla workflow to build a site without relying on detailed instructions for every step
- Build a business Web site

Step 1: Installation

As always, building a Joomla site starts with the installation. Remember the two installation methods we recommended in Chapter 2:

- **One-click.** Using the automatic installer provided by your hosting company.
- **Manual.** Downloading, uploading, and installing the files by yourself.

As in Chapters 2 and 12, go ahead and choose the method you feel most comfortable with. Here are two things to remember as you do the installation:

- Install Joomla into a subfolder called /business/. That means when this new installation is complete, you should be able to access the personal site from Chapter 12 in a subfolder called /personal/ and this new site in a folder called /business/.
- Remember not to install any sample data.

Step 2: Content

Now that our site is ready, we can start to add content. We use Joomla's CASh workflow:

- Categorize
- Add
- Show

Categorize

Let's plan out how our site could be organized. Here's how the categories could look. Figure 13.1 shows them organized graphically.

- About Us
- Our Services
- Our Portfolio
    - Websites
    - Logos
    - Brochures
- Our Staff
- Company News

Depending on how many services, products, clients, and staff members there are, we might need to consider adding more categories underneath. So, feel free to adjust those categories to meet your needs, but we're going to use them for this example.

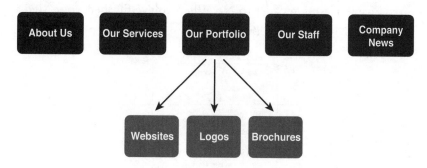

Figure 13.1   New categories for your business site

1. Log in to the administrator area of your new Joomla site and add all the five main categories and three subcategories that we suggested in Figure 13.1. Your Category Manager looks like Figure 13.2.

Figure 13.2   Category Manager with new categories
for your business site

2. Also to make sure the site stays as organized as possible, thus let's go to the Media Manager and do the following two things:

- Use the same structure to make folders for our images.

- To allow us to upload multiple images at once, click Options and set Enable Flash Uploader to No. When you've finished, your Media Manager looks like Figure 13.3.

Figure 13.3   Media Manager with new folders for your personal site

Add

Now let's write the articles for the site. The following list offers some ideas for articles to the categories. If you can, try to upload as many images as possible, particularly when it comes to your staff members and the portfolio categories. If you need help, you can always borrow the articles and images from http://www.joomlaexplained.com/business.

- About Us (Category)

  - Introduction (Article)

  - Business History (Article)

  - Location (Article)

- Our Services (Category)

  - Websites (Article)

  - Logos (Article)

  - Brochures (Article)

- Our Staff (Category)
    - Steve (Article)
    - John (Article)
    - Jane (Article)
- Company News (Category)
    - We're Hiring New Staff (Article)
    - We Just Launched a New Website for ACME Corporation (Article)
    - Come and Meet Us at the Big Web Conference (Article)
- Our Portfolio (Category)
    - Websites (Category)
        - ACME Corporation (Article)
        - ABC Non-Profit Organization (Article)
        - XYZ Business (Article)
    - Logos (Category)
    - Brochures (Category)

When the articles have been added, your Article Manager looks like Figure 13.4. It might be a good idea to set Featured to Yes for one of the articles so that it appears on your site's home page. You can see in Figure 13.4 that I did it for the Introduction article.

Show

Let's set up our menu links so that visitors can easily see our articles. Here's how we do it using the About Us category as an example. First, let's allow people to see all About Us articles:

1. Go to Menus, then Main Menu and click New.
2. Set these fields:
    - **Menu Item Type.** Category Blog
    - **Menu Title.** About Us
    - **Choose a Category.** About Us

Title ▲	Published	Featured	Category
ABC Non-Profit Organization (Alias: abc-non-profit-organization)	✓	○	Our Clients
ACME Corporation (Alias: acme-corporation)	✓	○	Our Clients
Brochures (Alias: brochures)	✓	○	Our Services
Business History (Alias: business-history)	✓	○	About Us
Come and Meet Us at the Big Web Conference (Alias: come-and-meet-us-at-the-big-web-conference)	✓	○	Company News
Introduction (Alias: introduction)	✓	✪	About Us
Jane (Alias: jane)	✓	○	Our Staff

Figure 13.4   Article Manager with new articles for your personal site

Now go ahead and repeat for Our Services, Our Staff, and Company News. Let's leave the Our Portfolio category alone for now—we have a special surprise for that later in the chapter.

After you've added the menu links to each Category Blog, your Main Menu should look like that shown in Figure 13.5.

	Title
Home (Alias: home)	
About Us (Alias: about-us)	
Our Services (Alias: our-services)	
Our Staff (Alias: our-staff)	
Company News (Alias: company-news)	

Figure 13.5   Your About Us menu links

By the time you're finished, the Main Menu should look like Figure 13.6.

If you go to the visitor area of your site, you should see the Main Menu module with all of your categories. Click on any category, and you see the articles in that category.

Finally, let's set the article options. For example, we don't really need the category name, author name, and published date on every page. We can turn this setting off by going to Article Manager and clicking on Options.

Figure 13.6   Main Menu links to all your categories and articles

Step 3: Components, Modules, and Plug-ins

Now it's time to add some more features to our business site using extensions.

Default Component: Contacts

Let's allow people to send an e-mail message to us. We use the Contacts component, and to create the form we use the CASh workflow. If you have more Staff members you could also decide to add more contact forms: perhaps one for each staff member.

1. **Categorize.** Go to Components, then Contacts, and then Categories and make sure that at least one category is in place. Uncategorized will be sufficient because we only have one contact form for this site.

2. **Add.** Go to Components, then Contacts, then Contacts, and click New. Add a contact form for yourself. Make sure to at least enter your e-mail address in here. To make the contact form easier to see, you might also want to click Display Options and set Display Format to Plain.

3. **Show.** Go to Menus, then Main Menu and make a menu link to your new contact form. When you're finished, it should look like Figure 13.7.

Installed Component: Zen Portfolio

Rather than simply using a plain article to show our company's portfolio, it would be a good idea to use a photo gallery instead. That would really enable us to show images of our work clearly. So let's add a photo gallery to our site. Before we start, make sure you have done two things already:

- Created the Our Portfolio category with subcategories. In our example those were Web sites, Logos, and Brochures.

- Added articles with images to the various subcategories.

Let's look for an extension that's capable of turning the work we've done into an attractive display.

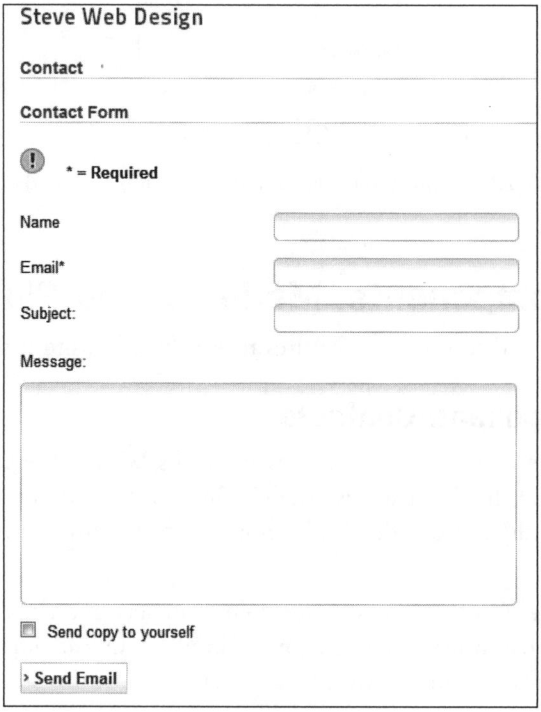

Figure 13.7   A contact form on your business site

Step 1: Research

Go to http://extensions.joomla.org and on the left-hand side under the Categories list, click Directory & Documentation, and then click Portfolio. Using our criteria, Portfolio Zen looks promising. Figure 13.8 shows how it looks on the Joomla Extensions Directory.

- **Rating.** Four of five stars, although it doesn't have many votes.
- **Compatibility.** Joomla 1.5 and 1.6
- **Commercial or Non-Commercial.** Non-Commercial
- **Extension Types.** Component

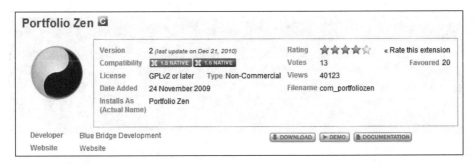

Figure 13.8   The Portfolio Zen Extension on http://extensions.joomla.org

- **Important Links.** The demo looks good although there are no support links.
- **Reviews.** They are almost all really positive.

Step 2: Download
Click the Download link and download the 1.6 version of Portfolio Zen.

Step 3: Upload
Log in to your Joomla site and install the file you just downloaded.

Step 4: Use
Go to Menus, Main Menu and click New. Set these fields:

- **Menu Item Type.** Portfolio Zen and Default Layout
- **Menu Title.** Our Portfolio
- **Category.** Our Portfolio

When you've successfully saved your menu link, you can go to the visitor area of your site, and each photo should look like Figure 13.9. Above the images you'll see a list of categories used by Portfolio Zen, and below the images you'll see numbers allowing you to move from one image to the next.

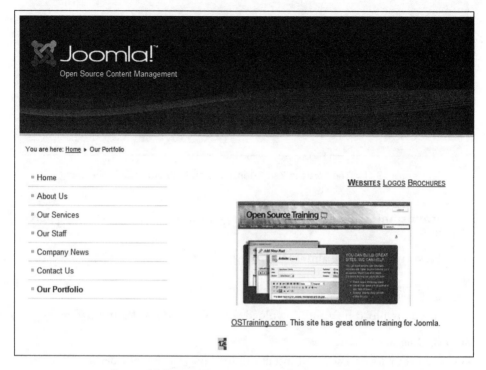

Figure 13.9   Portfolio Zen showing your Our Portfolio
articles in a slideshow

Default Modules: Most Read Content

Let's set up three modules that will be useful for our business site. Here are three modules to create, together with the settings I recommend:

- **Search.** This allows people to easily find what they're looking for on our site:
  - **Title.** Search
  - **Position.** position-6
- **Latest News.** This allows visitors to see our recent Company News.
  - **Title.** Latest Company News
  - **Position.** position-6

- **Popular Company News.** This allows people to see which Company News articles have received the most visits.

    - **Title. Popular Company News**

    - **Position.** position-6

    - **Category.** Company News

After you've created all three modules, you can see them all in action as in Figure 13.10.

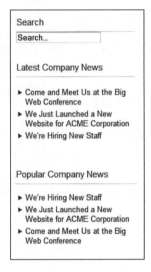

Figure 13.10   Three new modules on your Company News page

Installed Module: GTranslate

Now it's time to add an extra module to our site. One extra feature that might be useful is adding automatic translations so that potential customers can read the site in their own languages. The translations probably won't be perfect, but they should be understandable and therefore useful. If you need to manually translate the text on your site to ensure accuracy, turn to Chapter 15, "Joomla Languages Explained," for more details.

Step 1: Research

Go to http://extensions.joomla.org and on the left-hand side under the Categories list, click Languages, then Automatic translations. Let's look for an extension that matches our criteria. One that stands out is GTranslate shown in Figure 13.11.

- **Rating.** Four and a half out of five stars and plenty of votes.
- **Compatibility.** Joomla 1.5 and 1.6.
- **Commercial or Non-Commercial.** Non-Commercial.
- **Extension Types.** Module.
- **Important Links.** The demo is live on the developer's Web site and looks good. There's also a support forum available.
- **Reviews.** They are mostly positive.

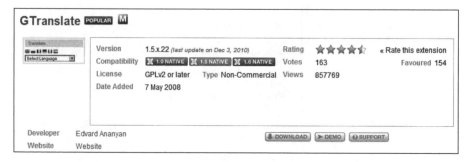

Figure 13.11   The GTranslate extension on http://extensions.joomla.org

Step 2: Download

Click the Download link, and you are taken to the developer's site. You have to register to download the file.

Step 3: Upload

Log in to the administrator area of your site and upload the file you just downloaded.

Step 4: Use

Go to the Module Manager and open the GTranslate module. Fill in at least these details:

- **Title. Translate This Page**
- **Published.** Published

- **Position.** position-6
- **Module Assignment.** On all pages

Go to the visitor area of your site, and you see the module in action as in Figure 13.12.

Figure 13.12   The GTranslate module on your site

Default Plug-in: User Profile

This task allows us to collect information about users when they register on our site. There are many reasons why you might ask people to register. For example, you might want to entice visitors to register and give you their details in exchange for free information or downloads. Also, registering is a popular way to reduce spam if you allow visitors to submit content on your site. See Chapter 14, "Joomla Users Explained," for more information on this.

1. Go to Extensions then Plug-in Manager and click on the red circle next to the User – Profile plug-in so that it turns to a green check mark.

2. Go to the visitor area and look for the Login Form module in the left column. Click on the Create an account link at the bottom of the module, and you see a screen like that in Figure 13.13.

3. To remove any of these fields or to make them required, go to Extensions then Plugin Manager and click on the User – Profile plug-in link. On the right-hand side in the Basic Options area, you can decide what information you collect from users.

Installed Plug-in: JPlayer

It would be great to add some multimedia to our site. One easy way to do that is to install a plug-in that allows us to use videos from YouTube.

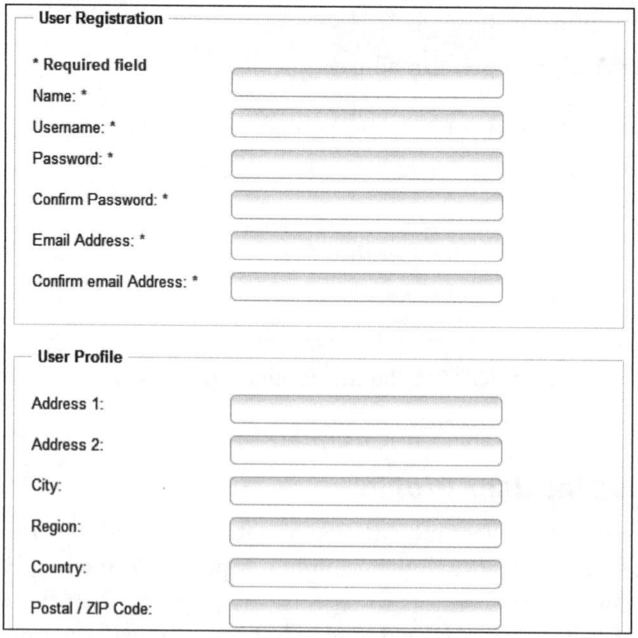

Figure 13.13   The User Profile plug-in working on your site

Step 1: Research

Go to http://extensions.joomla.org, and on the left-hand side under the Categories list, click Multimedia, Multimedia Players, and then Video Players & Gallery.

Let's look for an extension that matches our criteria. One that stands out is JPlayer shown in Figure 13.14.

- **Rating.** Four and a half out of five stars and plenty of votes.
- **Compatibility.** Joomla 1.5 and 1.6.
- **Commercial or Non-Commercial.** Non-Commercial.
- **Extension Types.** Plug-in.
- **Important Links.** There's a demo, support, and documentation available.
- **Reviews.** They are almost all positive.

Step 2: Download

Click the Download link and get the version for Joomla 1.6.

Figure 13.14   The JPlayer Extension on http://extensions.joomla.org

Step 3: Upload

Log in to the administrator area of your site and upload the file you just downloaded.

Step 4: Use

Go to the Plugin Manager and enable the Content – JPlayer module. Now it's ready to use. Here's how the JPlayer plug-in allows us to easily put YouTube videos on our site:

1. Go to YouTube.com and browse for a video.

2. Get the identifying code of the video. Often it will look like this: http://www.youtube.com/watch?v=vb2eObvmvdI. You're looking for the code after ?v=, so in this case the code we need is vb2eObvmdvI. This can be a little confusing because there can also be extra code at the end such as &feature=player_embedded. Be sure not to gather that extra code, just the approximately 12 letters and numbers in the identifying code.

3. Take that code and paste it into an article in this format: {youtube}vb2eObvmdvI{/youtube}. You can see an example in Figure 13.15.

Figure 13.15   Placing a YouTube video in a Joomla article using JPlayer

4. Go to the visitor area of your site, and you see the YouTube video as in Figure 13.16.

Figure 13.16   The JPlayer plug-in showing a YouTube video on your site

Step 4: Templates

We have one final step to finish our business site: a new template. Let's go through our workflow to get a new template:

Step 1: Research

Search for and evaluate the template with these criteria. The Roonix template from a company called Pixel Point Creative is one that's worth trying. Here's a link: http://roonix.pixelpointcreative.com/.

- **Compatibility.** Joomla 1.6
- **Commercial or Non-Commercial.** Commercial
- **Design.** Clean and professional-looking
- **Complexity.** Not too many elements
- **Documentation.** Some documentation with the demo
- **Support.** Only for paid users

Step 2: Download

Go ahead and download the Joomla 1.6 version of Roonix. You can find the download link here: http://www.pixelpointcreative.com/template.html. You need to right-click on the downloaded file and extract it because it has both the 1.5 and 1.6 versions in one file.

Step 3: Upload

Upload the Roonix_J16.zip file and make it the default template. Go to the visitor area, and your site looks like Figure 13.17. OK, so clearly we have some work still to do!

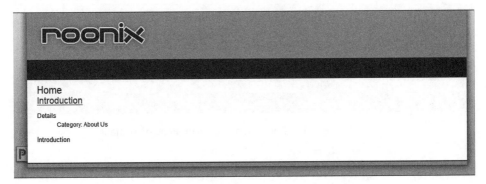

Figure 13.17   The Roonix template live on your site

Step 4: Modules

To place our modules, we need to find out where the module positions are on this template:

1. Go to the Template Manager, click Options, and set Preview Module Positions to Enabled.

2. In the Template Manager, click the Templates tab, scroll down to Roonix, and click Preview. You should see a lot of positions! Figure 13.18 shows some of them:

   Here are some ideas for where you can move the modules:

   - **Main Menu.** Move to the menu position. Also while you're editing the module, set Show Title to Hide and set Show Sub-menu Items to Yes. Those two options allow us to have a drop-down menu.

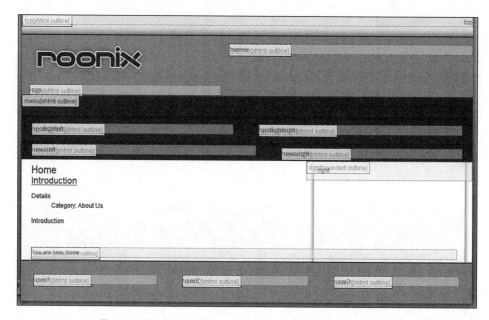

Figure 13.18   The Roonix template with module positions

- **Latest Company News, Popular Company News, Translate This Page and Login Form.** Move to the Right position. While you're editing these modules, you can take advantage of a useful extra option that some templates allow: module suffixes. What are module suffixes? If you put a small piece of text inside each module, the template will redesign that module in a certain way. For example, if you enter blue, the template might get a blue background. To make this work, open each module, look in the Advanced Options, and enter either red or blue in the Module Class Suffix boxes. This template does support module suffixes as an added feature: If you put those colors in that options box, it will automatically design those modules with that color.

- **Search.** Move to the top position. Also set these options:

  - **Show Title.** Hide.

  - **Box Label.** Just put your cursor in here and hit space. That removes the Search label that normally appears next to the box.

  - **Module Class Suffix.** Search.

When you've moved your modules, the visitor area should look a lot better, as in Figure 13.19.

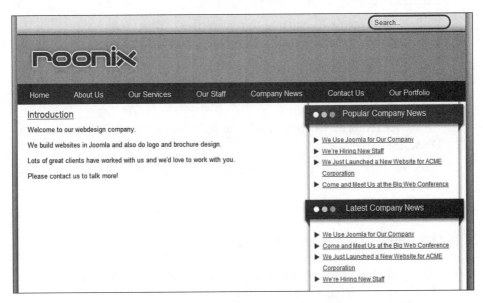

Figure 13.19   The Roonix template with your modules in the correct position

There are some more module positions we haven't used. For example, there's more room in the footer, and you could easily add more modules into the User 2 and User 3 positions. Fortunately, if we don't use those positions, the template will hide them automatically so you won't see any empty space.

Step 5: Modify

First, let's change the template's options:

1. Go to the Template Manager and click on Roonix – Default.

2. There's one key option for this template: You can choose to have it in red or blue.

The final task is to replace the logo. Some templates make this easy, but with others this can be the trickiest part of installing the template.

There are two ways you can change the logo on the Roonix template. This first way involves using FTP software such as Filezilla. Some of you might have used this to install Joomla in Chapter 2 or at the beginning of this chapter.

1. Log in to the site using your FTP software.

2. Browse through your Joomla site folders using this URL: templates/roonix/images/red/redLogo.png.

3. Upload your own redLogo.png to replace this existing redLogo.png file. Do make sure to use a capital L in redLogo.png as files on the server are case-sensitive.

Alternatively you can use the Media Manager to upload your logo. Here's how you can do it:

1. Go to the Template Manager, click the Templates tab, and click on Roonix Details.

2. Click Edit css/red.css if you're using the red design or blue.css if you're using blue.

3. Scroll down just a little way until you find this line:

```
#logo {
background: url(../images/red/redLogo.png) no-repeat;
}
```

4. Change the middle part of this line so that it looks like the following code. We changed ../images/ to ../../../images/ so that the template looks in a different location—in the Media Manager folder rather than the template folder.

```
#logo {
background:url(../../../images/logo.png) no-repeat;
}
```

5. Save this file and now if you go to the Media Manager you can upload any logo.png, and it will work for you. I have a sample logo ready at http://www.joomlaexplained.com/chapter13.

After you've changed your logo, you should hopefully be able to see a completed Joomla personal site for yourself as in Figure 13.20.

Figure 13.20   Your completed business Joomla site

What's Next?

Congratulations! You've now built three complete Joomla sites! You used the Joomla workflow to successfully build a city site, a personal site, and a business site. Here was the workflow you used:

Step 1: Installation

Step 2: Content

Step 3: Extensions (Components, Modules, and Plug-ins)

Step 4: Templates

So far you have learned the essential Joomla basics, and you'll use them in every site you build. If that's all you need, you can stop right here.

However, if you're ready to move on to some more advanced topics, we have three more in this book. Turn the page, and let's find out more.

14

Joomla! Users Explained

During the first 13 chapters of this book you learned everything that is essential to know about Joomla.

For example, it would be difficult to use Joomla if you didn't understand how to organize, add, and show content (Chapter 4, "Joomla Content Explained"). It would also be difficult to use Joomla if you didn't know the purpose of components (Chapter 7, "Joomla Components Explained"), modules (Chapter 8, "Joomla Modules Explained"), plug-ins (Chapter 9, "Joomla Plug-ins Explained"), or templates (Chapter 10, "Joomla Templates Explained"). You'd also be stuck if you didn't know how to add extra features to your site (Chapter 11, "Adding Joomla Extensions Explained") or how to put all these pieces together to build a real site (Chapter 12, "Putting It All Together: Personal Site," and Chapter 13, "Putting It All Together: Business Site").

These final three chapters are different in several ways:

- The information in these chapters is useful, but you don't absolutely have to know it to use Joomla.

- We're not going to build another example site throughout these chapters. We're just going to use our business site from the previous chapter as a base to work from.

- There won't be a long practice area at the end of each chapter. Particularly in Chapters 15 and 16, we set up things once on our Joomla site and won't need to do it again.

This chapter shows you how to manage multiple users on your site. This is useful if you have a lot of people logging in to your site and doing different things, but you can skip this chapter if your Joomla site only has a few users.

Chapter 15, "Joomla Languages Explained," shows you how to translate your site into more than one language. This is useful for many people whose visitors speak more than language, but you can skip this chapter if you're building your site in just one language.

Chapter 16, "Joomla Site Management Explained," shows you how to keep your site safe, secure, and updated. This is useful if you're going to be responsible for running and managing your Joomla site, but you can skip this chapter if you have a Web designer or technical person who is doing this for you.

We use our business site for these three chapters. So before you begin any of the three chapters, bring up your new Joomla business site you created in Chapter 13.

In Chapter 13, we built a business Web site using everything we've learned in this book so far. We used many parts of the Joomla administrator area, but you probably noticed that we skipped over some areas entirely. That was deliberate. Some of Joomla's features are more important than others, and some require more experience with Joomla. In fact, we actually skipped over one entire area of the main drop-down menu: Users. That area is the focus of this chapter.

Things You Can Do After Reading This Chapter

- Understand Joomla's three default access levels that control what people see on your site

- Understand Joomla's eight default user groups that control what people can do on your site

- Modify those access levels and user groups to meet the unique needs of your site

Imagine you are running a business site and you have many different types of visitors. Here are some fairly simple examples:

- **The general public.** They're just curious and want to browse around your site.

- **Registered users.** They want to log in to comment on your blog posts and maybe to access special offers.

- **Administrators.** They want to add content, move modules, add menu links, and do whatever else they need to manage the site.

Each of these types of visitors needs different permissions for different areas of the site. For example, we don't want to allow the general public to comment on our blog posts because we'd get too much spam. Also we don't want to allow any registered user to modify our site.

How do we give different permissions to different types of visitors? That's the question we're going to answer in this chapter.

One of the major improvements in Joomla 1.6 is the ability to have detailed control over what users can and cannot do on your site. The new system is often known as Access Control Levels, or ACL for short. We recommend three different ways to approach access control:

- **Method 1.** Using Joomla's default setup to control what people can see.

- **Method 2.** Using Joomla's default setup to control what people can do.

- **Method 3.** Modifying Joomla's default setup to create your own lists of what people can see and do. This is the most complex way of handling users. This method could merit a book by itself, so we're going to introduce you only to its most important features.

Carefully choose the method that is right for you. If you are at all unsure, err on the side of caution and choose the simpler step. Things can get pretty complicated if you add a lot of access control, each with different choices for what users can and cannot do.

What People Can See: Joomla's Access Levels

First, let's see how we can control what our site visitors can and cannot access on our site.

1. We use the business site from Chapter 13, so go ahead and log in to the administrator area of that site.

2. Click on Article Manager under Content in the main drop-down menu. You can see all of the articles that you added in the previous chapter as in Figure 14.1. Notice that there's a column called Access that we haven't mentioned yet. Every article has the same entry: Public. That means these articles are all available to the general public. Any visitor to our site can access every one of these articles.

3. Click on the article you wrote called Brochures, and you see the same article editing screen we used so often throughout the book. You can see there's an Access field here too. Click on that Access field, and a drop-down menu appears as in Figure 14.2.

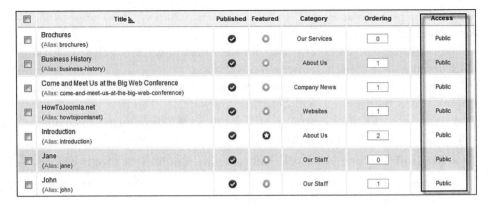

Figure 14.1   The Article Manager in your business site

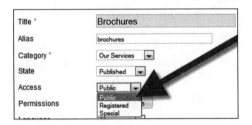

Figure 14.2   The Access field inside an article

Public is the default choice, but there are two other options: Registered and Special. Here's what the three options mean:

- **Public.** Accessible to anyone who visits the site
- **Registered.** Accessible only to people who create an account and log in to the site
- **Special.** Accessible only to the users who will maintain the site. This covers everyone from Authors who can only write content all the way up to Super Users who can control everything on the site.

Let's see how those options work in practice:

1. Select Registered as the choice for the Access drop-down and click Save & Close.

2. Go to the visitor area of your site. See if you can find that Brochures article you just saved. You can try the search box. You can try clicking on Our

Services in the menu. You can look all around the site, but you won't find the article.

3. Now, look for the Login Form module on the right-hand side of your site as in Figure 14.3. Log in here using the same username and password that you use for the administrator area.

Figure 14.3   The Login Form module as shown to visitors

4. After you've logged in successfully, you can see that the Login Form module has changed. The module no longer shows the information the general public needs such as how to register or recover a forgotten password. Now it just shows you a welcome message and a Log Out button as in Figure 14.4.

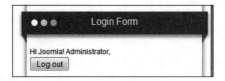

Figure 14.4   The Login Form module as shown to logged in users

5. Now find the Brochures article. You should be able to successfully find it by using the search box. Also if you click on Our Services in the menu, you can see the article as in Figure 14.5.

Figure 14.5   The Brochures article

6. Also in Figure 14.5 you see a pencil icon next to each article. That allows you to edit the article directly from here. Click on the pencil, and you can edit the article as in Figure 14.6. You see this pencil because you are now part of the Special access level and have the right to edit the article. The pencil didn't show before you logged in because we definitely don't want to allow any ordinary members of the public to do this.

From here you can edit the text and change a variety of options for the article, including the category, publishing dates, and more.

That's the concept behind access levels: You can give different access permissions to different people on your site. The public sees one version of the site, and people at the different access levels see different versions of the site. Let's see how far this goes by looking at the administrator area again:

1. Go back to the administrator and go to Main Menu under Menus in the main drop-down. You can see that Access is an option for all of your menu links as in Figure 14.7.

Figure 14.6   Editing the Brochures article from the visitors area

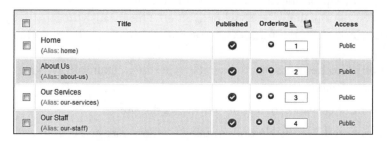

Figure 14.7   Viewing the Main Menu with Access options

2. Now go to Category Manager under Content in the main drop-down. You can see that Access is an option for all of your categories as in Figure 14.8.

3. Move on to the Module Manager under Extensions in the main drop-down. You can see that Access is an option for all of your modules as in Figure 14.9.

	Title	Published	Ordering ≜ 🖺	Access
☐	Uncategorised (Alias: uncategorised)	✓	○ [1]	Public
☐	About Us (Alias: about-us)	✓	○ ○ [2]	Public
☐	Our Services (Alias: our-services)	✓	○ ○ [3]	Public
☐	Our Portfolio (Alias: our-portfolio)	✓	○ ○ [4]	Public

Figure 14.8   Viewing the Category Manager with Access options

	Title	Published	Position ≜	Ordering	Type	Pages	Access
☐	Main Menu	✓	menu	[1]	Menu	All	Public
☐	Breadcrumbs	✓	position-2	[1]	Breadcrumbs	All	Public
☐	Banners	○	position-5	[1]	Banners	All	Public
☐	Popular Company News	✓	right	[1]	Most Read Content	All	Public
☐	Latest Company News	✓	right	[2]	Latest News	All	Public
☐	Translate This Site	✓	right	[3]	GTranslate	All	Public
☐	Login Form	✓	right	[4]	Login	All	Public
☐	Search	✓	top	[1]	Search	All	Public

Figure 14.9   Viewing the Module Manager with Access options

You can keep on moving through your administrator area, but you see the same Access option almost everywhere you go. This means you can control who sees what for most of the features on your site from articles to menu links to modules.

Let's try another example. Remember the three definitions we gave earlier? Here they are again:

- **Public.** Accessible to anyone who visits the site

- **Registered.** Accessible only to people who create an account and log in to the site

- **Special.** Accessible only to the users who will maintain the site. This covers everyone from Authors who can only write content all the way up to Super Users who can control everything on the site.

In the Brochures article example, we logged in as a Super User who is at the Special access level. That's why we were able to edit the articles. Let's try another example, this time at the Registered level . Here's how we're going to do it:

1. Click on the Translate This Page module.

2. Change the Access option to Registered and click Save & Close.

3. Click on Log Out in the top-right corner of the screen. You are taken to the front of your site. Notice that the Translate This Page module is no longer accessible.

4. Now register as an ordinary visitor to your site. Find the Login Form and click on the Create an account link. If you enabled the User–Profile plug-in in Chapter 13, you see a lot of fields including address, city, and phone number. The only key fields to fill in are Name, Username, Password, and Email address as in Figure 14.10. Enter a Username and Password that you can remember.

User Registration

* Required field
Name: *

    Test Account

Username: *

    testaccount

Password: *

    ••••••••••

Confirm Password: *

    ••••••••••

Email Address: *

    test@joomlaexplained.com

Confirm email Address: *

    test@joomlaexplained.com

Figure 14.10   Registering on your site

5. You get a message saying, "Your account has been created and an activation link has been sent to the email address you entered. Note that you must activate the account by clicking on the activation link when you get the email before you can login." Follow those instructions and click on the link to activate your new account.

6. When you do click on the link, you see another message. As in Figure 14.11, this one says, "Your Account has been successfully activated. You can now log in using the username and password you chose during the registration." You can use the login box under the message to log in.

7. After logging in, you can now see the Translate This Site module as in Figure 14.12. To test that this works, you can try logging out. If the Translate This Site module disappears again, you know that you were successful.

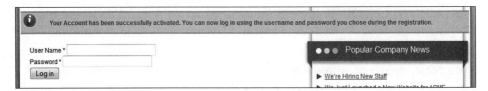

Figure 14.11   Confirming the new user account Translate This Page

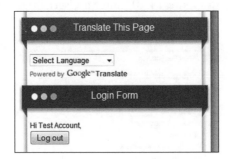

Figure 14.12   The Translate This Page module and the Login Form
module

There's one final and important thing to note about the Public and
Registered level concerning the administrator area rather than the visitor area.
Here's how to see that difference in action.

Go to the administrator area of your site and try to log in using the test
account. You get a message saying you don't have permission like the one in
Figure 14.13. Why were you denied access? It's because users can only access the
administrator area if a current user has given them access. This is a security feature, and you should think carefully about who you allow to access the administrator area.

So these are key differences among the three basic user levels:

- **Public.** Anything with this setting is accessible to anyone who visits
  the site.

- **Registered.** Anything with this setting is accessible only to people who
  have accounts and are logged in to the site.

- **Special.** Anything with this setting is accessible only to people trusted to
  maintain and run the site.

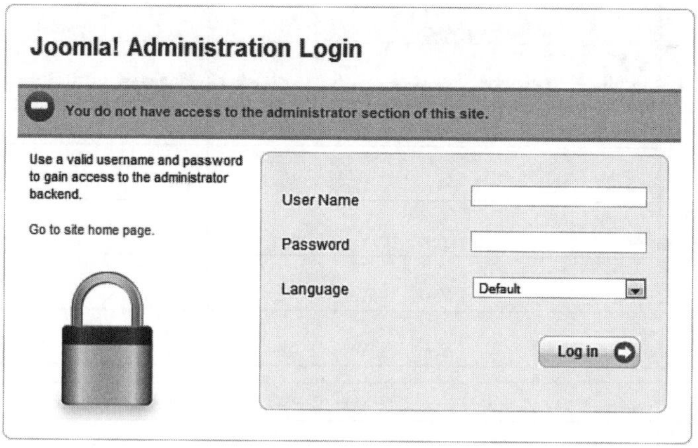

Figure 14.13   Access denied for the administrator area

Method 2: What Users Can Do: Joomla's User Groups

The three access levels (Public, Registered, and Special) work great for many sites. However, for some sites you want to do more than control what users can access: You also want to control what users can do.

Joomla comes with eight examples of user groups. There are Public and Registered, which correspond directly to the Public and Registered access levels that we just saw. The added examples are inside the Special access level. These groups are Author, Editor, Publisher, Manager, Administrator, and Super User.

With thanks to Brian Teeman from http://brian.teeman.net, Figure 14.14 is a chart of these groups and what they can and cannot do:

You can see that each of those user groups build on each other. Each one has slightly more permissions that the last.

You can also see that only three of these user groups are allowed to access the administrator area: Manager, Administrator, and Super User. These three groups are particularly useful. You've seen the Super User group throughout this book. Let's see how different the Manager and Administrator groups are. Let's log in as those two groups. Here's how we do it:

1. Go to User Manager under Users in the main drop-down menu.

2. Click on Demo User, uncheck the box next to Registered, and then check the box next to Manager.

	Public Registered					Special		
	Public	Registered	Author	Editor	Publisher	Manager	Administrator	Super User
View "public" content	Yes	Yes	Yes	Yes	Yes	Yes	Yes	Yes
View "registered" content	—	Yes	Yes	Yes	Yes	Yes	Yes	Yes
View "special" content	—	—	Yes	Yes	Yes	Yes	Yes	Yes
Create new content	—	—	Yes	Yes	Yes	Yes	Yes	Yes
Edit own content	—	—	Yes	Yes	Yes	Yes	Yes	Yes
Edit all content	—	—	—	Yes	Yes	Yes	Yes	Yes
Publish new content	—	—	—	—	Yes	Yes	Yes	Yes
Access the Administrator page	—	—	—	—	—	Yes	Yes	Yes
Create new users	—	—	—	—	—	—	Yes	Yes
Install extensions	—	—	—	—	—	—	Yes	Yes

Figure 14.14   Access denied for the administrator area

3. Click Save & Close and then Log out in the top-right corner.

4. Now go back to the administrator area and log in using the Demo User account.

5. You see a screen like Figure 14.15. Many of the drop-down menu options are gone. The Manager group has the ability to add and organize content. They can also use some of the components. However, they have very little ability to modify the site. They can't change the site's layout because they don't have access to the templates, modules, or menus. They also can't change any key settings because they don't have access to the Site Configuration screen or the Users link in the main drop-down menu.

   Do you have any people updating your site who always make mistakes? Are you that person who always makes mistakes? If so, the Manager group is a great place to put them. They can add content safe in the knowledge that they really can't make any serious errors.

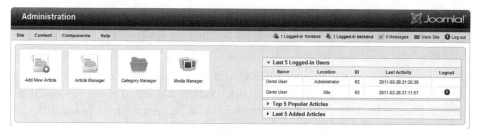

Figure 14.15   What the Manager group can see
in the Joomla administrator area

Now let's see what the Administrator group is like:

1. Click Log Out again and log in to the administrator area using the main Super User account you've been using through the book.

2. Go to User Manager under Users in the main drop-down menu.

3. Click on Demo User then uncheck the box next to Manager and check the box next to Administrator.

4. Click Save & Close and then Log Out in the top-right corner.

5. Log in again to the administrator using the Demo User account.

6. You now see a screen like Figure 14.16. The Administrator can do almost everything that the Super User can do.

Figure 14.16   What the Administrator group can see
in the Joomla administrator area

There is only one feature that the Administrator doesn't have access to. Go to User Manager under the Users link from the drop-down menu, and you see the users on the site.

Remember how your Super User account was able to control the Demo Site user? The opposite is not true. Because you are logged in as the Demo Site user, you won't be able to click on the Super User account. That's because the Administrator can't edit the Super User, can't control them, and can't demote them to a lower group. They also can't create a Super User.

The Administrator group is great if you want to maintain final control over the site but only give access to people who really know their way around Joomla. It's possible to make a lot of mistakes at the Administrator level, so be careful who you place in this group. For example, an Administrator can easily change the template, delete modules, upload extensions, and generally make a mess of the site. Of course, be even more careful about who you place in the Super User group. Super Users can do anything and everything on your site. So for security reasons, I highly recommend that you put only a very small number of people in this group and place everyone else in the lower groups.

Method 3: Creating Your Own Access Controls

In Method 1, you saw three access levels: Public, Registered, and Special.

In Method 2, you saw eight user groups: Public, Registered, Author, Editor, Publisher, Manager, Administrator, and Super Users.

In Method 3, you see how to change everything about those access levels and user groups. You also see how you can create your own versions of them.

Setting Up a New User Group

Let's give you an idea of how you can set up your own access controls. The example we use is someone whose only task is to add the latest news about the company. This is a role I've heard several students in our class describe: For example, they want to give someone from the marketing department the ability to write articles but only in one category. Here's how we do it.

Step 1: Create a User Group

First we need to create the user group called Company News Writer:

1. Log in to your administrator area with your Super User account.

2. Go to Groups under Users in the main drop-down menu.

3. Click New in the top-right corner, and you see a screen like Figure 14.17. There are two fields to enter here:

- **Group Title.** Set this to Company News Writer.

- **Group Parent.** This choice is harder. My advice would be to choose the group that is closest to the one you want to create. Almost certainly you need to go back a few pages to Figure 14.14 and see what permissions you want to give to this group. In our example, Author is a good choice. We just want people in the Company News Writer group to log in, write content, and edit their own content. No other permissions are necessary. If we choose Author, this new group automatically gets the Author's permissions.

Figure 14.17   Creating a new user group

4. After you save your new group, you can see it listed in the tree underneath the Author, as shown in Figure 14.18.

Figure 14.18   Your new user group

Step 2: Decide the Permissions

Second, we need to decide exactly what people in the Company News Writer group can and cannot do. Each area of the site has its own permissions, so we need to go to the area that we're focusing on. In this example, we focus on controlling which categories the users can write in, so we need to go to the Category Manager.

Go to Category Manager under Content in the main drop-down menu. Your screen should look like Figure 14.19.

Figure 14.19   The Category Manager screen

Here's what we need to do: We need to stop people in the Company News Writer group from creating content in all the categories except Company News. Because we based the Company News Writer on the Author group, they currently have permission to create content in every category. We need to disable the content creation permission for the Company News Writer in all the categories except Company News. Let's see how that's done:

1. Click on the Uncategorized category. We don't want the Company News Writer to create any content in this category, so we deny them permission to do that. Scroll down to the bottom of the page, and you see the Category Permissions area. Click on Company News Writer as in Figure 14.20.

2. You can see five available permissions:

   - **Create.** The users can create new articles in this category.
   - **Delete.** The users can delete articles in this category.
   - **Edit.** The users can edit any articles in this category.
   - **Edit State.** The users can publish and unpublish articles in this category.
   - **Edit Own.** The users can edit their own articles in this category.

▼ Category Permissions

Manage the permission settings for the user groups below. See notes at the bottom.

| ▶ Public |
| ▶ ┝ Manager |
| ▶ ┝┝ Administrator |
| ▶ ┝ Registered |
| ▶ ┝┝ Author |
| ▼ ┝┝┝ Company News Writer |

Action	Select New Setting [1]	Calculated Setting [2]
Create	Inherited ▾	✔ Allowed
Delete	Inherited ▾	⊖ Not Allowed
Edit	Inherited ▾	⊖ Not Allowed
Edit State	Inherited ▾	⊖ Not Allowed
Edit Own	Inherited ▾	✔ Allowed

| ▶ ┝┝┝ Editor |
| ▶ ┝┝┝┝ Publisher |
| ▶ ┝ Super Users |

Figure 14.20   The Category Permissions area of the Uncategorized category

Fortunately, by choosing to base Company News Writer on the Author group, the permissions are already close to what we want: The users can Create and Edit Own. However, we need to make one change to deny these users permission to Create in this particular category. Go ahead and set Create to Denied as in Figure 14.21.

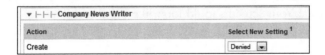

▼ ┝┝┝ Company News Writer	
Action	Select New Setting [1]
Create	Denied ▾

Figure 14.21   Changing permissions for the Company News Writer users

3. The change won't take effect immediately, so click Save and come back down to this area. The Create setting now shows as Denied as in Figure 14.22.

▼ ┝┝┝ Company News Writer		
Action	Select New Setting [1]	Calculated Setting [2]
Create	Denied ▾	⊖ Not Allowed

Figure 14.22   New permissions for the Company News Writer users

4. Repeat the process for the other categories, except for the Company News category. It's worth noting one part of this in particular. If you choose Denied for a main category, all the subcategories automatically inherit those settings. So in Figure 14.23, you won't have to edit all four categories. Just set Our Portfolio to Denied, and the others automatically inherit those same permissions.

Figure 14.23   Subcategories and permissions

Step 3: Create the User

This third step is the easiest. We just need to set up the user account and place them in the Company News Writer group. Here's how we do it:

1. Go to User Manager under the Users menu in the main drop-down.

2. Click New and set up a new user. Give the user a Name, Login Name, and Password. Most importantly, remember to set the user group at the bottom of the page. Your screen should look like Figure 14.24.

Step 4: Test

The final step in this process is to check that we set everything up correctly. Let's do that and introduce you to a new feature at the same time. We're going to allow the Company News Writers to submit content from the front of the site.

1. Go to Main Menu under Menus in the main drop-down menu.

2. Click New and set these fields:

   - **Menu Item Type.** Create Article

   - **Menu Title.** Write Company News

   - **Access.** Special

   - **Parent Item.** Company News

3. Save the menu link and go to the visitor area of your site.

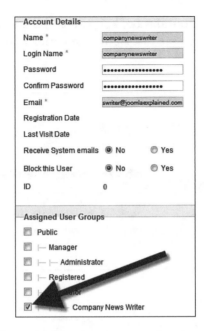

Figure 14.24   Creating a new Joomla user

4. Log in via the Login Form module and using the companynewswriter account you just created.

5. You should now be able to hover over the Company News menu and see your new menu link underneath as in Figure 14.25. If you don't see this, go back to the administrator area, go to the Module Manager, open Main Menu, and set Show Submenu items to Yes.

Figure 14.25   Write Company News menu link

6. You see the same article screen as earlier in the chapter. The main difference now is with the Category option. The user should only be able to choose Company News as in Figure 14.26.

7. If you really want to test this thoroughly, try logging out from the companynewswriter account and logging in with the Super User account

you've used throughout this book. If you go back to the Write Company News menu link, you see that all the categories are now available as in Figure 14.27.

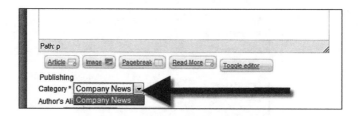

Figure 14.26   Writing a Company News article as a Company News Writer user

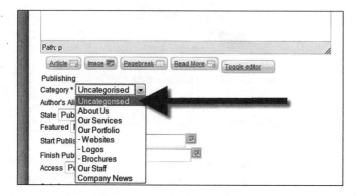

Figure 14.27   Writing a Company News article as a Super User

So that's the process for setting up a new user group on our site. To recap, here is the workflow we used:

Step 1: Create a User Group

Step 2: Decide the Permissions

Step 3: Create the Users

Step 4: Test

Creating a Chief Editor for Our Site

Now that we know how the process works, let's try that one more time. In this next example, we create a Chief Editor for our site. This person has the power to enter our administrator area to create, edit, and delete any article. However, they won't be able to do anything else. We don't want them changing the template, moving modules, or redesigning our site in any way. Here's how we go about setting up that user.

Step 1: Create a User Group

First we need to create the User Group called Chief Editor. We cannot apply permissions directly to an individual user, so first we need to set up a group to put them in:

1. Log in to your administrator area as the Super User.

2. Go to Groups under Users in the main drop-down menu.

3. Click New in the top-right corner and set these two fields:

   - **Group Title.** Chief Editor.

   - **Group Parent.** As before, choose the group that is closest to the one you want to create. Go back a few pages to Figure 14.14 and see what permissions you want to give to this group. In this example, Manager is a good choice. That group can log in and manage content. The only change we need to make is to deny the new group access to the components area. Figure 14.28 shows what our screen should look like.

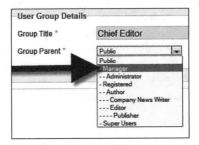

Figure 14.28   Creating a new user group

4. After you save your new group, you can see it listed alongside the others (see Figure 14.29).

Figure 14.29   Your new Chief Editor user group

Step 2: Decide the Permissions

Second, we need to decide exactly what people in the Chief Editor group can and cannot do. In this example, we're focused on stopping the Chief Editor users from having any access to the components. We need to visit the components we have installed and set the Chief Editor's access to Denied.

1. Let's start by going to Banners under Components in the main drop-down menu.

2. Click on the Options button in the top-right corner and then the Chief Editor area. Your screen should look like Figure 14.30.

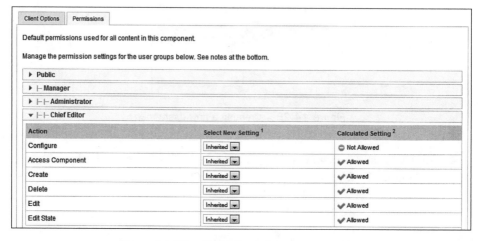

Figure 14.30   The Banners Permissions screen

3. All we need to do here is deny them access, so go ahead and set the Access Component field to Denied. The change won't take effect immediately, so click Save and come back down to this area to check that permissions are now set to Denied as in Figure 14.31.

▼ ├─ ├─ Chief Editor		
Action	Select New Setting [1]	Calculated Setting [2]
Configure	Inherited [▼]	⊘ Not Allowed
Access Component	Denied [▼]	⊘ Not Allowed

Figure 14.31   Denying access to the Banner component for Chief Editor users

4. Repeat the process for the other components: Contact, Newsfeeds, Search, and Weblinks.

Step 3: Create the User

Now we need to set up the user account and place them in the Chief Editor group. Here's how we do it:

1. Go to User Manager under the Users menu in the main drop-down.

2. Click New and set up a new user. Give her a Name, Login Name, and Password. Most importantly, remember to set the user group at the bottom of the page. Your screen should look like Figure 14.32.

Step 4: Test

The final step in this process is to test and see whether we've set up everything correctly. Doing this is relatively simple for the Chief Editor user. You simply need to log out and log in again to the administrator area using the Chief Editor account. If you want, testing is even easier if you open a separate Web browser. For example, if you're using Firefox you can open up Internet Explorer, or if you're using Safari, you can open up Chrome. In one browser you can be logged in as the Chief Editor and testing the account, and at the same time in the other browser you can be logged in as the Super User and making any changes you need.

If everything is set up correctly, you should see a screen like Figure 14.33 when you're logged in as a Chief Editor. Users can see the Site drop-down link from where they can edit their profile. They can see the Help drop-down link also. Otherwise the only thing they can do is manage content.

Figure 14.32   Creating a new Joomla user in the Chief Editor group

Figure 14.33   The Administrator area as seen by the Chief Editor

What's Next?

Congratulations! You've now been through three methods for controlling Joomla users. Each method is more flexible but also more complex than the one before. Particularly with Method 3, things can become really powerful but also complicated. In this chapter, we only scratched the surface of what Method 3 could achieve on large sites. However, my advice is the same as at the beginning of the chapter: Keep it simple. Managing three user levels or eight user groups is not too hard. Managing twenty-three user levels or twenty-eight user groups could become very complex. Err on the side of simplicity.

If you do need to use Method 3 to create a detailed set of user permissions on your site, we have a collection of videos and tutorials links to help you out. Go to http://joomlaexplained.com/chapter14 to find that information.

In the next chapter, we turn our attention to multilingual sites. You see how Joomla can allow you to add and manage translated content. Turn the page and see how to do it.

15

Joomla! Languages Explained

In Chapter 14, "Joomla Users Explained," you saw a new feature in Joomla 1.6: You can create your own access controls.

In this chapter, you see another new feature: the ability to run your site in more than one language. Visitors can click a button and change from one language to another.

It's worth noting something important before we begin:

- Joomla translates the default text such as Log In, Log Out, Create an Account, and Forgot Your Password in the visitors area and Global Configuration, Article Manager, Components, and Extension Manager in the administrator area.

- Joomla does not automatically translate text you enter. Joomla allows you to type in English, Spanish, and Chinese versions of your articles, but it won't actually do the translation for you. You still have to write the translated text yourself. If you want automatic translations (which tend to be of fairly low quality), look for an extension such as the GTranslate module that we installed in Chapter 13, "Putting It All Together: Business Site."

As with every previous chapter, I recommend that you follow a workflow to get started. The workflow is in fact identical to the one we used to create a new Joomla site. Remember that our Joomla workflow went like this:

Step 1: Installation

Step 2: Content

Step 3: Extensions (Components, Modules, and Plug-ins)

Step 4: Templates

Translating a site is a similar process. Think of what we're about to do as building a new site. We build a new site in our new language inside our existing

English site. Our workflow for building a translated site follows exactly the same pattern:

- **Installation.** Find and install the new language.
- **Content.** Categorize, add, and show articles in the new language.
- **Extensions.** Create versions of components and modules in the new language.
- **Templates.** Assign different template styles to different languages.

Let's use that workflow now to translate our site. The example we use in this chapter is translating our business site so that it appears in both English and Spanish.

Things You Can Do After Reading This Chapter

- Find and install new languages
- Enable the module and plug-in that Joomla requires to allow extra languages
- Translate your content
- Translate your extensions
- Apply different templates to different languages

Step 1: Installation

In earlier chapters, you saw four types of extensions that add features to your Joomla site:

- Chapter 7: Components
- Chapter 8: Modules
- Chapter 9: Plug-ins
- Chapter 10: Templates

There is actually a fifth type of extension: Languages.

The Joomla community has a large number of Translation teams that work to translate Joomla into their languages. As I write this, 64 languages are available for Joomla, from common languages such as Spanish, French, Hindi, and Chinese to rarer languages such as Dari, Khmer, Montenegrin, and even Esperanto. Let's see where those translations are so that we can download the Spanish translation.

1. You can find these languages alongside the other extensions at http://extensions.joomla.org. When you're there, find the Categories menu on the left-hand side, click Languages, and then click Translations for Joomla as in Figure 15.1.

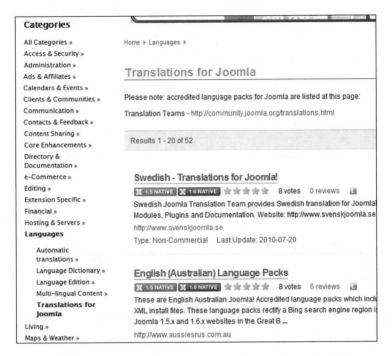

Figure 15.1   Translations for Joomla on the Joomla Extensions Directory

2. Unlike other extensions, there is also a dedicated page elsewhere on Joomla.org. Because these extensions are created and maintained by the Joomla community, this translations page is located at http://community. joomla.org/translations.html. Visit this page; it looks like Figure 15.2.

3. At the top of the page in Figure 15.2, there's a sentence saying, "Joomla1.6 language packs are available here: Joomla! 1.6 Translation Packs." Go ahead and click on that link Joomla 1.6 Translation Packs.

4. Now you see a page with links to all the available translations for Joomla 1.6. We want to enable Spanish on your site, so scroll down until you find the Spanish Translation Community area as in Figure 15.3.

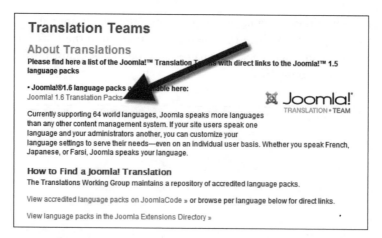

Figure 15.2   Joomla Translations page at http://community.joomla.org/translations.html

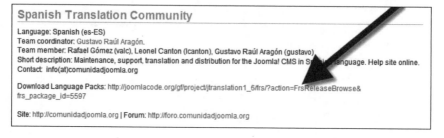

Figure 15.3   Spanish Translation Community area

5. On the page shown in Figure 15.3, click on the link next to Download Language Packs.

6. You now see a page like the one in Figure 15.4.

7. Click on any of the top three links shown in Figure 15.5. This downloads the Spanish translation files to your computer.

8. Go to the administrator area of your Joomla business site that we created in Chapter 13 and used in Chapter 14.

9. Go to Extension Manager under Extensions in the main drop-down menu.

10. As we've done many times in this book, install the extension you just downloaded. In our example here, click Browser, find the file with a name like es-ES_joomla_lang_full_160v1.zip, and click Upload & Install.

Release Name ↓	Release Date ↓	Filename ↓	File Size ↓	Download Count ↓
Spanish_es-ES_lang_packs	2011-01-10 18:00:00-06	es-ES_joomla_lang_full_160v1.zip	215 KB	1409
		es-ES_joomla_lang_full_160v1.tar.gz	127 KB	170
		es-ES_joomla_lang_full_160v1.tar.bz2	99 KB	74
		tinymce_lang_pack_es_3.3.9.3_1.6.tar.gz	11 KB	138
		tinymce_lang_pack_es_3.3.9.3_1.6.zip	26 KB	489
		tinymce_lang_pack_es_3.3.9.3_1.6.tar.bz2	10 KB	61

Figure 15.4   Spanish Translation download area

Figure 15.5   Spanish Translation download links

11. Go to Language Manager under Extensions in the main drop-down menu.
    You see a screen like Figure 15.6. Although English remains the default
    choice, Spanish should now be an option.

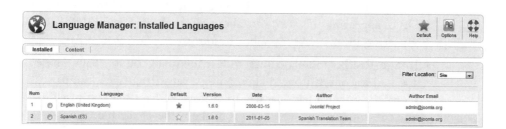

Figure 15.6   The Language Manager in your administrator area

12. This setting in the Language Manager allows us to translate our default
    Joomla text into Spanish. However, to actually translate our articles, menus,
    and modules, we need to complete one more task: Set up a New Content
    Language. Inside the Language Manager, click on the Content tab, and you
    see a screen like Figure 15.7.

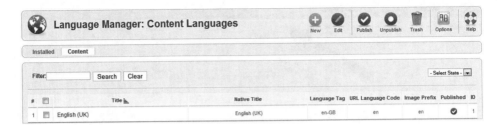

Figure 15.7   The Content tab in the Language Manager

13. You can see that Spanish is missing from here, so we need to add it. Click on New, and you see a screen like Figure 15.8. Here are the fields you need to fill in:

- **Title.** Set this to the name of the new language in the site's main language. So in this example, English is currently our site's main language; therefore, enter Spanish (as opposed to Español).

- **Title Native.** This is the name your new language uses for itself. So in this example, use Español.

- **URL Language Code.** This appears in your site's URLs for all pages in this language. So in this example, we could decide to use "en" for English and "es" for Spanish. That would lead to our English URLs appearing this way: /en/about-us/ and our Spanish URLs appearing in this way: /es/sobre-nosotros/.

- **Image Prefix.** Joomla comes with many small country flags. These are used for our visitors to click on to change languages. Joomla shows the Spanish national flag to visitors. Perhaps the best place to find the combination you need is in the name of the file you download. For example, we downloaded a file called es-ES_joomla_lang_full_160v1.zip, so the language we need is es.

- **Language Tag.** This is likely to be the trickiest field to fill in. We need two sets of two letters here: two lowercase letters for the language followed by two uppercase letters for the country. For example, en-GB is for British English, en-US for United States English, es-ES is for Spanish from Spain, and es-MX is for Spanish from Mexico. As with the previous field, the best place to find the combination you need is in the name of the file you download. For example, we downloaded a file called es-ES_joomla_lang_full_160v1.zip, so the language tag we need is es-ES.

Figure 15.8   Creating a Spanish Language entry

14. Before we go any further, let's test to see whether Spanish is working effectively on our site.

Go to the Installed tab in the Language Manager. You see that English currently has the gold star in the Default column. To make Spanish the default language for our visitor area, click on the star next to Spanish so that it now has the gold star as in Figure 15.9.

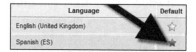

Figure 15.9   Changing the language for your site's visitor area

15. Visit your home page— Joomla's default text has changed to Spanish and the search box says Buscar rather than Search. But the most obvious change is in the Login Form as in Figure 15.10. Remember that we can change the title of the Login Form module by going to the Module Manager, so that name is still in English. So far, we are only changing Joomla's default text.

Figure 15.10   The Joomla login form in Spanish

16. Now go back to your administrator area and go to the Language Manager. Look for the Filter Location box on the right side of the page as in Figure 15.11.

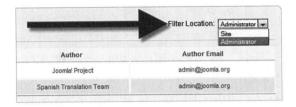

Figure 15.11   Changing the language for your site's administrator area

17. You see two options: Site and Administrator. We just changed the default language for Site. Let's do the same for Administrator. Select Administrator from this drop-down and then click on the star next to Spanish. It will be immediately obvious if you've done the right thing: The whole administrator area should now be in Spanish as in Figure 15.12.

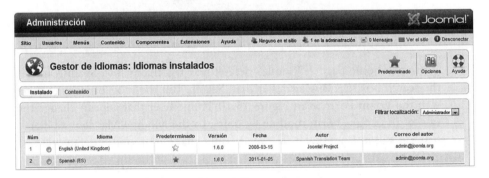

Figure 15.12   Your site's administrator area in Spanish

Great! We now know that Spanish is a working language on our site. Before we go on, I'm going to undo the last few steps and move my Site and Administrator languages back to English. That's going to remain the default language for my site. Go ahead and do the same unless you feel more comfortable in Spanish.

There are also two default Joomla extensions that we need for visitors to switch between the languages on our site: a plug-in called Language Filter and a module called Language Switcher. Let's enable both of those:

1. Go to Plug-in Manager under Extensions in the main drop-down menu and enable the plug-in called System – Language Filter.

2. Go to Module Manager under Extensions in the main drop-down menu and click New.

3. Choose Language Switcher as the type of module you're creating and then here are the settings you need:

   - **Title. Language Switcher**

   - **Show Title.** Hide

   - **Position.** Banner

4. Save the new module and go to the visitor area of your site. You see the British and Spanish flags next to your logo as in Figure 15.13.

Figure 15.13   Your visitor area with the Language Switcher module

If you click on the flags, you notice two things change:

- **Login Form and Search.** We noticed these language changes earlier in the chapter.

- **URLs.** For example, if you click the British flag the URL might be example.com/en, and if you click the Spanish flag the URL might be example.com/es/.

However, the articles and menu links don't change. That's because we haven't told Joomla which articles and menu links are English and which are Spanish. That's what we're going to do now.

Step 2: Content

Building our site in Spanish or any other language is exactly the same as building it in English. We use exactly the same workflow:

- Categorize
- Add
- Show

An Example of How Translation Works

Before we use our entire workflow, let's show an example. We have an English article on our home page. Let's add a Spanish version for when people click on the Spanish flag:

1. Go to the Article Manager and open up the Introduction article that is on our home page.

2. Change the Language field from All to English as in Figure 15.14, and then save this article.

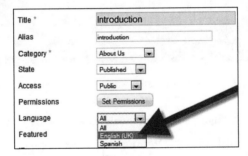

Figure 15.14   Changing the language setting for an article

3. Now you can create the Spanish version of the article. If you don't know enough Spanish to do this, you can always run your original English text through a tool like http://translate.google.com/. Also, don't forget these settings:

   - **Language.** Spanish
   - **Featured.** Yes

Your article should look like Figure 15.15.

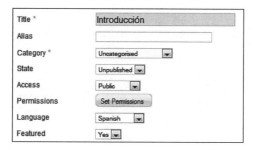

Figure 15.15   Changing an article in Spanish

4. Go to the visitor area of your site. Click on the Spanish flag, and you see the home page change from the Introduction article to the Spanish article you just created, as in Figure 15.16.

Figure 15.16   Your new Spanish home page

That was a fairly straightforward example, but you can see that it works.

Categorize

We need to start by creating Spanish categories for our articles and also by telling Joomla that our English categories really are only for English. Here's how we do it:

1. Go to Category Manager under Content in the main drop-down menu. We now need to create our Spanish categories.

2. Click New and create a new category called Sobre Nosotros (which means About Us in Spanish). Remember to set the Language setting to Spanish as in Figure 15.17.

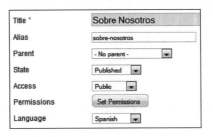

Figure 15.17   Creating a new category in Spanish

3. Repeat this for any category you want to translate into Spanish. It's important to note that you don't have to translate every category, every article, every menu link, or every module. If you have more content in English than Spanish, that's not a problem. You don't have to have a translated version of everything on your site.

4. Finally, we need to tell Joomla that our existing categories are in English. At the moment their Language setting is All, which means that Joomla uses them for both English and Spanish. Open up each English category and change the Language setting to English. When you've finished, your Category Managers should look like Figure 15.18 with some categories labeled English and some labeled Spanish.

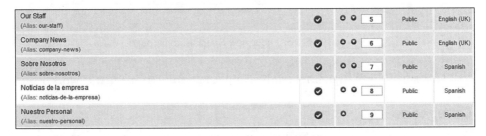

Figure 15.18   Your Category Manager with both
English and Spanish categories

Add

We repeat the same process with each article. We create our new Spanish articles and then change the Language setting of our English articles to English.

1. Go to your Article Manager, click New, and create your new articles in Spanish. Just don't forget these two things:

   - **Language.** Change this drop-down to Spanish.

   - **Category.** Choose one of the Spanish categories you created.

2. In your Article Manager, open each English article and change the Language drop-down to English.

When you're finished, your Article Manager should look like Figure 15.19 with both English and Spanish articles side-by-side.

Ubicación (Alias: ubicacion)	✓	○	Sobre Nosotros	0	Public	Joomla! Administrator	2011-02-27	0	Spanish
Utilizamos Joomla para Nuestra Empresa (Alias: utilizamos-joomla-para-nuestra-empresa)	✓	○	Noticias de la empresa	0	Public	Joomla! Administrator	2011-02-27	0	Spanish
We Just Launched a New Website for ACME Corporation (Alias: we-just-launched-a-new-website- for-acme-corporation)	✓	○	Company News	2	Public	Joomla! Administrator	2011-02-13	1	English (UK)
We Use Joomla for Our Company (Alias: we-use-joomla-for-our-company)	✓	○	Company News	0	Public	Joomla! Administrator	2011-02-14	0	English (UK)

Figure 15.19   Your Article Manager with both English
and Spanish articles

Show

The final step when creating our Spanish content is the same as when creating our English content: making menus and menu links. Also as with categories and articles, we need to tell Joomla that our English menu links really are only for the English part of the site.

Remember all the way back in Chapter 6, "Joomla Menus Explained," when we were introducing menus for the first time? I said that menus were like categories because they had the same purpose. Menus organize your menu links, whereas categories organize your articles. Well, they need to be treated the same way here. We created separate categories for our Spanish articles, and so let's create separate menus for our Spanish menu links.

1. Go to the Menu Manager link under Menus in the main drop-down menu. Click New and create a new menu called Spanish Main Menu.

2. Go to your Spanish Main Menu under Menus in the main drop-down menu. Click New and create your new menu links in Spanish. Just don't forget to change the Language drop-down to Spanish.

3. Go to your Main Menu, open each English menu link, and change the Language drop-down to English.

When you're finished, your Spanish Main Menu should look like Figure 15.20.

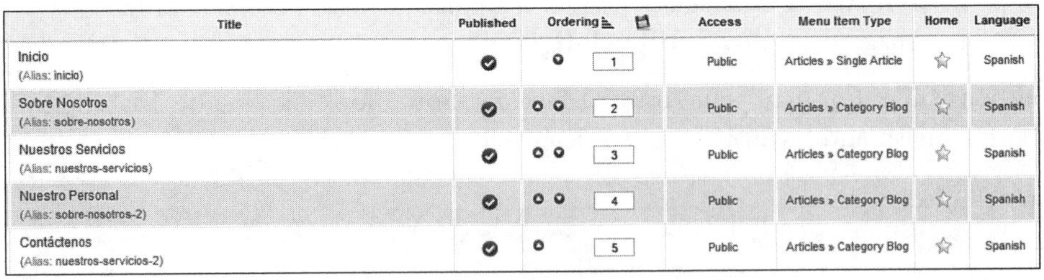

Title	Published	Ordering		Access	Menu Item Type	Home	Language
Inicio (Alias: inicio)	⊘	○	1	Public	Articles » Single Article	☆	Spanish
Sobre Nosotros (Alias: sobre-nosotros)	⊘	○ ○	2	Public	Articles » Category Blog	☆	Spanish
Nuestros Servicios (Alias: nuestros-servicios)	⊘	○ ○	3	Public	Articles » Category Blog	☆	Spanish
Nuestro Personal (Alias: sobre-nosotros-2)	⊘	○ ○	4	Public	Articles » Category Blog	☆	Spanish
Contáctenos (Alias: nuestros-servicios-2)	⊘	○	5	Public	Articles » Category Blog	☆	Spanish

Figure 15.20   Your Spanish Main Menu with both
English and Spanish menu links

At the moment, we do have different content on our home page with each language. We are using the default home page and simply changing the articles that show. It's worth noting that you can have completely different home pages for different languages. For example, imagine that your site sells books in English: You could place your shopping cart on the home page so that it's easy for visitors to find them. However, if you don't have a Spanish translation of the books, it doesn't make sense to have the shopping cart on the home page for Spanish-speaking visitors. Here's how to create a different home page for different languages:

1. Find the menu link that you want to use for the home page in the site's default language. In this case, we choose the home page for English-speaking visitors.

2. Check the box next to the menu link you've chosen and click Home in the top-right corner. The menu link now has a gold star beside it in the Home column.

3. Choose a menu link that you want to use for your Spanish home page. Make sure that the menu link has these two settings:

- **Language.** Spanish
- **Default Page.** Yes

4. Save the menu link, and you see that the Spain flag appears beside it. In Figure 15.21, you can see a Spanish home page link next to a normal home page with a gold star.

Title	Published	Ordering		Access	Menu Item Type	Home	Language
Home (Alias: home)	⊘	○	1	Public	Articles » Featured Article	★	All
Inicio (Alias: inicio)	⊘	○ ○	2	Public	Articles » Single Article		Spanish

Figure 15.21   A home page link in English and another home page link in Spanish

Step 3: Extensions (Components, Modules, and Plug-ins)

The third step in creating the Spanish side to our site is translating the extensions. Joomla allows you to create new language versions of your components and modules. You probably won't need to translate your plug-ins. Some occasional plug-ins may have a language setting for you to change, but none of the default plug-ins do.

Components

The only components we need to translate are the ones that follow the Categorize, Add, Show workflow. That means Banners, Contacts, Newsfeeds, and Weblinks.

We follow the same process as we did for content:

1. Follow the Categorize, Add, Show workflow to add Banners, Contact, Newsfeeds, or Weblinks in Spanish.

2. Open any existing Banners, Contact, Newsfeeds, or Weblinks in English and change their Language setting to English.

Here's an example using Contacts. Currently we use the Contact component for one contact form that is linked to from Contact Us link in our Main Menu.

Categorize

1. Go to Contacts under Components in the main drop-down menu and then click on Categories.

2. Either create a new category here for Spanish contacts or, if you only have one or two contact forms, you could leave the Uncategorized category as it is.

Add

1. Go to Contacts under Components in the main drop-down menu. Click New and create a new contact form in Spanish. Remember to set the Language option to Spanish.

2. Open the existing contact form and set the Language option to English.

Show

1. Go to Spanish Main Menu under Menus in the main drop-down menu. Click New and create new menu link to your Spanish contact form. By now I hope you're remembering to set the Language option to Spanish.

2. Go to Main Menu under Menus in the main drop-down menu. Click on the existing main link to the English contact form and set the Language option to English.

That's the process. Repeat it as many times as you need to translate the content inside your components.

Modules

Modules are a little easier and quicker to translate than the components in the previous part of the chapter. All we need to do is make a copy of the existing module and then duplicate it.

Here's how we can create translations of our modules, using the example of our two main menus:

1. Go to Module Manager under Extensions in the main drop-down menu. Select the box next to Main Menu and click Duplicate in the top-right corner as in Figure 15.22.

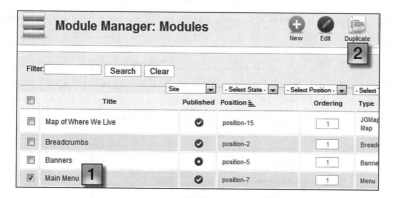

Figure 15.22   Creating a duplicate copy of a module

2. Click on the name Main Menu (2), which is the name of the new module. Enter these settings and then click Save & Close:

- **Title.** Spanish Main Menu

- **Language.** Spanish

- **Select Menu.** Spanish Main Menu

3. Open the Main Menu module and set the Language option to English.

That's it. Repeat the process for any module you want to translate into Spanish.

Some modules don't need any translating. Some modules, such as Search and Breadcrumbs, share these two features:

- The title isn't shown to the public.

- They don't require you to type in any content.

Step 4: Templates

The final way that you can translate your site is to have different template styles for different languages. There are reasons you might want to do this, including

- To make it clear to people which language they are browsing in by having different colors or designs on the site when different languages are enabled. At the simplest level, you might have a blue background for the English pages and a red background for the Spanish pages.

- Your template includes text inside images. There's no easy way to replace that text with text.

To make this change, go to your Template Manager under Extensions in the drop-down menu. Click on Beez2 – Default. You see that there's an option labeled default as in Figure 15.23. If you choose a language in here, this template style appears on every page where that language is chosen.

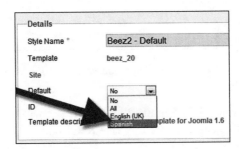

Figure 15.23   Assigning a template style to an individual language

Finally, you might not be completely finished yet if you chose a template style for English with one set of module positions and choose a completely different style for Spanish with a different set of module positions. If your English and Spanish template styles are very different, you need to go back to your Module Manager and assign the English modules to their correct positions and the Spanish modules to their correct positions.

What's Next?

We have one final, important topic to cover in this book. If you are the person responsible for your site, you need to know how to keep your site safe and secure. Among other things, you need to know how to protect your site and update it to the latest version. Turn the page, and we show you how to successfully manage your Joomla site.

16

Joomla! Site Management Explained

Are you going to be responsible for maintaining your Joomla site? If so, this chapter is for you. This chapter shows you how to keep your site safe, secure, and updated.

Many of you will have other people to take care of these tasks for you. You might have a Web design company, colleagues in the IT department, or other experienced people to help you out. If that's you, then you can happily skip this chapter.

However, if you are the person responsible for your site, then you need to know how to keep your site safe and secure. Among other things, you need to know how to protect your site and update it to the latest version.

Things You Can Do After Reading This Chapter

- Update your site
- Update your extensions
- Disable or uninstall extensions
- Use additional measures to protect your site
- Back up your site
- Understand the Global Configuration screen

Updating Your Site

Treat your Joomla site as you treat your car.

All cars need regular maintenance and so do all Joomla sites. With a car, you need to pump up the tires, change the oil, change the battery, or do other fixes. With a Joomla site, you also need to apply fixes. Fortunately the most important of these fixes can be applied automatically using Joomla's update system.

Before we show you how to use Joomla's update system, you need to understand what you're updating to. Joomla's updates are based on version numbers as described in the following section.

An Overview of Joomla Version Numbers

Back in Chapter 1, "Joomla Explained," we talked a little about Joomla's version numbers. Some of the key points we mentioned are

- At the time of writing, there are three major version of Joomla:
  - Joomla 1.0 was released in 2005 and is no longer supported.
  - Joomla 1.5 was released in 2008 and will be supported until April 2012.
  - Joomla 1.6 was released in 2011 and is the version we used in this book.
- More versions will be released. In fact, there's a good chance that by the time you're reading this book, the latest version of Joomla will be 1.7, 1.8, or something even higher.
- Different versions don't mean huge changes. New versions of Joomla are like new models of cars. This year's Toyota, Ford, or Honda might have small improvements or tweaks over last year's model, but it's instantly recognizable as the same car, and you'll have little problem moving from one to the other. Now that you've almost finished this book, you should be able to pick up a site using 1.0, 1.5, 1.6, or even a future version and be able to successfully use it.

Now let's get a little more specific about version numbers. Essentially there are two types—major versions and minor versions.

Major Versions

Major versions have large intervals between releases and often add important new features to Joomla.

- **Numbering.** 1.0, 1.5, and 1.6 have been released, and in the future we can expect 1.7, 1.8, 1.9, 2.0, 2.1, and so on.
- **Reason for new major versions:** To add new features.

- **Importance.** Is it important to use the latest major version? It's useful but not essential. Because new major versions are released to add new features, there are no security problems if you don't upgrade. However, each major version is only supported by the Joomla team for so long, so yes, it's generally best to use the latest major version if possible.

- **Release dates.** Previously these versions were released whenever they were ready, but now the Joomla team has committed to releasing them every six months. That means the future release schedule looks like this:

  - Joomla 1.7: July 2011

  - Joomla 1.8: January 2012

  - Joomla 1.9: July 2012

  - Joomla 2.0: January 2013

- **Updating.** Unfortunately, it can be difficult to update from 1.0 to 1.5 and from 1.5 to 1.6. The more complicated the site, the more difficult it is to update. However, the Joomla Team has promised to make updates much easier in the future, starting with the move from 1.6 to 1.7. At the time of writing, the update process hasn't been finalized, but when firm details are available we'll publish them at http://joomlaexplained.com/updates.

Minor Versions

Minor versions are released irregularly but often and provide small fixes to existing features.

- **Numbering.** Each major version has minor versions such as 1.6.0, 1.6.1, 1.6.2, 1.6.3, and so on. For major versions that are out for a long time, these can add up so that the final version of 1.0 was 1.0.16, and the current version of 1.5 is 1.5.23. The current version of 1.6 is 1.6.3.

- **Reason for new minor versions.** To fix security problems and bugs.

- **Importance.** Is it important to use the latest minor version? Yes, absolutely. Because new minor versions are often released to fix security problems, it is vital to make sure you're using the latest version.

- **Release dates.** These versions are released approximately every one to two months, or as needed.

- **Updating.** In Joomla 1.6 you can update directly from your site's administrator area.

What Version Do I Have?

Now that we understand what the numbers mean, let's see how to apply updates.

Go to the administrator area of your site and look at the bottom of the screen. You can see what version number you currently have. In Figure 16.1 the site is at version 1.6.0.

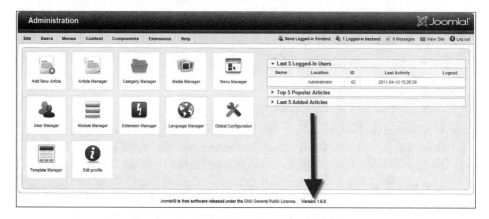

Figure 16.1   The version number of your Joomla site

How Do I Get Notified About Updates?

The best place to get update news is via Joomla Security News. You can sign up to get e-mail notification of updates by visiting http://www.joomla.org/download.html. The e-mail sign-up box is shown in Figure 16.2. If you're an RSS user, you can sign up for RSS notification at http://feeds.joomla.org/JoomlaSecurityNews.

So you've signed up for the Joomla Security News and you get information about a new Joomla version. What do you do? Let's see how you can update to the latest version.

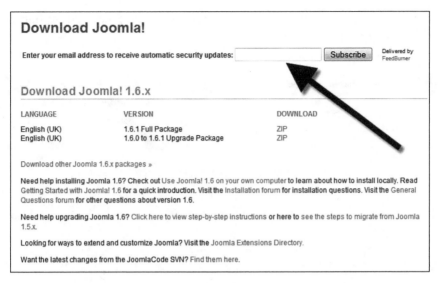

Figure 16.2   Getting e-mail notification of Joomla updates

How Do I Update?

The site shown in Figure 16.1 is using 1.6.0, which is definitely out-of-date. We mentioned earlier that at the time of writing, version 1.6.2 is out so we definitely need to update. Fortunately Joomla 1.6 has new a feature that allows us to update Joomla directly from our site's Extension Manager. Here's how we do it:

1. In the administrator area of your site, go to Extensions in the drop-down menu, then Extension Manager.

2. Click on Update under the Extension Manager heading. You see a screen like the one in Figure 16.3.

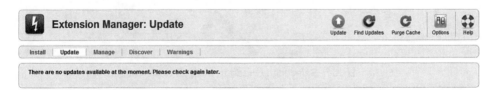

Figure 16.3   The Update area of your Extension Manager

3. To check to see if updates are available, click on the Find Updates button as in Figure 16.4.

Figure 16.4   Checking to see if your site can be updated

4. You now see a list of the available updates for your site as in Figure 16.5.

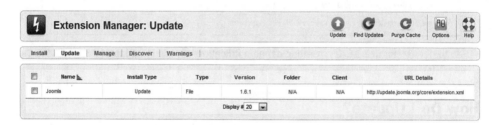

Figure 16.5   Available updates for your site

5. If there are available updates, you can apply them by checking the box next to the listed update and clicking the Update button as in Figure 16.6.

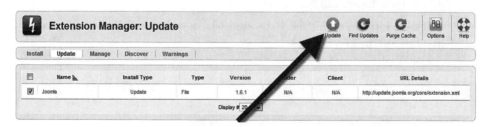

Figure 16.6   Selecting upgrade to apply to a Joomla site

6. You then see a message saying "Updating file was successful," as in Figure 16.7.

Figure 16.7   A successful update to the latest Joomla version

7. You can double-check to see whether the update has been successful by looking at the version number at the bottom of the page as in Figure 16.8.

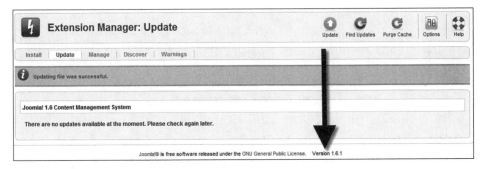

Figure 16.8   The new Joomla version number
showing in the administrator area

Updating Your Extensions

Just like every piece of software ever written, Joomla is not perfect. It's constantly being updated and improved. The same is true for your site's extensions. So, to keep your site safe, you may need to update your extensions as well as the main Joomla version. Components, modules, and plug-ins need regular updates. Templates may occasionally need them, but they are likely to be much less frequent.

Joomla 1.6 has the new feature we've just seen that allows us to update our site from the Extension Manager. The same new feature also applies to extensions. It's worth noting that not all extensions have been rewritten to take advantage of this yet, but let's see how it works for extensions that use it.

We test how extension updates work using a module called Tweet Display Back, which allows us to show our Twitter posts on our site. To show how this works, we need to do something that isn't normally advised: Download an old version.

1. Go to http://extensions.joomla.org and search for Tweet Display Back. In the category tree, it is under Social Web and then Twitter Display. The Tweet Display Back module is shown in Figure 16.9.

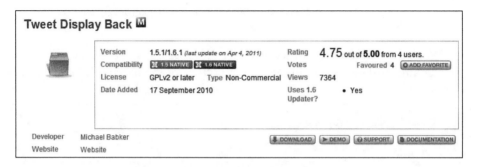

Figure 16.9   The Tweet Display Back page on http://extensions.joomla.org

2. Click Download to get to the developer's Web site. Click on the link that says "Head over to the Files Repository and get your copy today!" as shown in Figure 16.10.

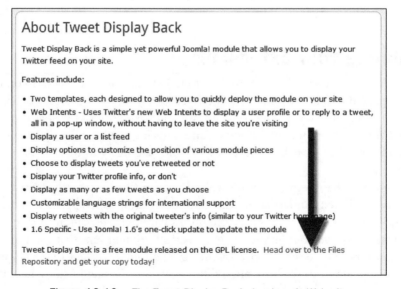

Figure 16.10   The Tweet Display Back developer's Web site

3. After clicking on the link, you are taken to http://www.joomlacode.org, which is an official site used to host many Joomla extensions. Click on the name TweetDisplayBack1.6.x as shown in Figure 16.11.

Package Name	Latest Release	Maturity	Files	File Size	Downloads
TweetDisplayBack1.6.x	1.6.1	5 - Production/Stable	mod_tweetdisplayback_161.zip	17.58 Kb	90
TweetDisplayBack1.5.x		5 - Production/Stable	mod_tweetdisplayback_151.zip	17.04 Kb	31
TweetDisplayBack1.1.x	1.1.10	6 - Mature	mod_tweetdisplayback_1110.zip	57.08 Kb	474
TweetDisplayBack1.0.x	1.0.10	Mature	mod_tweetdisplayback_1010.zip	55.84 Kb	184

Figure 16.11   The Tweet Display Back download area

4. You now see current and older versions of the module. Look at the Release Date column and pick the second most recently released file. In Figure 16.12 that is version 1.6.0. Click on the filename for the version you've chosen and download it to your desktop.

Release Name	Release Date	Filename	File Size	Download Count
1.6Beta2	2011-03-11 17:00:00-06	mod_tweetdisplayback_16beta2	17 KB	152
1.6Beta	2011-03-05 17:00:00-06	mod_tweetdisplayback_16beta.zip	55 KB	77
1.6.1	2011-04-03 17:00:00-05	mod_tweetdisplayback_161.zip	18 KB	90
1.6.0	2011-03-28 17:00:00-05	mod_tweetdisplayback_160.zip	17 KB	59
1.2Beta	2011-01-28 17:00:00-06	mod_tweetdisplayback_12beta.zip	53 KB	202

Figure 16.12   Tweet Display Back files hosted on http://www.joomlacode.org

5. Log in to your Joomla site's administrator area. Go to the Extension Manager and install the Tweet Display Back extension into your site.

6. Inside the Extension Manager, click on the Update tab as you did earlier in this chapter.

7. Click on the Find Update button as you also did earlier in this chapter. Afterward, you see that available updates include Tweet Display Back as in Figure 16.13.

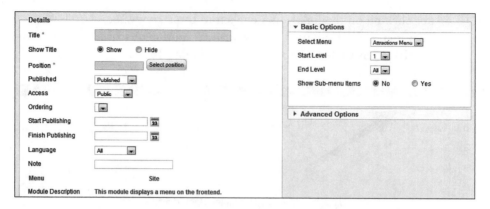

Figure 16.13   Tweet Display Back updates available in your Joomla site

8. Select the update and click the Update button. You now see the message saying "Updating module was successful," as shown in Figure 16.14.

Figure 16.14   Updating the Tweet Display Back module

If you ever want to know the version of an extension, you can click on the Manage tab in the Extension Manager. You see a screen like the one in Figure 16.15 with a list of all your installed extensions and details on each one.

Now, it's worth noting again that this method of updating doesn't work for all extensions. This feature is new in Joomla 1.6, and not every extension takes advantage of it yet. If your extension doesn't allow updates via this method, the best thing to do is check the documentation available for the extension. Here are three common ways for older extensions to update:

- Some extensions can be updated by downloading the new version and installing it. The extension automatically recognizes and overwrites the older version, leaving all your data intact.

- Some extensions have their own automatic update tools inside their own parts of the administrator area. For example, the Admin Tools extension that we discuss in the next section of the chapter can be updated by going to the Admin Tools link under Components in the main drop-down menu.

- Some much older extensions might ask you to uninstall the existing version and install the new version. We haven't yet covered how to uninstall extensions, but the next section of the chapter shows you how to do it.

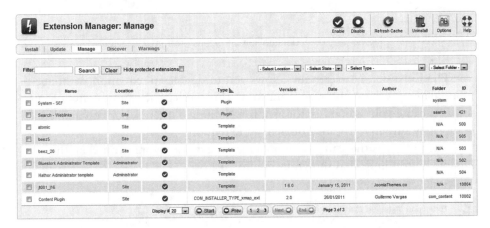

Figure 16.15   A list of all your installed extensions in the Extensions Manager

Disabling or Uninstalling Your Extensions

For security reasons, it's important to uninstall any extensions that you're not using. If extensions are unused you're also more likely to forget about updating them. Older extensions that haven't been regularly updated are more likely to suffer from security holes. Here's how you can remove those unused extensions:

1. In Extension Manager, click on the Manage tab and you see the screen shown previously in Figure 16.15.

2. Scroll down to find the extension you want to uninstall or type its name into the search box.

3. Check the box next to the extension and click the Uninstall button as in Figure 16.16.

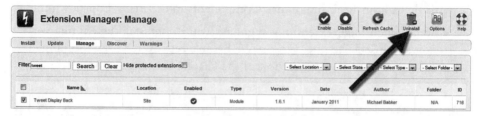

Figure 16.16   Uninstalling an extension from your site

The Extension Manager also allows you to disable an extension without uninstalling it. Why would you want to do this? Perhaps the most common reason is because your administrator area is becoming cluttered, but you aren't completely sure if you want to delete an extension.

The process is the same as uninstalling an extension, only you click the Disable button instead as shown in Figure 16.17.

Figure 16.17   Disabling an extension on your site

Additional Measures to Protect Your Site

There are some extensions available on http://extensions.joomla.org that add extra security features to your site. One of the best is called Admin Tools. Here's how to use it:

1. Go to http://extensions.joomla.org and search for Admin Tools. In the category tree, it is under Access & Security, then Site Security, and then Site protection. The Admin Tools page is shown in Figure 16.18.

Figure 16.18   The Admin Tools page on http://extensions.joomla.org

2. Click Download go to the Admin Tools developer's Web site. You see the Admin Tools category as in Figure 16.19. Click on the black View Releases in This Category button.

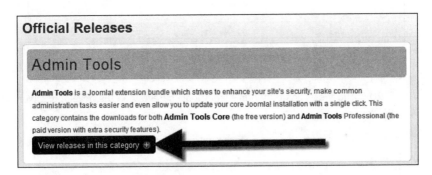

Figure 16.19   The Admin Tools category on the developer's Web site

3. Scroll down and click on the black View Files button as in Figure 16.20.

4. Scroll down and click on the blue Download Now button as in Figure 16.21.

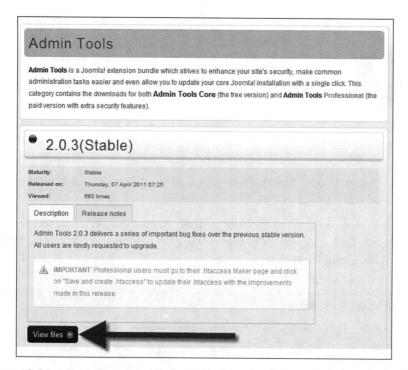

Figure 16.20   The View Files button in Admin Tools category on the developer's Web site

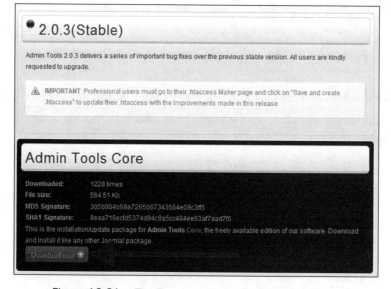

Figure 16.21   The Download Now button for Admin Tools

5. Log in to the administrator area of your site and install Admin Tools. Go to Components in the main drop-down menu and click on Admin Tools. You see a screen like Figure 16.22.

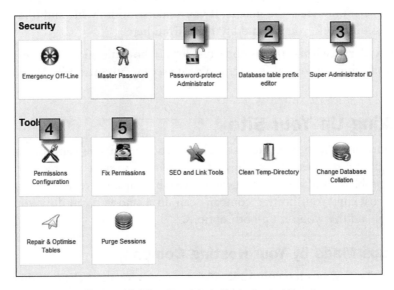

Figure 16.22   The Admin Tools Control Panel

Here are five of the important security features it provides:

- **Password-Protect Administrator.** By default, anyone can access the administrator login form for any Joomla site. All they have to do is add the word /administrator onto the end of the site's URL. This feature allows you to put an extra username and password in front of the administrator area and greatly decrease the chance of someone guessing your login, or using an automated script to try and find it.

- **Database Table Prefix Editor.** If you installed Joomla manually, you were able to choose part of the prefix Joomla used when adding your data to the database. By default this is jos_. However, many people who try to hack Joomla sites assume that jos_ is being used, and this gives them a head start in finding weaknesses. This feature allows you to change it to something other than jos_.

- **Super Administrator ID.** This is similar to the database table prefix. Joomla's main user account (the one you've been using throughout this book) is identified in the database with the number 42, and knowing that gives hackers a head start. This feature allows you to change the number.

- **Permissions Configuration.** Just like the features on your Joomla site, all the files and folders on a Web server have permissions that decide who is allowed to access and use them. To take a simple example, your /images/ directory allows Joomla users to upload and view images, but general visitors can only view the images. If you understand how file and folder permissions work, you can modify them from here.

- **Fix Permissions.** If you don't understand how file and folder permissions work, this feature can set them to a safe setting automatically.

Backing Up Your Site

It's important to keep your site secure, but even the best sites can run into problems, and even the best site administrators can make mistakes. To recover from serious problems and errors, you need to have backups. There are two main ways to make backups: Your hosting company can do it, and you can do it yourself. I recommend that you set up both options. ·

Backups Made by Your Hosting Company

Many of the best hosting companies make backups for their clients. Some of the best ones, such as http://www.rochen.com which hosts the main Joomla.org sites, not only make the backups but also give you the ability to restore a backup in place of the current site. Some others make the backups but require that you contact them and ask for the backup to be restored. Finally, some hosts won't make any backups at all available to you as they create backups to recover from server failure and not your mistakes.

It's important that you know the backup policy of your host, whether it's good, mediocre, or bad.

Backups Made by You

The same developer who created the Admin Tools extension also created a useful extension for backing up and restoring your Joomla site. The name of the extension is Akeeba Backup. We show you how to use it so that you can back up sites by yourself. Here's how to use Akeeba:

1. Go to http://extensions.joomla.org and search for Akeeba Backup. In the category tree, it is under Access & Security, then Site Security, and then Backup. The Akeeba Backup page is shown in Figure 16.23.

Figure 16.23   The Akeeba Backup page on http://extensions.joomla.org

2. Click on the download link for Akeeba and you are taken the developer's site. Getting to the Akeeba Backup download is similar to the way you reached the Admin Tool's download. Click on the Akeeba Backup name, click on the black View Files button, and then click on the blue Download Now button under Akeeba Backup Core. The link is shown in Figure 16.24.

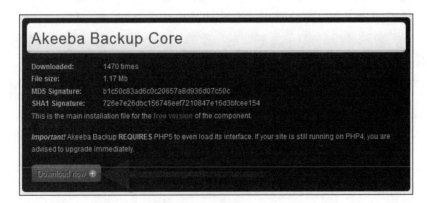

Figure 16.24   The download link for Akeeba Backup

3. Install Akeeba Backup; then go to the Components link in the drop-down menu and click on Akeeba Backup. You see a screen like the one in Figure 16.25. Check to see that the message on the right-hand side of the page says Akeeba Backup is ready to back up your site. If it does, click on Backup Now to start the back-up process.

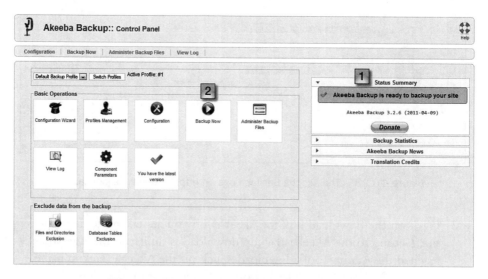

Figure 16.25   The Akeeba Backup administrator area

4. After clicking on Backup Now you see a screen like the one in Figure 16.26. Click on the Backup Now! Button to start the backup.

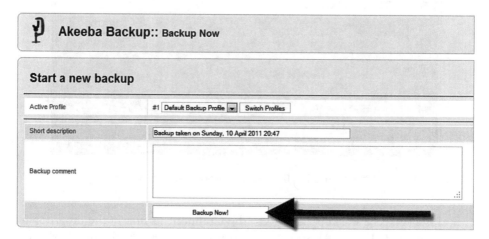

Figure 16.26   Starting the backup using Akeeba Backup

5. During the backup process, Akeeba Backup shows a progress bar as in Figure 16.27 and tells you what it's working on.

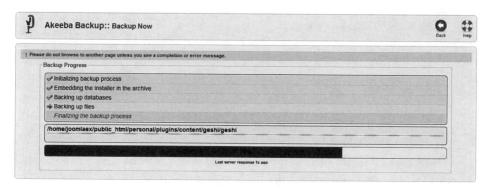

Figure 16.27   A backup in progress with Akeeba Backup

6. When the process is over, you see a message saying Backup Completed Successfully as in Figure 16.28. Click on Administer Backup Files to go and download your backup.

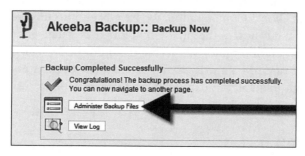

Figure 16.28   A backup successfully completed with Akeeba Backup

7. You now see a list of your backups. Look under the Manage & Download column and click on the name of the file (see Figure 16.29). That downloads it to your desktop. From there you can store the backups in a safe place on your hard drive or elsewhere.

Remember that all hosting is different, and you might run into problems while creating backups. If you do, the Akeeba Backup Web site at http://www.akeebabackup.com is an excellent source of information. It has further documentation on how you can use the extension in more advanced ways. For example, you can create backups automatically and send the backups to remote storage provided by companies such as http://www.amazon.com and http://www.dropbox.com.

Figure 16.29   Downloading a successfully completed backup

The Akeeba Backup site also provides a file called Akeeba Kickstart, which allows you to extract and restore the backup that you made.

The extension is thoroughly documented at http://www.akeebabackup.com and is well worth exploring further if you want to make sure that your site has safe and regular backups.

Global Configuration

There is one final, important part of the Joomla administrator area that we haven't covered: Global Configuration. We have been into this area occasionally during this book, but now is the time to explore it in detail. Go ahead and click on Global Configuration under Site in the main drop-down menu, and you see a screen like the one in Figure 16.30. There are many options in here, so I won't take you through them all but explain those that are the most useful and important.

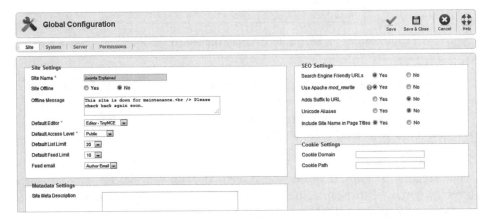

Figure 16.30   The Global Configuration screen

Taking Your Site Offline

One of the most useful options available inside Global Configuration is the ability to take your site offline. You can use this setting while you're getting a site ready for launch or if you want to take it offline while making improvements. Here's how you use it:

1. In Global Configuration, check the box setting Site Offline to Yes. You can use the Offline Message box to write a message to show visitors. When you're finished, click Save & Close (see Figure 16.31).

Figure 16.31   Taking your Joomla site offline

2. Go to the visitor area of your site, and your site looks like Figure 16.32. People who don't have a username and password at a sufficiently high level won't be able to log in.

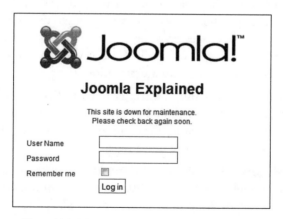

Figure 16.32   Your Joomla site in offline mode

3. Enter your username and password that you normally use to get into the administrator area of your site. You now can see, edit, and browse around your site without any restrictions.

4. As soon as you're ready to make your site live again, go to the administrator area and Global Configuration, set Site Offline to No, and click Save & Close.

5. If you want to change the logo that people see when the site is offline, go to the Media Manager. You need to replace a file called joomla_logo_black.jpg. Delete that file and upload a new image with that same name. If your company has a different name such as logo.jpg, you need to rename it to joomla_logo_black.jpg.

Metadata Settings

To be honest, I'm including these options because they cause confusion, rather than because they are useful. We get a lot of questions about them from our students in class. We normally tell them not to touch the settings at all and just leave the default choices in place. The settings are shown in Figure 16.33, and here's a rundown of what they do:

- **Site Meta Description.** I mentioned the meta description back in Chapter 5, "Joomla Content Editing Explained." This text may appear under your site title in search engine results. However, to be worthwhile, each description needs to be unique for the page it's on. Therefore, I recommend leaving this field blank because no single description can correctly apply to all the pages on your site. Instead, make sure to fill in the Meta Description inside each article. Even if you don't, search engines read the text on your site and create a description.

- **Site Meta Keywords.** Also in Chapter 5, I said that search engines now entirely ignore keywords included in your metadata because so many people tried to misuse that feature for spam. It's much more important to have keywords in your main article text instead.

- **Content Rights.** This tag shows information about who holds the copyright for the content on the site. Often copyright information is complex enough that the best thing to do is include a link in here to a full page of copyright information.

- **Show Title Meta Tag.** This setting can be left as Yes. It shows the title of the page, plus the site name, inside the metadata.

- **Show Author Meta Tag.** This setting can also be left as Yes. It shows the author of the content, as listed in the article, inside the metadata.

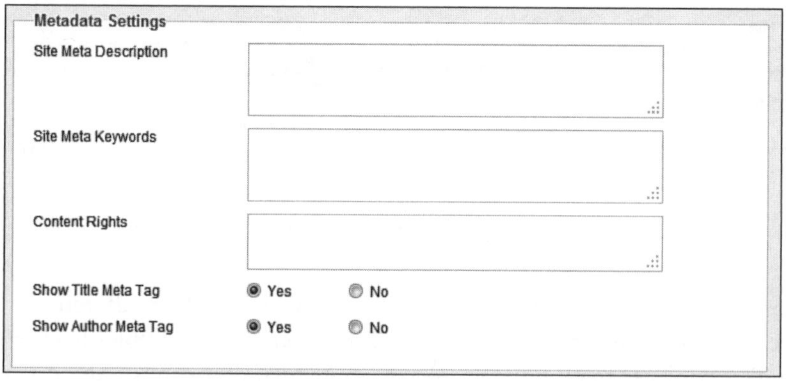

Figure 16.33   Metadata Settings in Global Configuration

Changing Your Site's URLs

So, we dismissed the Metadata Settings as having little impact on your site's search engine rankings. However, these next settings will likely have a greater impact and will also make your site more usable for visitors. We now explain how to change Joomla's URLs.

I have two warnings before we begin:

- These settings are more responsible for people saying "Help, my site has crashed!" than anything else in the history of Joomla. Fortunately the fix is simple: If you change any of these settings to Yes and your site starts producing broken links, simply change the settings back to No again. At the end of this section we have some suggestions for making these settings work if they cause problems on your site.

- It is best to get these settings right before you launch your site. If you change them later, they can cause broken links and frustration for your visitors.

To change your URLs, look inside your Global Configuration for the SEO Settings as shown in Figure 16.34.

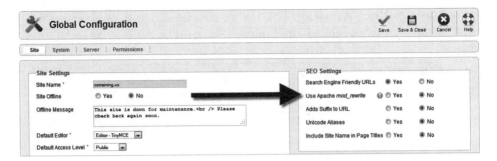

Figure 16.34   SEO Settings in Global Configuration

Four of these settings modify the URLs on your site. The difference between choosing Yes or No can be major. Here are two examples for the same article. The choices are cumulative, so you must turn on Search Engine Friendly URLs before turning on Add Suffix to URLs.

- **Search Engine Friendly URLs.** This setting radically shortens and improves the URLs.

  - **Yes.** http://www.joomlaexplained.com/index.php/2-category-name/1-article-name

  - **No.** http://www.joomlaexplained.com/index.php?option=com_content&view=article-name&id=1:joomla&catid=2:category-name&Itemid=101

- **Use Apache mod_rewrite:** This setting removes /index.php/ from the URLs.

  - **Yes.** http://www.joomlaexplained.com/2-category-name/1-article-name

  - **No.** http://www.joomlaexplained.com/index.php/2-category-name/1-article-name

- **Adds Suffix to URL.** This setting adds .html to the end of the URLs.

  - **Yes.** http://www.joomlaexplained.com/2-category-name/1-article-name.html

  - **No.** http://www.joomlaexplained.com/2-category-name/1-article-name

- **Unicode Aliases.** This setting is only for people running their sites in a language other than English.
  - **Yes.** Your URLs show in the characters of the native language. For example, Greek Web sites will have URLs using Greek characters, Arabic Web sites will use Arabic characters, Chinese Web sites will use Chinese characters, and so on.
  - **No.** Your URLs will be show in A-to-Z characters only.
- **Include Site Name in Page Titles.**
  - **Yes.** If you look at the top of your browser and in search results, the title shown will be in this format: Your Site Name – Your Page Title. For example, in Figure 16.35 the title is Joomla Explained – Joomla on a Mac. Your Site Name is taken from a field inside Global Configuration.
  - **No.** The title of the page in your browser and your search results will simply be the title shown on your page. Your Site Name won't be included.

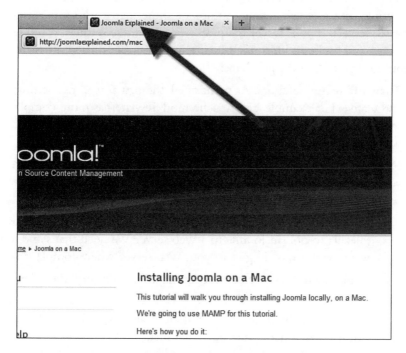

Figure 16.35   The impact of the Include Site Name in Page Titles setting in Global Configuration

Here are my recommendations for those settings:

- **Search Engine Friendly URLs.** Yes. This setting radically shortens and improves the URLs.

- **Use Apache mod_rewrite.** Yes. This makes the URLs shorter, and /index.php/ doesn't add anything useful to the URLs.

- **Adds Suffix to URL.** No. We're not building HTML Web sites any longer, and it doesn't make much sense to extend the URLs with .html.

- **Unicode Aliases.** No, if you're running your site in English or any language that primarily uses A–Z and 0–9 characters. If you're using a language with another character set, choose Yes if you think your users will prefer to use those characters rather than A–Z and 0–9.

- **Include Site Name in Page Titles.** Yes. It's important to show people what the name of your site is. However, make sure that your site name is short, accurate, and helps people indentify your site.

So, if these settings can produce much better URLs, why are they not all turned on by default? It's because not all hosting companies work well with these settings, and Joomla's default settings are those that work on the largest number of servers. If your server has problems with these settings, you'll see blank pages and broken URLs on your site until they are turned off. So what can you do if you see these problems?

- **Turn off some settings.** As mentioned, the first three SEO settings are cumulative. For example Use Apache mod_rewrite has more complex requirements to work than does Search Engine Friendly URLs. So, try turning off some of the settings such as Use Apache mod_rewrite.

- **Rename the htaccess.txt file to .htaccess.** This is a useful feature for your URLs but also for your site's security. Here's how the file can be renamed:

  1. Back in Chapter 2 we showed how to use FTP software such as Filezilla to upload Joomla to a Web server. We need that same software for this task. Log in to your Web server where Joomla is hosted.

  2. In the main directory of your Joomla files, look for a file called htaccess.txt.

  3. Rename the file to .htaccess. If there is already a file called .htaccess, you need to rename that other file first.

- **If neither of the preceding two techniques works, go to http://www.joomlaexplained.com/urls, which has more details on enabling Joomla's URLs.** These settings are particularly difficult to make work on Windows servers.

Making Your Site Run Faster

There are two settings inside Global Configuration that make your site run faster and reduce the amount of work your site needs to do.

First, and simplest, is Gzip Page Compression. All those extensions and templates that you downloaded have used the same Gzip compression. It compresses all the files into smaller versions, without damaging them, so that they move around the Web more quickly. If your whole site is compressed, that means visitors get a compressed version of your site that reaches them more quickly and therefore takes less time to load. To change the setting, click on the Server tab and look for Gzip Page Compression inside the Server Settings box as shown in Figure 16.36. Change the setting to Yes.

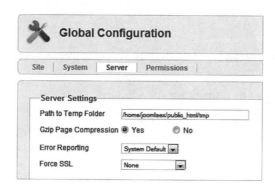

Figure 16.36   Gzip Page Compression settings in Global Configuration

Second, and a little more involved, is Cache. Whereas Gzip Page Compression makes your site much smaller, the Cache setting freezes it. What does that mean? Every time a visitor arrives at your site, Joomla needs to do a lot of work. It needs to check which template is being used, which modules are needed, which articles or components should appear on the page, and also check a lot of things to make sure the page displays correctly for the visitor. All those checks take time, and Joomla repeats the process for each new visitor. Cache solves that problem by freezing the page and delivering the same version to each visitor. Joomla doesn't have to re-create the page each time, so everything loads much more quickly.

The downside to Cache is that the information can become out-of-date if it freezes for too long. Joomla solves that problem by deleting the Cache after a fixed period of time and then creating a new, frozen version.

You can turn the Cache on by clicking on the System tab inside Global Configuration and changing the Caching setting to Yes. You can see the setting in Figure 16.37.

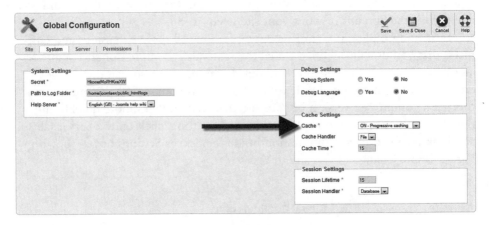

Figure 16.37   Cache settings in Global Configuration

Two more things to note about the Cache:

- It's not helpful if you're making a lot of edits on the site because every time you make an edit, you'll still be looking at the version from 15 minutes ago.

- You can reset the Cache at any time by going to Site in the main dropdown menu, and then going to Maintenance and clicking on Clear Cache. The link is shown in Figure 16.38.

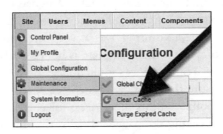

Figure 16.38   Clearing the cache

Staying Logged In for Longer

This final setting is useful for those of you who will do a lot of work on your Joomla site. If you're not active on the site, for example, if you step away for a cup of coffee, you'll be logged out after 15 minutes. You then need to log in again. If you'd like to stay logged in for longer, you can change that time by clicking on the System tab and going to the System Settings fields as shown in Figure 16.39. Don't make this number too high, but you can certainly change it to 60 or 120 minutes.

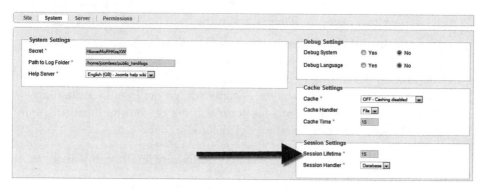

Figure 16.39   Changing System Settings in Global Configuration

What's Next?

Congratulations! You've reached the end of *Joomla! Explained.*

So what's next?

- **Practice.** The only way to get better at Joomla is to build Joomla sites. Decide on your first Joomla project and start practicing.

- **Practice now.** You will forget most of what you've read in this book. That's human nature and doesn't make me a bad teacher or you a bad learner. The longer you wait to practice Joomla, the more you'll forget. Why not get started right away?

- **Learn more.** I guarantee that there are things you will come across while using Joomla that haven't been included in this book. This book has only a limited number of pages, and we've tried to focus on only the most important things about Joomla. However, one of the great things about Joomla being so popular is that almost every problem you run into has been encountered by other people. Many of those people will have asked for or posted solutions to their problems online. If you ever get stuck, here are the first two places you should go to for help:

- **http://www.google.com.** If you get an error message or encounter a problem, type it directly into a search engine, and there's a good chance you'll find a solution.

- **http://forum.joomla.org.** The Joomla forums have around 2.5 million posts at the time of writing, so there are a lot of solutions to be found. Search for a solution to your question, and if you don't find it, write a new post. There's sure to be someone able to help you.

- **Join the Joomla community.** Joomla doesn't rely on money; it relies on people like you. Whether you attend a local Joomla event, post solutions you find on the forum, or even say thank you to someone who's helped you, there are many easy ways to become part of the Joomla community. The more you rely on Joomla for your Web site or your business, the more it will benefit you to become part of the community.

I hope to see you around in the Joomla community, and I wish you all the best in your use of Joomla!

Index

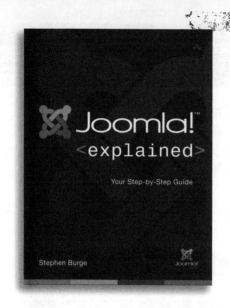

FREE Online Edition

Your purchase of **Joomla! Explained** includes access to a free online edition for 45 days through the Safari Books Online subscription service. Nearly every Addison-Wesley Professional book is available online through Safari Books Online, along with more than 5,000 other technical books and videos from publishers such as Cisco Press, Exam Cram, IBM Press, O'Reilly, Prentice Hall, Que, and Sams.

SAFARI BOOKS ONLINE allows you to search for a specific answer, cut and paste code, download chapters, and stay current with emerging technologies.

Activate your FREE Online Edition at www.informit.com/safarifree

STEP 1: Enter the coupon code: YGLWEBI.

STEP 2: New Safari users, complete the brief registration form.
Safari subscribers, just log in.